AF207395

THE REVOLUTION IS FOR THE CHILDREN

ENVISIONING CUBA Louis A. Pérez Jr., editor

THE REVOLUTION IS FOR THE CHILDREN

The Politics of Childhood in
Havana and Miami, 1959–1962

Anita Casavantes Bradford

The University of North Carolina Press Chapel Hill

© 2014 THE UNIVERSITY OF NORTH CAROLINA PRESS
ALL RIGHTS RESERVED
MANUFACTURED IN THE UNITED STATES OF AMERICA
DESIGNED BY KIM BRYANT AND SET IN MILLER BY CODEMANTRA

The University of North Carolina Press has been a member of the Green Press Initiative since 2003.

Library of Congress Cataloging-in-Publication Data
Casavantes Bradford, Anita.
The Revolution is for the children : the politics of childhood in Havana and Miami, 1959–1962 / Anita Casavantes Bradford.
    pages cm. — (Envisioning Cuba)
ISBN 978-1-4696-1152-5 (pbk.) — ISBN 978-1-4696-1154-9 (ebook) (print)
1. Cuba—History—Revolution, 1959—Social aspects. 2. Children—Government policy—Cuba. 3. Children and politics. 4. Children—Cuba—Social conditions—20th century. 5. Children—Florida—Miami—Social conditions—20th century.
6. Cubans—Political activity—Florida—Miami—History—20th century. 7. Political refugees—Florida—Miami—History—20th century. I. Title.
F1788.C2617 2014
972.9106'4—dc23   2013041141

18 17 16 15 14   5 4 3 2 1

For my *nena*—
la maravillosa Ana Sofía

CONTENTS

ILLUSTRaTIONS

ACKNOWLEDGMENTS

This book has been a collaborative effort. Almost ten years ago at Texas A&M University, Kingsville, Richard Hartwig and Nirmal Goswami encouraged me to begin thinking seriously about the politics of childhood in Cuban history. Since then, I have been fortunate to enjoy their continued encouragement and friendship.

This book also benefited from the contributions of a number of exceptional faculty members at the University of California, San Diego (UCSD). Luis Alvarez, who continues to inspire me with his fierce intellect and zen-*zapatista* spirit, gave selflessly of his time to pore over every word of the manuscript in its multiple iterations, giving special attention to developing its analytical framework. David Gutiérrez has challenged, harangued, and supported me every step of the way, raising questions and critiques that prompted me to reframe several of the book's key arguments. Thanks also to Daniel Widener, John Skrentny, Mark "the Captain" Hanna, and Nayan Shah for their support of the book—and to Christine Hunefeldt, whose wisdom, compassion, and generosity are a model for women in academia.

A number of other readers at the University of California, Irvine, and elsewhere contributed their vast knowledge and experience to this book. I am grateful beyond words to Raúl Fernández, who fact-checked every footnote, provided important research materials, and told me marvelous stories about his own Cuban childhood during the early revolutionary years. Special thanks to Félix Masúd-Piloto and Silvia Pedraza, who subjected the manuscript to several rigorous readings; their detailed constructive criticism strengthened the book's argument, organization, and style. Jorge Duany also graciously took time to read the manuscript and provided thoughtful comments, for which I am truly grateful. My gratitude also goes out to the inestimable Vicki Ruiz for her guidance and unwavering confidence in my work during the past few years.

Generous financial support helped bring this book to completion. The University of California, San Diego, provided travel research grants in 2008 and 2009; the UCSD Latino Studies Research Initiative also provided two grants during 2009 and 2010. The Cuban Heritage Collection

(CHC), University of Miami Libraries, provided support for three months' research during the fall of 2010 and winter of 2011. Special thanks to Maria Estorino, Annie Sansone-Martínez, and Rosa Monzón for their warmth and assistance navigating the CHC's rich and varied collections. The UC-Cuba Multi-Campus Initiative also provided grants for travel to Cuba during the spring of 2011 and funding to present chapters from this book at a number of conferences and workshops. My thanks and affection go out to my UC-Cuba family for accompanying me and this book on its journey to publication. The University of California Office of the President provided me with the precious gift of time, in the form of a two-year Presidents' Postdoctoral Fellowship, to thoroughly revise the book. Thanks to Kimberly Adkinson and Sheila O'Rourke in the Office of the President for their unfailing advocacy, and to my UC-President's colleagues and mentors, especially Sylvanna Falcon and Douglas Haynes, for their encouragement during the revisions process.

I am especially grateful to Louis A. Pérez for expressing an early interest in the book, and to Elaine Maisner, senior editor at the University of North Carolina Press, for shepherding the book from inception to completion.

I also wish to thank Father John Paul Forté and my Catholic community at the UCSD Newman Center, especially Gloria Kim, Jennifer Ehren, and Gabriela Ponce, the Park Terrace crew (including Charlie and Orlagh), and of course *tía abi* Beth, for the many ways they helped this book reach its final form. My husband, Mike, has listened patiently, provided essential technical assistance, and cheered me on each day. Last but certainly not least, I extend my thanks to the remarkable María Covadonga Pato for caring for, educating, and loving my precious *nena* Ana Sofía during the revisions process.

The credit for all that is good in this book belongs to the people mentioned here and to others too numerous to name who also helped it reach publication. Any errors or shortcomings contained within its pages I claim entirely for myself.

THE REVOLUTION IS FOR THE CHILDREN

THE POLITICS OF CHILDHOOD IN CUBA'S REVOLUTION AND EXILE

No real understanding of the past is possible if children are excluded.
—Paula S. Fass, "Is There a Story in the History of Childhood?"

Since 1959, the Castro regime has based its legitimacy on the assertion of a unique moral imperative, expressed in the slogan "La Revolución es para los niños [The Revolution is for the children]." This highly normative claim alludes most directly to early revolutionary successes in providing education and health-care services to hundreds of thousands of Cuban children whose needs had been neglected during the era of the U.S.-dominated republic. It nonetheless has roots that extend further into the island's history. Fidel Castro's famous statement evokes the even better-known words of José Martí, leader of Cuba's late nineteenth- and early twentieth-century independence struggle, who declared in 1898 that the third and final battle to wrest the island's liberation from Spain would be fought "for the children, since they are the ones who know how to love— they are the hope of the world."[1]

Castro's oft-repeated slogan simultaneously appropriates the patriotic power of Martí's memory and frames the Revolution's leaders as sharing his special concern for the well-being of the island's youngest citizens. Anti-Castro Cubans, however, have laid their own discursive claims to Martí's legacy. As early as 1960, counterrevolutionaries declared them-selves the true inheritors of his moral vision, even as a rapidly growing exile community in Miami sought to portray itself as heroic defenders of Cuban children, innocent victims of Castro-communist indoctrination, oppres-sion, and deprivation. These mutually antagonistic discourses resurfaced in November 1999, when five-year-old Elián González was discovered shipwrecked off the coast of southern Florida. During the following six months, U.S. federal district court deliberations on the boy's immigra-tion and custody status dominated the news in Havana and Miami and provoked extreme emotional responses among island and exilic Cubans alike. The heated transnational battle for custody of the small *balsero* was but the latest and best-publicized manifestation of a preoccupation with children that has been central to the multiple strains of Cuban nationalism that have emerged since the island's independence.

During the twentieth century, the politics of childhood—the strategic deployment of morally and emotionally resonant representations of childhood in the pursuit of power or resources, accompanied by efforts to press the bodies and minds of flesh-and-blood children into the service of broader political, social, and cultural objectives—has played a starring role in Cuba's national life. Beginning before 1898 and continuing throughout the republican era, North American politicians and journalists repeatedly used an infantilizing parent-child metaphor to characterize relations with the island nation and to justify their dominance of its political and economic life.[2] At the same time, the competing nationalist visions of pro- and anti–United States, conservative and progressive, black, white, elite, and working-class Cubans were also frequently and forcefully expressed through child-centered discourses and images. Cuban political and religious leaders, social reformers, and civic activists also recruited and trained children to assume a much celebrated role in a wide range of nation-making projects. Children's persistent visibility in the mass media and in public life dramatically articulated Cubans' frustrated aspirations to modern nationhood and propelled the island toward a second nationalist revolution in 1959. In subsequent years, it also spurred the processes of political polarization that led to the fragmentation and reformation of the republic into "Two Cubas" centered on the cities of Havana and Miami.[3]

This book engages the history of the Cuban Revolution and exile as a single transnational site in which to interrogate the complex uses and abuses of children and the figure of the child in the construction and maintenance of modern nation-making projects. It focuses on the crucial political work performed by symbolic representations of childhood and flesh-and-blood boys and girls between 1959 and 1962, a historically unprecedented four-year period during which Cubans rejected a discredited republican model of nationhood and the quasi-colonial relationship with the United States that buttressed it, embarking on two new and mutually antagonistic nationalist endeavors: on the island, the establishment of revolutionary socialism, and in southern Florida, the creation of a counterrevolutionary exile community. Although focusing on the pivotal years between the Revolution's triumph and the Cuban Missile Crisis, this book frames these four years as a powerfully generative moment in which to explore an ongoing dynamic that has played a constitutive role in twentieth-century Cuban and Cuban American history and in the history of U.S.-Cuban relations.

The book asks a series of interrelated questions, located on the interstices linking the fields of U.S., Cuban, and hemispheric Latina/o history, that seek to uncover the little-explored relationships between children and the modern nation-state and between the Cuban/Cuban American experience and the transnational life stories of other Spanish-speaking peoples in the United States. It begins by asking what role the politics of childhood have played in creating, enforcing, and contesting the asymmetrical relationship between Cuba and the United States, an asymmetry that—as in other Latin American nations—limited the sovereignty and efficacy of successive republican governments and drove the island toward revolution. How did children's centrality to propaganda, public debate, and political action influence the Revolution's radicalization after 1959? Conversely, how did the radicalization of Cuban society change children's role in propaganda and politics? What role did symbolic and actual children play in dissent on the island, in the exodus to Miami, and in relations among the U.S. government, Cuban refugees, and the anti-Castro movement? And how did the politics of childhood help create a privileged "Golden Exile" (to quote Alejandro Portes's much borrowed phrase) that mainstream Americans and exiles themselves continue to imagine as having little in common with other U.S. Latina/os?[4]

These questions, though inextricably intertwined with events and themes that transcend this book's periodization, are best answered through an analysis of the period between 1959 and 1962, a key juncture in U.S., Cuban, and hemispheric Latina/o history during which the politics of childhood achieved a dramatic salience on the island and in the United States. During these four years, Fidel Castro rapidly transformed a broadly based moral crusade to remove dictator Fulgencio Batista from power and renew the Cuban Republic, reshaping this movement into a socialist Revolution; as Castro did so, children played an important role in his efforts to create and maintain political consensus, mobilize support for revolutionary initiatives, and marginalize dissenting voices. Castro also used child-centered discourses and flesh-and-blood children to pursue a new strategic alliance with the Soviet Union, a process that contributed to the breakdown of relations with the United States and provoked growing opposition to his increasingly paternalistic and authoritarian leadership. The politics of childhood thus simultaneously spurred the radicalization of the Revolution and became a means by which many of Castro's original middle-class, urban, and Catholic supporters articulated their resistance to the rapidly evolving revolutionary nation-making project, at the same time as the Revolution's ever greater interventions into the realms of childhood, family life, and education motivated as many as 200,000 Cubans to flee the island.[5]

When they arrived in Miami, anti-Castro refugees and their North American allies drew on a counterrevolutionary politics of childhood to explain the origins of the exile community in terms that harmonized impoverished and dislocated Cubans' immediate needs with the federal government's Cold War foreign policy objectives. In tandem with covert efforts to spur middle-class out-migration from the island, politicians, civic actors, and journalists spread the idea that freedom-loving refugees sought asylum in the United States to protect their sons and daughters from the horrors of communism. This exile "creation myth" simultaneously discredited Cuba's nascent socialist experiment, reinforced North Americans' commitment to their own democratic-capitalist nation-making project, and warned other Latin American governments about the threat of communist subversion throughout the hemisphere. Its discursive power helped ensure that anti-Castro Cubans would benefit from a virtually unrestricted immigration status and would receive historically unprecedented levels of financial assistance for their resettlement in the United States, laying the groundwork for a policy of strategic generosity toward refugees fleeing communist regimes around the world.[6] Media attention to refugee children also helped secure sympathy and support for Cuban exiles from Miami's white majority—a welcome by no means inevitable—by downplaying their racial and cultural similarities to other Latina/os, working-class immigrants, and minorities and emphasizing their anticommunist politics and the middle-class Christian family values they shared with mainstream Americans.[7]

Exile leaders also relied heavily on the politics of childhood to negotiate the terms of their asymmetrical relationship with the U.S. intelligence agencies that sponsored the anti-Castro movement, to promote unity and solidarity among an initially politically heterogeneous refugee population, and to mobilize all of the community's resources in the struggle to overthrow the Revolution. After the April 1961 Bay of Pigs invasion and the October 1962 Missile Crisis failed to bring down Castro, however, exiles' dreams of a triumphant homecoming began to recede. Miami Cubans nonetheless clung to their belief that exile had been the right choice—a necessary evil to be endured in order to safeguard the well-being of their sons and daughters—and remained committed to securing the next generation's return to the *patria*. In the coming years, the exile community would continue to turn to the politics of childhood in order to make sense of their losses—of home, dignity, and homeland—even as they turned increasingly to their own sons and daughters for the inspiration and strength to begin building new lives in the United States.

CHILDHOOD AND NATION-MAKING IN THE TWO CUBAS

The persistent linkages between children and Cuban aspirations toward modern nationhood make the conjoined Two Cubas—revolutionary and exilic, territorial and diasporic—a uniquely powerful site in which to analyze the politics of childhood. These links have encompassed at least a century of struggle against first Spanish and then U.S. dominance and provoked a dramatic clash between the democratic-capitalist and socialist nation-making projects after 1959. Although this theme resonates through the last two centuries of Cuban and U.S. history, however, and indeed through the very history of modernity, historians and social scientists have not paid sufficient attention to childhood as an active force in national life, on the island or elsewhere.

Since the 1962 publication of Philippe Ariès's *Centuries of Childhood*, historians of childhood have acknowledged that childhood, like other identities, including those of race, class, gender, and sexuality, is constructed socially.[8] Child-centered scholarship during the 1970s embraced Ariès's assertion that modern notions of childhood did not acquire widespread social or cultural significance until at least the sixteenth century, but the scholars focused on interpreting his argument about the changing meaning of childhood within the "private" realm of family life. Scholars built on Ariès's work in studies that portrayed the premodern family as instrumental, authoritarian, and lacking in affective ties and that insisted on the progressivism and moral superiority of the modern family. Subsequently, in a critique that began to emerge in the 1980s, historians sought to disprove Ariès by insisting that parental awareness of childhood, in all its distinct ages and stages, special needs and vulnerabilities, was documented all the way back to antiquity.[9]

This generative scholarship nonetheless failed to respond to the central challenge posed by Ariès's work, which opened the door to wider-ranging critical analysis of the ways understandings and practices of childhood have been influenced by changing political, legal, social, and cultural structures. Although they asked important questions about children in the past, first-wave historians of childhood clung to dichotomous notions of public and private that their feminist contemporaries had only recently begun to challenge. In doing so, they reinforced—perhaps unintentionally—a gendered logic that relegated childhood to the private sphere even as it reinscribed women's traditional association with privacy. Early histories of childhood thus shored up patriarchal understandings of women's and children's dependence and isolation in the domestic realm while reinforcing the connections between masculinity, adulthood, and national life.[10]

During the 1990s, historians began to consider how children's experiences have been shaped by events and processes originating outside in the public sphere. More recent scholarship has analyzed how modern notions of children as "blank slates" and malleable future citizens—the building blocks with which modern nations could be constructed—led to greater state involvement in the education and social control of young people by the late 1800s. Historians have also considered how government officials and reformers in Canada and the United States identified children as a focal point for campaigns to confront social problems produced by industrialization, racial tensions, urban poverty, and immigration.[11] They have focused new attention on how children's lives were impacted by the rise of fascist and communist nation-making projects in twentieth-century Europe.[12] A small body of work has also begun to consider the omission of children from colonial and modern Latin American history.[13]

However, much of this scholarship approaches children peripherally, through studies of demography, household economics, and childrearing practices, as well as social policy, law, and education. Despite gender historians' and cultural theorists' efforts to draw attention to the ways notions of domesticity and womanhood, and by extension childhood, have undergirded modern nation-making projects, feminist scholar Barrie Thorne has observed that both traditional and critical scholarship remains "deeply and unreflectively centered around the experience of adults."[14] Moreover, those few scholars who do take children seriously often persist in framing them primarily as beneficiaries or victims of social change and state intervention, rather than as agents of change in their own right.[15] Reluctant to theorize children as political actors, historians have yet to engage in substantive debate about the importance to national life of children and discursive representations of childhood.

To date, the scarce scholarship on Cuban children reflects these limitations. Louis Pérez's historical analyses of public education, changing consumption patterns, and popular culture in republican-era Cuba offer glimpses into children's lives as a means of illustrating his broader argument about North American influence on the prerevolutionary island.[16] In *Cuba in the American Imagination* (2008), Pérez explores how turn-of-the-century North American politicians and journalists used child-centered metaphors to characterize Cuba as ill-prepared for independence, thereby justifying U.S. imperial ambitions toward the island. The study is nonetheless focused, as its title indicates, on representations of childhood originating in the United States. Moreover, since it is primarily a study of the way North Americans imagined their relationship with Cuba, the book does not consider the influence of actual Cuban children on the trajectory of the nation they were understood to represent.

Critical studies of revolutionary children are also limited. Cuban and international sources from this period, written in support of the new regime's claim that the Revolution was *para los niños*, offer a vivid record of the tangible benefits it provided to rural and working-class young people; however, they neglect to explore the impact of revolutionary initiatives on the lives of middle- and upper-class Cuban children and those from anti-Castro families. Most of these works also accept without question the Revolution's self-designation as the exclusive benefactor of the island's children, failing to acknowledge the extent to which the legitimacy of the Castro regime relied on its close relationship with the island's youngest citizens.[17] More recently, social scientists have analyzed revolutionary efforts to place young people at the center of a new socialist ideology and culture on this island. These studies nevertheless focus on top-down policies and initiatives directed at children, neglecting the active role played by symbolic representations of childhood and flesh-and-blood boys and girls in the Revolution's socialist nation-making project. Lillian Guerra's recent book, *Visions of Power in Cuba: Revolution, Redemption and Resistance, 1959–1971*, while not primarily focused on children, nonetheless begins the work of analyzing their centrality to what she calls the "grand narrative" of the Revolution and their critical role in the Castro government's ongoing struggle to create and control public discourse on the island, thereby ensuring the regime's long-term survival.[18]

Children also remain understudied in the fields of hemispheric Latina/o history and studies. They are present, though not the primary focus of analysis, in social and cultural histories of Mexican and Puerto Rican women in the United States.[19] They also make fleeting appearances in the history of Mexican American Los Angeles, as targets of early twentieth-century Americanization campaigns, as the subject of moral panics about juvenile delinquency among poor and racialized youth, and as victims of police-sanctioned violence and legal discrimination.[20] Children also appear, albeit peripherally, in histories of U.S. Latina/o struggles to overcome educational segregation and inequality.[21] Recent scholarship has also analyzed how the North American media has constructed Latina fertility—and, by extension, Latina/o children—as a racialized threat to the nation.[22] Children nonetheless play a minor role, and usually a passive one, in these studies.

The small body of literature on Cuban American history pays even less attention to children—a startling omission, in light of their ongoing importance within the exile worldview.[23] Sociological and political studies of the exile community allude more frequently to the ways the Revolution's radicalization threatened traditional notions of Cuban family life and childhood and accelerated emigration from the island; however, the few works focused specifically on children are dedicated to documenting the experience of unaccompanied minors whose parents, fearing communist indoctrination in Castro's schools, sent them into foster care in the United States through "Operation Pedro Pan."[24] In *The Lost Apple: Operation Pedro Pan, Cuban Children in the U.S., and the Promise of a Better Future* (2003), political scientist María de los Angeles Torres approaches Operation Pedro Pan as a case study on how modern notions of childhood influenced U.S.-Cuban relations and Cold War foreign policy.[25] Torres insightfully analyzes the children's importance in the struggle among Cuba, the United States, and the Soviet Union but gives minimal consideration to the intentions and actions of young Cubans caught up in the Cold War contest for their nation's destiny. Moreover, missing from her analysis—and from the other previously mentioned studies—is the recognition that Cuban children were not simply victims of the Revolution but rather played an active role in the competing nation-making projects around which the Two Cubas were organized.

THE CHILD AS NATION-MAKER:
THEORIZING THE POLITICS OF CHILDHOOD

Despite the paucity of scholarship on Cuban children, Cuba—both the territorially bounded nation and its diasporic counterpart—offers historians and social scientists a uniquely rich site in which to examine the powerful role played by the politics of childhood in shaping the destiny of modern nations. Both on the island and throughout the world, representations of childhood and flesh-and-blood children have been central to the processes of nation-building, state formation, and the ongoing construction, performance, and policing of national identity, unity, and stability. Children have played a constitutive role in the ideological labor through which different actors have pursued a range of modern nation-making projects, starring in the historical myths and metanarratives through which nations have been given concrete expression, bestowing legitimacy on leaders or hastening their delegitimization, and reinforcing or contributing to the destruction of institutions within which the range of political beliefs and possibilities have been contained and national trajectories determined.[26]

These complex nation-making projects have been negotiated not only in the spheres of politics, law, civil society, and the market but also within the underexamined spaces of spirituality and myth, morality and emotion, narrative and memory—the realms in which our most fundamental understandings and experiences of both nationhood and childhood originate.[27] Scholars have accordingly begun to recognize that the nation is a social construction, as historically contingent as notions of what constitutes a child.[28] In line with Benedict Anderson's reenvisioning of the nation as an "imagined community" created in large part through the media-facilitated circulation of a shared discourse of nationality, this book moves beyond ahistorical and territorially based definitions of nationhood. It uses the term *nation* as both a category of analysis and a description of a collection of social, cultural, and political practices by which people negotiate their identities and memberships in different communities and make sense of their lives, themselves, and others.[29] According to this definition, the nation is not a static or self-evident entity contained by clearly demarcated borders. Rather, it is an ever evolving construct, produced via multiple and multivalent interactions between institutions and individuals, in both the discursive and material realms, constantly in flux as a result of human efforts to create and contest its boundaries.

This definition deliberately foregrounds the contingency and amorphous quality of nationhood, focusing less on what the nation is or is not and more on how it is "done" through a wide range of nation-making projects. Decoupling the nation-as-practice from the nation-as-territory allows us to pay closer attention to how these nation-making projects have influenced and been influenced by the same discursive relations of power—including the hierarchies of race, class, gender, and sexuality—that also determine how childhood has been understood, experienced, and represented in different historical moments and spaces.

Moving away from territorial notions of nationhood also allows us to begin, somewhat paradoxically, to imagine the nation as a transnationally/ translocally constituted phenomenon.[30] This is not to suggest that globalizing forces have diminished the nation-state's power to control access to the rewards and benefits of citizenship—an enduring reality that continues to impose severe limits on the life chances of Latin American refugees, undocumented migrants, and their children in the United States.[31] This book nonetheless frames the history of the Cuban Revolution and exile within a singular transnational field, challenging practices of methodological nationalism that equate society and nation with the state and assume that countries are the natural unit for analysis.[32] It reads Cuban and U.S. archival sources gathered during seven research trips to Havana and Miami between 2000 and 2011 as a single record of the transnational/translocal historical process by which residents of two geographically and ideologically divided but nonetheless mutually constituting Cuban communities made surprisingly similar use of symbolic and flesh-and-blood children in the pursuit of mutually antagonistic nation-making projects.

This transnational approach accounts for the historical intimacy of U.S.-Cuba relations, the presence of Cuban diasporic communities in southern Florida and New York (smaller numbers also settled in New Orleans, Philadelphia, and elsewhere) for more than 150 years, and the important role played by U.S.-resident Cubans in the island's political, economic, and cultural life. It maintains that the severing of formal relations between the United States and Cuba in 1961 failed to curtail the cross-border forces and actors driving the politics of childhood in Havana and Miami, as evidenced by the continued movement of revolutionary and counterrevolutionary print, television, and radio messages across the Straits of Florida.[33] It further demonstrates that even after the 1962 Missile Crisis, a transnational and translocal politics of childhood, bolstered by ongoing migration, phone calls, letters, gifts and remittances in kind, and return travel by exiles to the island after the 1970s, continued to shape the competing nation-making projects of the Two Cubas.

New understandings of the nation-as-practice are complemented by this book's definition of childhood as a socially constructed identity that attributes historically contingent meanings to physiological, cognitive, and psychosexual differences associated with age. Just as we cannot "see" raced or gendered difference except through our socially mediated knowledge of the body, children cannot be identified outside of the specific discursive contexts in which they are always enmeshed.[34] This has inevitably led, in Cuba and elsewhere, to conflict and confusion over who is and is not recognized as a child. In different historical moments and spaces, the line separating childhood from adulthood has shifted in response to changing relations of power articulated through notions of race, class, gender, and sexuality and negotiations between domestic and international political, legal, and economic structures and forces. It has also responded to changes in the institutions of science and health care, religion, the family, media, and schools.

This book thus does not focus on a strictly defined age group. Recognizing that definitions of childhood are tied to the purposes for which children and their representations are deployed, it includes in its analysis all young people considered "children" by those seeking to make use of them in the pursuit of broader nation-making goals. Much of the historical data and analysis presented in the following pages accordingly focuses on school-age Cuban boys and girls between five and sixteen years old, but attention is also given to the early childhood years and to students up to the age of eighteen. The book also refers to university students when relevant, in recognition of the fact that Cuban and Cuban American youth, like all young people, have been profoundly shaped by their earlier experiences. Their inclusion in this story reminds us of the impossibility of completely separating childhood from adulthood in historical analysis.

Historians and cultural theorists who analyze the discursive production of raced and gendered identities provide us with additional theoretical tools for understanding the complex relationship between experience and representation in the politics of childhood. Stuart Hall argues that posing representations of race as outside of and opposed to concrete lived experience obscures the way the two are intimately linked to one another. David Roediger similarly calls for "a healthy refusal to imagine a choice between experience and representation" in his study of white racial formation. He uses the phrase "textured scholarship" to describe work that takes seriously the material bases of experience as well as the representations that correspond to them.[35] Since childhood is also a socially constructed identity, powerfully linked to notions of race, class, gender, and sexuality, this book demonstrates its own commitment to "texture" by drawing only the most tentative heuristic distinction between flesh-and-blood children and symbolic representations of the child.

This distinction nonetheless allows us to ask more precise questions about why and how knowledge about children is produced, contested, and naturalized. It makes visible the frequency with which representations of children, though embodying historically contingent understandings of childhood, appear in dominant public discourse in the figure of a symbolic "everychild" that reinscribes hegemonic notions of this stage of life. Moreover, it reveals the extent to which the figure of the child has stood in as a symbolic proxy for the nation, incarnating its shared virtues, values, and aspirations, as well as its vulnerabilities and anxieties—and marking the boundary between those who do and do not belong to the community it represents.

In the Two Cubas as in many modern nations, the politics of childhood has been organized around a number of recurring metanarratives—for example, the child as the building block of the future—and motifs that have long preoccupied the nation's political leaders, intellectuals, artists, social reformers, and journalists. Throughout the twentieth century, the archetypes of the child as problem, as innocent victim, and as virtuous *vocero* of national conscience have been deployed in Cuban political discourse to justify actions taken on the child's behalf and, by extension, on behalf of the nation. They have also played a starring role in broader campaigns to discredit and suppress competing nation-making projects. The figure of the child, in its multiple iterations, has had an equally powerful influence on the structures, institutions, and practices that shape the lives of flesh-and-blood Cuban children, whose minds and bodies have been consistently targeted by adults for care and protection, training and mobilization, indoctrination and control.

Moreover, the symbolic child has frequently been implicated, on and off the island, in efforts to discipline individual boys, girls, and adults who have expressed nonnormative ideas, beliefs, or identities, or to denounce behaviors that threaten the interests of those in positions of power. This book thus pays close attention to the complex interactions between the lived experiences of Cuban children, excavated from memoirs, biographies, material culture, and oral histories, and to the meanings attributed to them in government, church, and civic proclamations, curriculum documents, political iconography and cartoons, newspapers, periodicals and photographs, and other forms of propaganda. It also seeks to expose the often deliberate misrepresentations of children in the public sphere that are made possible by the structural and individual inequalities between adults and children, and to consider the historical consequences for both the territorial and diasporic Cuban nations and their children.

This book also uses the lenses of race, class, and gender to frame important questions about those who have and have not been empowered to engage the politics of childhood in the public sphere, as well as about the nature of the competing nation making projects that have been expressed through strategic representations of childhood. On and off the island, members of the elite and middle classes have traditionally enjoyed greater access to civil society and political decision-making processes. Many anti-Batista insurgents and members of Castro's provisional government were white, urban Catholics from privileged families. Moreover, in spite of Cuba's historically high rates of literacy relative to other Latin American nations, and the well-documented patterns of enthusiastic media consumption by

Cubans of all social classes even before the Revolution, the civic sphere in which revolutionary discourses were created and contested between 1959 and 1962 remained a largely middle-class space, a site in which privileged urban citizens debated the future of the Revolution before Castro's 1960 campaign to suppress non-state-sponsored institutions, associations, and expression.[36]

It is thus not surprising that counterrevolutionary opposition to the Revolution's radicalization was most common among, though not exclusive to, privileged Cubans. Accordingly, though initiatives to redefine the lives of poor, working-class, and urban children were central to the Revolution's self-definition, the early child-centered political struggles that accompanied its turn toward socialism and sparked the emergence of the exile community were largely fought—on both sides of the Straits of Florida—by members of the Cuban middle class primarily concerned with middle-class children.

Issues of gender were also implicated in the politics of childhood in Havana and Miami. Though women played a significant role in the campaign to overthrow the Batista dictatorship, they were underrepresented in Castro's provisional government and assigned supporting roles in initiatives dedicated to what *machista* revolutionaries considered "women's work." In most cases, the ground-level work of organizing services and programs for young children was done by women. For example, though the revolutionary government prioritized the creation of daycare centers, neither Fidel Castro nor Education Minister Armando Hart attended many opening ceremonies at the new *círculos infantiles*. Given their frequent and visible presence at the inauguration of primary, middle, and high schools, especially those in converted prisons or military forts, this absence is all the more striking. It speaks to the gap between the Revolution's groundbreaking rhetoric of sexual equality and the persistence among the new regime's leadership of a patriarchal Latin American worldview that would reinforce gendered assumptions about the care and education of the island's youngest children at the same time as it underwrote Fidel Castro's increasingly paternalistic relationship to his supporters.[37]

Moreover, the majority of the journalists at the state-sponsored newspapers and magazines that played such a crucial role in the dissemination of revolutionary discourses of childhood were men, often writing columns for women about children's initiatives to which the journalists had little connection. A similar dynamic shaped the counterrevolutionary politics of childhood in Miami, where women played a starring role in the care, protection, and education of exile children, although men occupied most of the leadership positions in exile organizations and media outlets that deployed child-centered discourses in support of the anti-Castro movement.

Though concerned primarily with the use and misuse of the symbolic figure of the child in nationalist politics, this book also asks important questions about flesh-and-blood children's participation in national life. In line with social and cultural norms that proscribe young people's voicing their opinions or making their own decisions, children have historically been barred from participating in formal electoral politics. Children in the Two Cubas and elsewhere have nonetheless been encouraged or compelled to perform other "adult" political duties—rallying at marches and demonstrations as well as participating in mass organizations, intelligence gathering activities, and even military service—in spite of, or perhaps because of, the multiple factors that limit their opportunities to exercise free will or speak on their own behalf.

THE POLITICS OF CHILDHOOD IN CUBA'S REVOLUTION AND EXILE

Since at least the 1898 war of independence and especially after the 1959 Revolution, Cuban children have been important political actors, if not always of their own volition or with full understanding of their actions. Those actions and the meanings attached to them within public discourse have nonetheless had enormous political consequences in both Cuba and the United States.[38] Their centrality to the competing revolutionary and exilic nation-making projects has converted the Cuban child into a nation-maker—and, since 1959, a nation-breaker—who has powerfully influenced the processes of polarization that led to the fragmentation and reformation of the nation into Two Cubas centered around the cities of Havana and Miami.

Approaching the transnational history of the Cuban Revolution and exile through the lens of the child as nation-maker makes visible the pervasive but largely unacknowledged role played by children in nationalist politics and the evolution of the modern nation-state. This is equally true in the history of the United States and other democratic-capitalist nations, where hegemonic notions of childhood continue to imagine it as a protected space of innocence, dependence, and play, as it has been in the socialist world since the 1917 Russian Revolution gave birth to an alternative vision of the nation-state, along with a distinct understanding of childhood that saw generational conflict as a primary engine of historical change and celebrated children as radical political actors.[39] Although tensions between these competing nation-making projects sparked the Cold War in which the politics of Cuban childhood would play out between 1959 and 1962, the presumed malleability of children and their centrality to national destinies has remained one of the fundamental notions around which democratic-capitalist and socialist visions of the future are organized.

This modern metanarrative is a powerfully unifying thread that sutures the politics of childhood in Havana and Miami.[40] It underlies this book's retelling of the story of the Cuban Revolution and exile, an alternative version that emphasizes continuities and recurring trends as much as moments of innovation and rupture. Moreover, this book offers a nuanced consideration of the powerful cultural forces that propelled the 1959 Revolution, forces that are not adequately acknowledged in the structural explanations offered by many scholars.[41] Attention to the contested site of Cuban childhood sheds new light on how the nation's self-definition evolved in the first four years after Fidel Castro's ascent to power, illuminating the processes of cultural change that made possible the Revolution's radicalization. It demonstrates that the revolutionary government's strategic interventions in the realm of Cuban childhood allowed a nation saturated in U.S. commodities, customs, and values to cast off foreign dominance and chart a new vision of the future that nonetheless resonated with historically Cuban aspirations. This book thus challenges the teleologies of collective memory and scholarship that portray the socialist revolution, which was not consolidated until 1961, as an event that sprang spontaneously and fully formed from the hearts of the Cuban people, rather than as a highly polarizing nation-making project that was constructed and contested in a specific historical context.

The theoretical lens of the child as nation-maker sheds new light on the emergence of opposition to the Revolution, the sites from which counterrevolutionary attacks were launched, and the specific strategies selected by the anti-Castro movement. Its focus on the politics of childhood allows us to move beyond class-based analyses in explaining resistance to the Revolution. The suspension of electoral democracy and takeover of private properties and businesses on the island undoubtedly contributed to the growing alienation of privileged Cubans by 1960; however, it was not inevitable that progressive middle-class parents, Catholic clergy, activists, and educators would become counterrevolutionaries, especially given their initial support for the anti-Batista insurgency and the Movimiento 26 de Julio (M-26-7). Without downplaying the importance of conventional political and economic factors to the deterioration of relationships

and the emergence of counterrevolutionary opposition, this book nonetheless demonstrates the powerful role played by children in the emergence of the anti-Castro movement on both sides of the Straits of Florida.
In doing so, it also provides evidence of how an exile community often
understood in ahistorical terms as politically monolithic and static in fact
developed an increasingly hegemonic anti-Castro and anticommunist
agenda over time.

In the pages that follow, this book also offers a new interpretation of the
connections linking events and actors in Havana, Washington, D.C., and
Miami and between exiles and other U.S. Latina/os. It demonstrates that
the U.S. government's support for the growing exile community, though
strategically couched in child-centered terms, was in fact largely motivated by Cold War geopolitical considerations; however, it also reveals the
shared assumptions about the relationship between childhood and the
nation and the future of democracy that underwrote the asymmetrical
relationship between the U.S. federal government and the anti-Castro
movement. It further analyzes the starring role played by children in creating the white, middle-class, and anticommunist identity that facilitated
exiles' acceptance by Miami's Anglo-American majority, many of whom
were initially predisposed to a racialized distrust of Cuban immigrants.
This book's focus on the politics of childhood thus generates new understandings of how Cuban Americans' distance from and position of privilege vis-à-vis other U.S. Latina/os were produced through struggle, rather
than immediately granted in recognition of presumed affinities between
the exile community and the U.S. mainstream.[42]

This book seeks to encourage critical consideration of how Cuban
Americans have and have not shared the experiences of other peoples of
Latin American origin in the United States. Recognizing that historically
contingent differences of power, prestige, and privilege, often linked to
the U.S. government's international relations and foreign policy objectives, have produced dramatic inequities between different Latina/os' life
chances, it nonetheless links the exceptionalist narratives of Cuban American history to other Latina/o stories. In subsequent chapters, the politics of childhood in Havana and Miami is consistently analyzed in light
of the shared Latin American experiences of U.S. imperialist incursion
and subordination to a powerful northern neighbor.[43] It is also framed
as playing a uniquely salient role in an otherwise familiar Latina/o story
of migration, marginalization and struggle, and collective reinvention in
the United States.[44] Viewed through the lens of the child as nation-maker,
Cuban and Cuban American history is clearly revealed as an integral,

if understudied, part of the broader field of hemispheric U.S. Latina/o history.

The politics of childhood, however, is not unique to Latina/os or Latin Americans. Children have been and continue to be central to nation-making projects around the world. Through its exploration of the politics of childhood in Havana and Miami, this book uncovers the shared modern meta-narrative that links children to the destiny of the nation in a wide range of nation-making projects. It also confirms that studies of childhood have much to contribute to our understanding of "adult" history, both domestically and internationally, in times of nation-building, expansion, imperialism, war, peace, and even revolution.

1
FOR THE CHILDREN

José Martí and the Politics of Cuban Childhood,
1898–1958

While living in exile in New York City in 1892, José Martí—poet, journalist, pedagogue, and revolutionary father of the Cuban nation—published an essay titled "Nuestra América." The now classic text is an eloquent statement of Latin American nationalist aspirations, offering an impassioned defense of the region's moral prerogative to pursue its destiny without outside interference. In morally and emotionally resonant language, Martí placed the notion of childhood at the heart of his argument in favor of his island's independence. Since Cubans, he argued, were "children of their progenitors whose vices and virtues they reflect," it was essential that they persevere without compromise in their almost thirty-year struggle for national self-determination. Only a total break from Spain would permit Cubans to move beyond the antidemocratic legacy of the fatherland and realize their individual and shared potential in the context of republican nationhood.[1]

A few weeks later Martí used similarly child-centered language in an essay for *Patria*, a journal founded to mobilize U.S.-resident Cubans and Puerto Ricans for the liberation of their homelands from Spanish colonial rule: "Having been born on Spanish soil is not what the oppressed inhabitants of the Antilles detest in the Spaniard; it is the aggressive and insolent occupation of the country where he embitters and atrophies the lives of his own children. The war is fought against the bad father, not the good one. . . . The Spaniard who detests the country of his children will be uprooted by the very war that he has made necessary. The Spaniard who loves his children . . . will safely live in the republic he is helping to create."[2]

José Martí's affection for young people and his belief in their innate goodness were already familiar to readers of his tender poems for and about children, including *Ismaelillo* and *Los Zapaticos de Rosa*. However, when Martí chose to articulate his expansive (if somewhat undeveloped) vision for Cuba's republican future through an equally evocative child-centered discourse, he gave birth to a visceral and particularly durable brand of nationalism that, while undergirded by a foundational Western metanarrative linking children to the destiny of the modern nation-state, would play a uniquely important role in the island's subsequent and competing nation-making projects. Even before the Spanish-Cuban-American War was launched, Martí's pro-independence writings had engendered a uniquely permeable Cuban politics of childhood in which a Rousseauian belief in the innate virtue of children and a Lockean notion of the child as tabula rasa would coexist in dynamic tension with repeatedly frustrated efforts to establish honest, effective, and egalitarian government on the island. This tension would be exacerbated by growing U.S. hegemony in Cuba after the end of the war in 1898, driven by the North American belief that Cubans' racial inferiority and political immaturity left them ill-equipped for independence.

As a result, debates about childhood became a powerful force in the island's national life throughout the first half of the twentieth century. Even as Cuban leaders increasingly turned to children to express competing political values and to exercise control over state and society, everyday citizens also relied on their understandings of childhood to measure the nation's progress toward modernity and assess their government's legitimacy—or lack thereof. Child-centered discourses similarly continued to reflect U.S. reservations about Cubans' political maturity and capacity for self-rule, as well as Cubans' own self-doubts about their ability to build a functional and moral republic for their children to inherit.

Between 1902 and 1959, conservative Cuban elites and a growing portion of the U.S.-allied middle class also relied on children to justify the political and economic structures that protected their wealth and positions of prominence in a society marred by instability, corruption, and raced, classed, and gendered inequality. At the same time, however, progressive Cubans continued to insist that discussions about childrearing, welfare, and education should be approached as Martí had framed them—as an integral part of the island's ongoing quest for sovereignty, democratic government, and multiracial social justice. These actors' overlapping and conflicting goals, expressed through morally and emotionally resonant representations of childhood and the targeting of actual children as a means of realizing a wide range of political, economic, social, and cultural objectives, came to comprise a republican politics of childhood that dramatically articulated the unfinished nature of the Cuban struggle for independence and helped propel the island toward a second nationalist revolution in 1959.

CHILDHOOD, THE SPANISH-CUBAN-AMERICAN WAR, AND U.S. OCCUPATION, 1898–1902

José Martí's writing reveals the extent to which the establishment of an independent multiracial Cuban republic depended on claiming, or rather reclaiming, the image of the child as a central trope of national identity. While many modern states had similarly drawn on the figure of the child in support of their nation-making projects, Martí's politics of childhood possessed a particularly visceral power originating in the dialectic between the liberatory discourse of the independence struggle and U.S. resistance to Cuban self-rule. This resistance was frequently expressed through a competing discourse of childhood that allowed North American commentators to dismiss *independentistas'* aspirations toward autonomy and self-determination.

As early as the 1820s, U.S. political leaders had identified Cuba for potential annexation. Annexationist interest grew during the decade preceding the U.S. Civil War, especially among southern politicians, who coveted the island's fertile agricultural land and saw its large African-origin slave population as essential to the expansion of their plantation-based society. Echoing the racialized and infantilizing discourses that had justified the expansionist Mexican-American War between 1846 and 1848, advocates of Cuban annexation stressed Cubans' racial inferiority, political and psychological immaturity, and incapacity to assume "adult" responsibility for the care and nurture of an independent republic. Expressing these sentiments in 1859, Richard Henry Dana's travelogue *To Cuba and Back* likened Cuba to "a child at play" with the idea of liberty but unable to achieve it, because its citizens lacked the qualities of the Anglo-Saxon race which were essential to self-government.[3]

Almost forty years later, poet Robert Manners similarly used discourses of childhood to emphasize Cuba's racially derived unsuitability for self-rule, to discount the hard-won victories that had brought Cubans' thirty-year independence struggle to its decisive moment by 1898, and to justify the last-minute intervention of the United States in the third and final war against Spain. Characterizing Cuba as "the loveliest child that Nature gave" into the protective care of the United States, Manners dramatized even while denigrating the vain efforts of "Cuba's valiant children" to establish an independent nation.[4] Echoing the theme of Cuba's vulnerability and inability to act decisively on its own, North American political cartoonists began to depict the island as a fair Spanish señorita in need of rescue by a heroically masculine U.S. military; however, after the war ended, cartoonists also turned to the figure of the child to counter the unexpected resistance of much of the Liberation Army to U.S. intervention.

North American political cartoons, like the discourses opposing Cuban independence that accompanied them, also reflected popular ideas about race that had informed U.S. relations with indigenous peoples during the era of westward expansion and animated increasing U.S. contact with non-white people and nations overseas.[5] To that end, more sympathetic cartoons depicting Cubans as eager for U.S. tutelage often featured docile white boys and girls; however, those that condemned *independentista* critiques of the ongoing U.S. military occupation frequently included dirty, half-naked, and ill-behaved black children. The North American media thus interpreted the multiracial insurgent leaders' desire to assume immediate control of their own government as a shocking display of ingratitude and—as is so often the case with a spoiled child throwing a temper tantrum—an irrational refusal to accept badly needed help from their (white) elders.[6]

Racialized and infantilized media representations also reinforced popular notions of the United States as a benevolent father, whose duty to protect and uplift "backward" nations—for their own good—exposed him to the immature resentments of the nonwhite peoples on whose behalf he selflessly acted. Most important, they justified U.S. military rule on the island in the immediate aftermath of the war as a measure taken to protect both U.S. and Cuban interests, lest the island fall into the hands of "an irresponsible government of half-breeds."[7]

In resisting these racially derived North American representations of Cuba, José Martí and other *independentista* leaders, including Antonio Maceo and Raimundo Cabrera, had already begun to formulate a counterdiscourse of childhood to mobilize support for a multiracial independence struggle.[8] Even as U.S. military officers, journalists, and politicians continued to represent Cubans as dark, childlike savages unfit for self-government, "the child featured in Cuban insurgent rhetoric . . . worked to create an antiracist Cuban nation—in direct opposition to the child featured in U.S. political rhetoric that upheld racial difference within and outside the United States."[9]

Martí had long drawn on child-centered language to argue that battle-weary Cuban patriots must continue their liberatory struggle unaided. His own years of exile in New York had opened his eyes to North American

This cartoon is one of many racialized portrayals of the nascent Cuban nation to appear in the turn-of-the-century U.S. media. These images critiqued Cubans' desire for independence while emphasizing their presumed incapacity for self-rule and need for American tutelage. *From* Chicago Tribune, *April 14, 1901.*

imperial designs on Cuba and exposed him to the persistent racial inequalities that continued to mar the U.S. republican project; as a result, he believed that accepting U.S. assistance would almost certainly impose unacceptable limits on the nascent Cuban Republic's sovereignty. Thus, although Cubans had once had "a childlike confidence in the certain help of the United States," Martí insisted that their collective coming of age—made manifest in the construction of an autonomous, multiracial, and egalitarian nation rested on winning the war against Spain without northern intervention.[10]

Martí further elaborated his understanding of the relationship between childhood and the nation within an explicitly egalitarian framework. Since he believed that liberty and equality were closely linked to literacy and culture, Martí's vision of a color-blind Cuban republic featured a comprehensive public school system that would prepare boys and girls for citizenship in a multiracial democracy. The success of the republican nation-making project rested on the care and education of these children since, he argued, "there will be no true growth for the nation . . . until the child is taught" to uphold its ideals. Within this vision, Cuban patriots would wage war to create the future nation "for the children," but the island's youngest citizens would also play a role—albeit a largely symbolic one—in constructing what Martí called "moral republicanism" since "they are the ones who know how to love."[11] These words converted children into an important mobilizing force in the independence struggle and a powerful symbol of the longed-for future nation that would continue to resonate with Cubans of widely varying political persuasions throughout the twentieth century.

The conclusion of the Spanish-Cuban-American War did not usher in the period of peace, prosperity, and self-determination of which nationalists had dreamed. In accordance with the terms of the 1898 Treaty of Paris, the Spanish Crown surrendered control of the island to the U.S. government rather than local leadership. Moreover, though the fourth clause of the Joint Resolution on Cuba (known as the Teller Amendment) had foresworn formal U.S. colonization of the island, it nonetheless provided for an unspecified period of North American occupation to pacify the war-torn society and postponed Cuban self-government to a date to be determined by their new overseers.

On January 1, 1899, the United States assumed formal possession of Cuba from Spain, and a military governor was appointed to oversee progress toward eligibility for self-rule—measured by a set of political, economic, social, and cultural preconditions to be established and evaluated exclusively by the island's new trustees. However, not all of them were committed to the idea of Cuban independence. For more than seventy-five years, many North American political leaders had clung to the goal of annexation, a pursuit that was central to the ideal of Manifest Destiny that continued to inspire the growth and expansion of the United States. High-ranking officials in the McKinley and Roosevelt administrations argued that the Teller Amendment, while prohibiting the annexation of Cuba as a result of the victory over Spain or as the consequence of U.S. military occupation, did not preclude the possibility of union at a later date.

These officials also pressed for policies that would facilitate the eventual acquisition of the island. These included the development of reciprocal trade agreements and national institutions compatible with U.S. political and economic structures, the recruitment and cultivation of local allies (especially among the islands' conservative, land-owning white elite), the suppression of Spanish colonial customs, and the widespread Americanization of Cuban society and culture—all of which were presented as necessary preconditions for self-government but would equally well serve the goal of the island's incorporation as a U.S. territory.

Leonard Wood, the island's military governor-general from 1900 to 1902, shared the belief that preparation for independence under North American tutelage might simultaneously serve as an impetus toward annexation. While rejecting the acquisition of Cuba by force, he nonetheless hoped that a brief experience of self-rule might satisfy the people's desire for "theoretical liberty" and remove their resistance to union with their northern neighbor.[12] Wood believed, as did many other U.S. military leaders and politicians, that the grounds for this eventuality must be laid through the cultivation of a critical mass of proannexationists on the island, a goal his administration pursued by targeting Cuban children. In line with Progressive Era thought stressing the close relationship between the care and education of the child and the construction of a modern, democratic, and prosperous nation, Wood's military government quickly set out to prepare the island for self-rule—in harmony with U.S. strategic and commercial interests on the island and without precluding the possibility of annexation—through the creation of a new system of public education geared toward the production of citizens aligned with North America.

Governor Wood's policies sought to remake Cuban society through the extension of U.S.-style education to all children in Cuba.[13] Modeled on their counterparts in the United States, new public schools set out to disabuse Cuban children of their Spanish cultural inheritance, replacing the Catholic instruction and rote learning methods that had dominated Cuban colonial schools with progressive pedagogical approaches designed to inculcate students with the "modern" values necessary to the smooth functioning of a democratic-capitalist society. These included the virtues of hard work, frugality, and self-discipline; respect for the law and property; civic engagement and prudent participation in electoral politics; obedience to duly constituted political authority; and adherence to a Protestant Christian spiritual tradition.

To that end, children in U.S.-occupied Cuba enrolled in coeducational schools modeled after the Ohio state system of public education, attended classes taught by teachers trained at special Harvard summer school programs for Cuban educators, and studied English, U.S. history, geography, and civics, in addition to other subjects taught with Spanish translations of U.S. textbooks. The role of Catholic clergy on local school boards and their influence in the public schools was strictly curtailed, and religious instruction was restricted to private schools, which continued to enroll a significant proportion of children from the island's elite white families.[14] However, even as U.S. officials and private citizens launched a new educational system to prepare Cuban children for citizenship in a modernizing nation, their perception of the island's people as racially inferior and immature gave them grave doubts about Cubans' ability to take charge of the education of their own children. Indeed, Cuban teachers sent to Harvard in 1901 were described in the U.S. media as "grown up children . . . who could not understand the significance of what they saw."[15]

Paternalist and racist though this educational campaign undoubtedly was, the effects of the military government's investment in Cuban schools were immediate and dramatic. In the first year of Wood's administration, the graft and political trafficking in lucrative teaching appointments that had characterized the Spanish colonial educational system was eliminated, teacher salaries were raised (in some cases exceeding those paid in the United States by as much as 80 percent), and school enrollments skyrocketed from 21,000 to over 100,000. By 1900, Cuba had a larger proportion of its overall population enrolled in school than Mexico, Argentina, Spain, France, or Japan. In 1902, the Ministry of Education dedicated 4 million pesos of public funds—four times more than Spain had spent in 1894—to educational programs and the construction of new facilities.[16] Moreover, this initial growth in enrollments was substantially consistent across Cuba's regions, including both urban and rural areas, and distributed more or less evenly among the island's white and black children.[17]

By the end of the occupation period, U.S. military administrators had clearly demonstrated their concern for the care and education of Cuban children and had placed enormous resources at their disposal. However, their efforts were motivated less by altruism than by long-range strategic considerations. With very few exceptions, most occupation officials saw the establishment of a North American–inspired public school system as a means of guaranteeing the nurture of future generations in line with U.S. interests, rather than as a way to support Cuban aspirations to national autonomy, balanced economic development, or social justice.[18]

At the same time, the significant presence of proindependence Cubans in school classrooms and administrative posts ensured that teachers and curricula also sought to instill in children their nationalist, antiracist, and anti-imperialist values. Graduates of this deeply bifurcated educational system would accordingly struggle to reconcile their patriotic education with their growing frustration at the extent to which the island's political and economic development continued to be curtailed by vestiges of Spanish colonialism and ongoing U.S. interference.[19] Thus, well before the establishment of the First Republic, children had been pressed into the service of U.S. efforts to consolidate political and economic control of the new nation, even as Martí-inspired *independentistas* struggled to retain control of the hearts and minds of the island's young people—and through them, to shape the destiny of their republic. This struggle for control of the island's educational system quickly transformed childhood into a site in which U.S. imperial designs, accommodated by a conservative U.S.-aligned Cuban elite, would inevitably collide with the more progressive nation-making project of the mixed-race Cuban middle and working classes.

CHILDHOOD AND THE FIRST REPUBLIC, 1902–1933

In 1901, the U.S. government withdrew its army from the island in anticipation of the declaration of the Cuban Republic. Formal independence, however, was made conditional on the acceptance of the deeply unpopular Platt Amendment to the Cuban Constitution, which gave the United States the right to intervene in the island's political affairs and established the U.S. coaling and naval base at Guantánamo. Despite widespread protests to the amendment, Senator Orville H. Platt (R-CT) dismissed Cuban demands for immediate and unconditional independence as the product of only the "most radical element of the Cuban electorate," "irresponsible as children . . . dazzled with the prospects of at last being their own masters."[20] Their desire for freedom summarily ignored, Cubans thus greeted the proclamation of their republic in 1902 with joy and bitterness, relief and disappointment, and, above all, a profound uncertainty about the true nature of the island's independence.

Perhaps more damaging to the Cuban national psyche than the Platt Amendment, however, were the stark ideological differences that divided the new republic's leadership and defined its competing nation-making projects. *Independentista* heroes, committed to Martí's modern-liberal political values and to the establishment of an egalitarian multiracial republic, occupied most elected positions in President Tomás Estrada Palma's inaugural government. However, U.S. oversight had ensured that the island's bureaucracy was dominated by conservative white elite Cubans, many of whom had opposed the break from Spain and now supported annexation. Those few among them who favored independence espoused a corporatist vision of the Cuban nation, organized by a strong centralized state that would ensure order and harmony by distributing its resources among the distinct sectors of society while preserving the raced and classed social hierarchies of the colonial era.[21]

Conservative elites clung to a colonial political culture that viewed Cuba as racially unequipped for self-government and remained deeply suspicious of the former slaves and poor whites who had risen to positions of prominence through their participation in the independence struggle. For many of these wealthy Spanish-descent Cubans, sovereignty and democratic government would lead inevitably to irrational mob rule by their mixed-race inferiors; only the firm hand of the "better classes" and their U.S. tutors could guide and protect the infant republic as it grew into adulthood. Elites in the government and bureaucracy thus used their new political power to infuse the island's emerging civil society with a discourse of "negative Cubanidad" that echoed U.S. racially derived doubts about Cubans' ability to govern themselves.[22] This discourse exposed the shadow side of Martí's liberatory politics of childhood, embedding a strain of self-doubt deep in the island's political culture that would facilitate its continuing dependence on and domination by its powerful North American father figure.

Buoyed by the initial euphoria of independence, more progressive Cubans persisted in hoping that their nation would rapidly develop into Martí's moral republic. These hopes were not totally unfounded. U.S. military occupation and investment had helped lay the foundation for democratic government and had rebuilt the island's war-ravaged infrastructure; a liberal constitution had been promulgated and universal suffrage granted, new roads and railroads had been built, and sugar mills were restored to operational condition. Spending on public health and schools had raised expectations that the next generation of Cuban children would be healthier, more educated, and better equipped to confront the challenges and opportunities of a modernizing economy and society.

However, many Cubans recognized that the alarming growth of U.S. investment in the island's economy and the United States's constitutionally guaranteed right to intervene severely limited the autonomy of their fledgling government. The 1903 U.S.-Cuban Reciprocity Treaty, which gave Cuban tobacco and sugar preferential access to the powerful northern market in exchange for reduced tariffs on U.S. imports, further exemplified the possibilities and perils contained in the new nation's increasingly intimate ties to the United States.[23] The resulting tensions between the imposition of a mediated sovereignty on the child republic and Cubans' deferred dreams of self-determination would engender ever greater collective frustration and self-doubt that played themselves out in the complex interaction between notions of childhood, adulthood, and nationhood, the strategic political deployment of the figure of the child, and the experiences of actual children.[24]

Resistance to the limitations imposed by the Platt Amendment and the Reciprocity Treaty produced different responses among different sectors of Cuban society. White elites quickly reestablished themselves in the U.S.-supported sugar industry and focused on recovering the wealth lost during the war, arguing that Cuba would only achieve full independence when its politically backward mixed-race masses had proved themselves worthy of full membership in the community of modern nations. This quest for modernity sparked initiatives to rationalize the island's political, judicial, and bureaucratic structures and introduce new systems of agriculture and land tenure. These initiatives also sought to promote scientific and technological knowledge and increase general levels of literacy, culture, and morality among the campesinos and working classes. Adopting the values and customs of the United States, the elites argued, would liberate Cuba from its backward colonial past; Cuba needed to turn away from its primitive, African heritage and eradicate the superstitions and customs that stood in the way of the republic's march toward modernity.

Memories of the multiracial independence struggle nonetheless remained a guiding force in early republican politics. The prestige of the Liberation Army's Afro-Cuban leaders and the Martían vision of "a new republic that would be not only politically independent but egalitarian and inclusive" contributed to the evolution of competing notions of nationhood by the end of Estrada Palma's first term as president. Within another decade, political instability and social upheaval, combined with the threat of another U.S. military intervention to restore order, helped justify the racially motivated repression of the Partido Independiente de Color in 1912, on the basis that its activities represented "a threat to the very survival of the republic." At the same time, the state's massive subsidization of immigration from Spain reflected elite beliefs that the key to the nation's development lay in "whitening" the population; left unchecked, the current trend toward "Africanization" would lead to political, economic, and cultural ruin.[25]

The political cleavage of the nation along classed and raced lines found expression in an elite-generated moral panic that inverted Martí's multiracial nationalist discourse by linking an imagined black threat to the Cuban nation with widespread fears of the danger that Afro-Cuban religious practices supposedly represented to children. Many whites and even some middle-class black Cubans feared African *brujería*—witchcraft—believing that it drew its power from rituals involving human sacrifice and even cannibalism; popular belief further held that *los negros brujos*, or "black wizards," especially coveted the cadavers of white children for use in their gruesome rites. During the first two decades of independence, Cuban journalists frequently reported the alleged kidnapping and murder of children, especially of small blonde girls, as part of African religious ceremonies.

Though lacking substantive evidence to corroborate the cases, media coverage and rumor repeatedly pointed at *los negros brujos* to explain the otherwise inexplicable illness or death of a white child. In 1906, the death of a young white girl in Pinar del Río was attributed to *brujería*; in 1907, another *brujo* was detained and his home searched following the death of a child, even though a doctor had previously certified that the death was caused by meningitis. When this finding was confirmed by an autopsy, the Cuban press nonetheless insisted on reporting the event as "*brujería* in Havana."[26] By 1922, child-centered discourses had been used with great effect to discredit Afro-Cuban claims to equal citizenship. Laws were passed to repress the practices of *brujería* and traditional medicine, and a resolution passed by the secretary of the interior banned all Afro-Cuban religious ceremonies and dances on the grounds that they were opposed to culture and civilization. Moreover, he further claimed, "experience showed" that they frequently "led to robberies, kidnappings, or killings of children of the white race."

The fears of elites and more conservative members of the middle class that Cuba's African heritage presented an obstacle to the achievement of modern nationhood, articulated through the moral panic over black witchcraft and the cannibalistic murder of white children, reflected and reinforced the associations Martí had drawn between children and the Cuban nation. His writings, however, had emphasized the children's importance to the construction of a moral multiracial republic; elite obsession with the small blonde victims of black wizards re-created white children as the exclusive embodiment of a modernizing Cuba threatened by African primitiveness and degeneracy, exacerbating the differences between the nation-making projects of conservative, U.S.-allied elites and the island's more progressive middle classes and mixed-race majority.

In spite of growing race- and class-based cleavages in their society, Cubans of all backgrounds nonetheless continued to share Martí's belief that the future of the nation depended on the education of all the island's children. The island's Afro-Cuban parents adhered passionately to this belief, tirelessly seeking access to an unsegregated public school system for their sons and daughters. By the 1920s, many young blacks had graduated from the public school system and were increasingly qualifying for skilled and professional jobs that offered new possibilities for social mobility. Exposure to the racist assumptions of elite Cuban and U.S. teachers and North American curricula, however, worked to estrange black children from their cultural heritage, producing a growing middle-class black community that sought to distance itself from African-derived customs and to use education as a point of access to a modernizing society.[27]

During the first two decades of the First Republic, as efforts to define the Cuban nation increasingly diverged along lines of race and class, North American politicians, entrepreneurs, and missionaries continued to bring Progressive Era notions of childhood and education to Cuba as part of a larger strategic effort to safeguard U.S. interests on the island. Their concern for the nation's young people, though in many cases well-intended, was directed at remaking Cuban society through interventions in the lives of children. At the same time, increasing U.S. political and economic hegemony in Cuba was reflected in the rapid succession of weak and illegitimate governments that alternately relied on North American patronage and chafed at external limitations on their autonomy.[28] Governmental inefficacy and political instability reinforced elite Cubans' doubts about their fellow citizens' capacity for self-rule and helped reinscribe normative assumptions—both on and off the island—about U.S.-Cuban relations and the "proper" roles of the United States as benevolent father figure and Cuba as a grateful and obedient child.[29]

As U.S. investment in the island's infrastructure, agricultural land, sugar mills, and mines continued to expand, many North American corporations sponsored the construction and operation of schools by organizations concerned with the ongoing inability of the Cuban public school system to provide adequate education to all children. In doing so, the companies underwrote the exposure of thousands of children to Anglo-American culture and values even as they anticipated the future commercial benefit represented by the cultivation of a new generation of workers trained in English and according to U.S. standards. With these goals in mind, the United Fruit Company provided Quaker and Methodist groups with land, building materials, and funds to establish schools in Holguín, Gibara, Banes, Puerto Padre, and Guaro. Hershey sponsored a Presbyterian school in Aguacate, and the Guantánamo and Constancia Sugar companies opened schools near mills.[30]

Protestant mission schools undoubtedly provided previously unavailable opportunities for Cuban boys and girls to improve their lives through study and vocational preparation, especially in remote rural sectors of the island. However, in appointing themselves caretakers of the nation's children, U.S. missionaries reawoke Cubans' nagging insecurities about their capacity for self-determination by making visible the republic's presumptive failure to take responsibility for educating its youngest citizens. They further contributed to the symbolic undercutting of Cuban nationhood—and, by extension, citizens' claims to adulthood—by questioning Cubans' fitness as parents. Missionaries criticized local childrearing practices, which they felt produced willful, selfish, and undisciplined young people, and sought to redeem Cuban children by exposing them to North American role models, curricula, and teaching methods. Methodist Edgar Nessman praised the "character building experiences" of student government and 4-H clubs: "It is exciting to watch the progress of youngsters brought up in an authoritarian culture as they learn to work together, each holding some responsibility for the success of the group." The Methodist Agricultural and Industrial School proclaimed as its mission the preparation of Cuban children "for democracy by trying to practice democracy at all levels within the school culture."[31]

However, the democratic values of North American educators frequently came into conflict with and were subordinated to the imperative of maintaining U.S. hegemony on the island. As a result, much of the preparation received by Cuban children—including future dictator Fulgencio Batista, who attended a U.S.-sponsored school in his rural hometown—was informed by explicitly antidemocratic thought. Teachers and curricula discouraged Cuban children from seeing themselves, their parents, or compatriots as qualified for the mature enjoyment of national self-determination. Textbooks rewrote the history of the Spanish-Cuban-American War, instructing students that their republic had come into existence as a result of heroic U.S. military intervention in their failed independence struggle. Geography and civics texts similarly emphasized Cuba's dependence on the United States and North Americans' faithful discharging of their moral obligation toward the island, and they reminded Cuban students of their corresponding duty to demonstrate gratitude to their northern benefactor.

This revisionist history also allowed North Americans to dismiss Cuban critiques of ongoing U.S. involvement in the island's affairs and frame as childish ingratitude their support for policies that placed national priorities above U.S. interests. In 1915, when the Ministry of Education repealed a law stipulating mandatory English-language instruction for Cuban children, an affronted journalist at the *Memphis Commercial Appeal* reminded readers that "it was the people of the United States who gave Cubans their freedom" and concluded that "Cuba has not been a grateful nation." The U.S.-expatriate newspaper *Havana Post* similarly observed that it "may seem to some to be rather ungracious . . . for the Cubans to cut the language of their deliverers from the public school curriculum."[32] These arguments relied on distorted historical memory to remind Cubans of their role as dependent children in perpetual debt to a benevolent northern father.[33] In doing so, they reinforced the ideological framework undergirding U.S. claims to the right of intervention in the island's affairs and bolstered their commitment to ensuring that the education of the next generation of Cuban citizens proceeded in line with U.S. interests.

Debates about the public school system—both its dominance by outside influence and its failure to meet the unceasing demands for more and better rural facilities—became increasingly politicized in the 1920s, when Cuban nationalists who had long called for the repeal of the Platt Amendment also began to insist that true independence would be impossible without the fulfillment of Martí's vision of democratic education for all children.[34] This new wave of nationalist ferment, expressed powerfully through child-centered discourses, helped propel Gerardo Machado to the presidency in 1925. Machado's initial populist appeal rested in large part on his much-publicized efforts to build schools; by 1926, student enrollments had reached a high of between 63 and 71 percent.[35] However, as the Machado administration quickly deteriorated into tyranny, the inability of any Cuban government to establish an autonomous and egalitarian nation without estranging local elites and angering the United States became heartbreakingly clear.

During the upheaval that came to be known as the Machadato, wealthy white Cubans and more conservative sectors of the middle class allied themselves with the dictator and U.S. leaders against socialist trade unions, peasant farmers, and a landless black underclass. The collision between elite Cuban nation-making projects and the aspirations of progressive, mixed-race, and working-class sectors of society sparked the brutal repression of the Cuban Socialist Party and an explosion of anti-U.S. sentiment that would eventually bring down the dictator.

This process was driven in large part by a generation of radicalized urban adolescents and young people who, although educated in U.S.-sponsored schools and mostly sympathetic to North American political ideals, had become disillusioned by northern efforts to curtail Cuban sovereignty. Frustrated to the point of violence by the gap between their vision of a moral republic and the increasingly embedded corruption and inefficacy of their government, they led a revolution that culminated in Machado's overthrow in 1933. Reinfusing—albeit briefly—Cuban politics and society with the virtue and idealism Martí had attributed to the island's youth, their dedication to the apostle of Cuban independence would contribute powerfully to establishing his vision as the singular legitimate expression of Cuban nationhood and ensure that the politics of childhood would continue to play a constitutive role in the nation's ongoing quest for self-determination.

CHILDHOOD AND THE SECOND REPUBLIC, 1933–1958

After the collapse of the Machado regime and the 1934 repeal of the Platt Amendment, conditions were once again ripe for Cubans to try to realize their competing visions of modern nationhood. Communists, peasants, and sugar workers, in tandem with a vibrant urban labor movement, struggled to revive Martí's aspirations for a multiracial and egalitarian republic, while U.S.-allied conservative forces sought to restore the relative order and stability of the pre-Machado republic, in part by granting significant concessions to workers. The concessions improved the living conditions of many working-class families but, together with the persistence of socioeconomic inequalities dating back to the colonial era, contributed to the growing salience of racial and class identities in Cuban society. Most Cubans nonetheless shared a new sense of resolve to resist U.S. hegemony on the island, to assert their right to self-determination, and to prioritize Cuban over North American interests.

This surge of nationalist sentiment was expressed through efforts to reduce North American influence on the education of Cuban children. A new government led by the left-leaning Partido Auténtico issued nationalist textbooks to replace North American materials in common use. Particularly offensive were U.S. textbooks that instructed children in a version of the Spanish-Cuban-American War that featured U.S. soldiers as the heroic rescuers of a failing Cuban insurgency, emphasizing the island's vulnerability, dependence, and continuing need for U.S. tutelage.[36] Cuban nationalists argued that North American textbooks alienated Cuban children from their history and culture and prevented them from developing the self-confidence and patriotic spirit that would allow future generations to exercise a more substantive national sovereignty than that enjoyed by their parents.

U.S. observers responded to the nationalist ferment on the island with indignation and disbelief. North American politicians and journalists reminded Cubans of their liberation by the U.S. military and ongoing dependence on U.S. benevolence and guidance, dismissing Cubans' pretensions to charting their own political course as expressions of immaturity and ingratitude. Journalist Henry Phillips decried Cuba as "the problem stepchild of the United States," adding that "while Cuba owes her very existence as a nation to the United States, her gratitude and friendliness have been of a most doubtful character."[37]

In spite of U.S. resistance to the upsurge in Cuban nationalism, the convening of a second Constitutional Convention in 1939 ensured that children would remain central to debate over the future of the republic. Cuban control over the education of Cuban children was accordingly enshrined in the 1940 Constitution, a progressive document that strongly reflected the Martían vision of a sovereign and egalitarian nation-state. It stated that all education would "be inspired in a spirit of Cubanness" and would have as its goal the nurture of "the conscience of the educated, love of fatherland, its democratic institutions and all those who have fought for them." The Constitution similarly required that teachers of Cuban literature, history, geography, civics, and government be Cuban by birth, and that textbooks be written by authors who had been born on the island. It further guaranteed the right of parents to choose public or private, secular or religious education for their children.[38]

Cubans overwhelmingly supported the provisions of their new Constitution. However, disagreement over the guarantee of the right to private education revealed that they had yet to resolve the conflict between the competing race- and class-inflected visions of the republic that had brought down the Machado regime. Decrying the dramatic increase in private school enrollments over the last decade, Communist Party leader Juan Marinello linked the expansion of private education to the growth of racial and socioeconomic inequality in Cuban society, asserting in 1940 that "all secondary and technical education of any value is dispensed in schools for white kids."[39]

Marinello's objections to the growth of elitist and racially exclusive private schooling were not unfounded. With the onset of the Great Depression, the island's primary export economy fell into dire straits, prompting severe reductions in education spending. The cuts disproportionately affected schools in rural areas and working-class neighborhoods, where teacher shortages and the deterioration of facilities, as well as increases in poverty and the numbers of working children, drove student enrollments to their lowest level in the entire republican era. At the same time, however, the number of private schools on the island began to multiply in response to the inadequacies of the public education system.

With the growth of the Cuban middle class by the end of the decade, the number of parents who made enormous financial sacrifices to enroll their children in private schools also expanded. These parents sought to ensure their children's future social mobility through an education that would prepare them for university and thus for white-collar jobs. Having children in private schools also signified many Cubans' aspiration to class mobility. Since attending a private school confirmed a child's, and his or her family's, membership in the upper classes of Cuban society, many parents of humble origin and means struggled to pay for the tuition, books, and uniforms that enhanced their children's and their own social standing.

By the time of the Constitutional Convention, then, widespread perceptions of private education as the key to both future success and present social status reinforced the raced and classed hierarchies that delineated the Second Republic's competing nation-making projects. Marinello and other progressive leaders argued that steps needed to be taken to combat class elitism and racial discrimination in private schools, which they condemned as antidemocratic, un-Cuban, and an obstacle to the achievement of authentic national autonomy and social justice. Supported by the Communist Party and several prominent Afro-Cuban societies, proposed laws to regulate private education attracted considerable public support; they died, however, in a Congress dominated by wealthy elites, most of whom had children enrolled in the capital's most exclusive schools.[40]

As a result, the growth of private education continued unchecked. By the 1950s, up to 35 percent of the primary school population attended private elementary schools; another 150 *colegios, academias,* and *institutos* provided private secondary education to thousands of middle- and upper-class Cuban adolescents.[41] The best of these predominantly Catholic institutions were clustered in the capital, but several religious orders opened schools in provincial cities as well. At the same time, while educational projects sponsored by U.S. entrepreneurs and missionaries continued to alleviate some of the pressures on understaffed and underfunded public schools, they never succeeded in providing access for all. Many children in rural areas attended classes in one-room huts with palm-thatched roofs and dirt floors—and counted themselves lucky to be studying at all. According to the 1953 census, only slightly more than half of all Cuban children attended school.[42]

The rapid expansion of private education not only made visible the persistent problems of racial and socioeconomic inequality that plagued Cuba; it also reinforced those inequalities, producing and policing a series of spatial and cultural boundaries between privileged private school students and their poor, rural, and dark-skinned public school counterparts. For children and their parents, the day-to-day experiences of life within those boundaries would normalize the hierarchical insertion of these boys and girls into a deeply stratified society after graduation. Observers of the "disproportionate increase of private school enrollments" thus increasingly worried that the persistent failure to provide all Cuban children with equal access to quality education would only "intensify social class divisions."[43] The continuing expansion of private education in a nation defined by a morally and emotionally resonant politics of childhood would inevitably be understood as yet another failure of the government to realize Martí's vision of a multiracial and egalitarian republic.

The prevalence of private schools also came to be seen as symbolic of U.S. dominance on the island and the ongoing limitations it placed on the nation's sovereignty. In spite of directives established by the 1940 Constitution, private school curricula continued to rely on North American materials. They also offered extensive English-language programs taught by native-speaking foreign teachers. In the best U.S.-affiliated schools in Havana, English songs, games, and activities were introduced as early as kindergarten, and by first grade children could recite their ABCs in both languages. Private schools also uniformly sought to prepare children—more often boys than girls—for postsecondary education at colleges and universities in the United States. Accordingly, throughout the 1940s and 1950s, public debate remained focused on the pressing need to reduce North American influence over Cuban education, both public and private.

Nationalist leaders decried the pernicious impact of U.S.-centric curricula on the national psyche, arguing that it limited the ability of Cuban children to develop a strong cultural identity or locate themselves within the framework of a meaningful national history. In 1949, Professor Plácido Lugris y Beceiro lamented that students were not being taught to value the achievements of their *mambí* forefathers. He challenged his fellow citizens to "ask any school-age child who were the men that sacrificed all . . . in order to give us a free and independent homeland and you will see that more than 50 percent don't know more than half a dozen names. Inquire then, who have been the Cubans in the arts, in sciences, or in sports who have carried the name of Cuba gloriously through other latitudes, and one won't even arrive at that limit." Lugris y Beceiro also chastised parents and educators for failing to inculcate Cuban children with an appropriately patriotic spirit, urging them to "make a list of the principal Cuban patriotic dates. Tell the child to explain what it is that each one commemorates and we will have an unpleasant surprise. . . . Something that we should be immensely proud of is almost completely unknown to school-age children."[44]

Nationalists also worried about the effect of U.S. popular culture on the formation of the next generation of Cuban citizens. As part of efforts to nurture pro-U.S. sentiment on the island, the Boy, Girl, and Cub Scouts had established thriving troops on the island by the 1920s. *Escoutismo*, or scouting, had quickly spread to the provinces, with branches in Matanzas, Cienfuegos, Camagüey, Banes, and Santiago de Cuba, as well as Havana. By the 1950s, approximately 2,500 Cuban girls and boys were part of the Scouts de Cuba. The Cuban branches of North American civic organizations like the Rotary and Lions Clubs also arranged activities for local members' children to expose them to the superiority of middle-class Anglo-Saxon American culture and values. Cuban children across the island participated in these U.S.-sponsored clubs, activities, and events. Some even celebrated North American holidays. Georgie Anne Geyer recalls that in Banes, the hometown of 1950s dictator Fulgencio Batista, "on the Fourth of July, the Americans and the Cubans held a huge picnic at the American Club."[45] American clubs in mill communities across the island invited well-positioned Cubans to join them for other celebrations, including Washington's Birthday and Thanksgiving.

North American culture especially permeated the daily lives of middle-class and elite Cuban children in Havana.[46] Many were voracious readers of translated U.S. comic strips and books, and radios broadcast U.S. programs like *Superman* and *Tarzan* into many Cuban homes. A 1956 survey also indicated that many of the capital city's young people attended movies at least once a week.[47] Hollywood deepened many Cuban children's education in the history and culture of the United States, reinforcing the North American values, social norms, and aesthetics that they had encountered at school and that their parents sought to emulate.

Middle- and upper-class Cuban mothers also sought to demonstrate their elevated social status by rearing their children in accordance with received notions of family life in the United States. They followed U.S. columnists' advice on nutrition and the most "modern" childrearing methods and read feature articles translated from U.S. women's magazines in local editions of *Bohemia* and *Vanidades*. These articles offered guidance on toilet training, grooming, play, disciplinary methods, and toy selection, linking modern parenting to the careful selection and consumption of North American goods.

However, given the republic's uneven economic development and dependency on the United States, privileged Cubans' aspirations toward the North American way of life were never entirely successful. Nor did these aspirations usually enable Cuba's middle-class and elite families to interact with expatriate North Americans as social equals. As a result, well-off Cuban children still felt inferior to their expatriate peers, who lived in a few elite neighborhoods and attended school and socialized almost exclusively with other expatriate children. Those children who benefited from a similarly high-quality education and a comparable standard of living were nonetheless often isolated from and envious of the Americanized world inhabited by expatriate children. These circumstances reinforced the Cuban elites' latent lack of confidence in their own cultural identity and limited their ability to take pride in their island nation.

Although unable to completely bridge the gap separating them from North Americans resident on the island, elite Cubans were nonetheless able to use U.S.-inflected notions of childhood to clearly distinguish themselves and their children from poor, working-class, and rural Cubans. Privileged Cubans employed a range of child-centered practices and performances to convert the bodies of their children into signifiers of the family's elevated social status. The foods that well-off boys and girls were served, the medicines or natural remedies with which they were treated (or which they were prohibited from taking) in times of sickness, and the clothes and shoes they wore all came to signify their elevated social status. The care of middle-class and elite children—often overseen by black nannies and domestics—thus became a site in which hierarchical social identities were created and reinforced, articulated through the North American cultural forms that dominated the lives of the well-off during the last prerevolutionary decade.

Social reformers also drew distinctions between the children of the middle and upper classes and those of the poor and working classes, whom they cast as disorderly or deviant, less victims of poverty and inequality than social problems to be solved. Rather than focusing attention on the dramatic discrepancies between the privileged Americanized childhoods of the middle and upper classes and the hunger, hardship, and illness that defined the lives of the majority of the island's youngest citizens, reformers often used these "problem children" to stigmatize the poor and explain away the imbalances and injustices created by a modernizing economy. Neglected children also became a focus for normative claims that inverted

Martí's argument linking the care and education of the child to the fate of the nation. Instead of viewing their disadvantage as a measure of the republic's failures—and as a serious obstacle to its democratic future—poor children and their parents became the focus of a campaign of defamation that framed them as saboteurs of the elite Cuban nation-making project.

Nowhere was this more obvious than in public discussion of the plight of street children. By the late 1940s, Habaneros had grown all too accustomed to the sight of young boys and girls begging on the streets of the capital. This did not, however, move them to explore the links between the growing numbers of displaced or abandoned children and the stagnation of the sugar industry, the increase of rural landlessness, and rapid urbanization. Middle-class social reformers chose instead to point the finger at their supposedly indifferent mothers and fathers. *Los problemas de la niñez actual*, a reformist tract based on Lugris y Beceiro's 1949 address to Havana's Guaimano Masonic Lodge, blamed the desperate situation of Havana's street wretches on the working classes, who "are those who procreate on the largest scale" and "have no consciousness of the responsibility that they contract" in becoming parents.

According to the tract, the unwanted children of the poor were "thrown onto the street," where they inevitably fell first into begging and later into delinquency—a condition to be abhorred less for the danger it posed to any individual child than for the threat it represented to public order. By portraying the failure of poor families to provide for their children as indicating a lack of individual or civic responsibility, the tract reinforced, though in an inverted fashion, Martí's belief that the well-being of the child and that of the nation were inseparable. Moreover, in attributing the existence of street children to the sexual appetites of a promiscuous working class, conservative reformers converted the ragged waifs who lined Havana's broad thoroughfares into pathetic symbols in a morality tale, reinforcing traditional notions of female chastity, Christian marriage, and patriarchal duty by illustrating the disastrous consequences to the individual or society straying from these precepts. They thus precluded the possibility of a more self-searching collective debate in which street children might come to be understood as the innocent victims of the landlessness and unemployment that had displaced and fragmented so many Cuban families—the human cost of the island's uneven development and structural dependence on the United States.

As a result, even well-intentioned reformers concerned with the plight of the nation's children frequently proposed individualistic solutions to the pressing social problems flowing from their nation's frustrated political and economic potential, formulating policies and programs that provided services to unsupervised and neglected children without addressing the roots of the nationwide phenomenon. In order to distract potential delinquents from wrongdoing, towns as small as Guara (population 4,500) and Perico (population 3,200) organized community baseball teams, and 1,600 boys between the ages of nine and thirteen played on sixty Cubanitos teams organized by the Asociación de Béisbol Infantil.

While some middle- and upper-class children belonged to this children' league, Cubanitos was created primarily in order to reach out to disadvantaged youth. Armando Villegas wrote that the league aimed to fight illiteracy and juvenile delinquency by taking boys "off the streets by way of baseball." Expressing the widespread belief that the problems of troubled and neglected boys—for delinquency was seen as an almost exclusively male phenomenon—were primarily the result of individual and familial shortcomings, Villegas proposed to improve their life chances by encouraging them to attend school, training them in self-discipline, and inculcating them with "character and good habits."[48]

These reformist initiatives, though problematic, were most likely well-intentioned. They were nonetheless never matched by a corresponding government commitment to the well-being of the island's most vulnerable young people. In his 1949 address to Havana's Guaimano Masonic Lodge, Lugris y Beceiro had called in vain for the creation of a federal Ministry of Child Welfare to study and respond to the needs of Cuban children. But he did not make this demand without misgivings; at the same time as he recognized the need for greater governmental assistance to disadvantaged boys and girls, Lugris y Beceiro feared that new policy initiatives in child welfare would simply create more opportunities for corrupt politicians to divert public funds into their own bank accounts and pay off patrons. "I confess frankly that I have an instinctive fear of the word [ministry]," he told his audience, "because I am afraid that it would quickly become a job factory to reward political favors, without any kind of practical result."[49]

Lugris y Beceiro's reservations were shared by many Cubans who had long criticized the graft, embezzlement, and patronage operating under the auspices of the Ministry of Education. They were complemented by the vestiges of a colonial era political culture that saw the problems of needy children as best addressed by the Church and private charities. It is not surprising, then, that government-administered welfare programs were underfunded, were poorly led, and enjoyed little public support. Prerevolutionary reforms thus made little difference in the lives of needy Cuban children.

During the final decade of the Second Republic, as government corruption and inefficacy and the precarious state of the island's economy became painfully evident to more and more Cubans, children were increasingly deployed to maintain an insupportable status quo. Pressed into the service of a conservative nation-making project that served North American interests and prioritized the needs of a propertied and U.S.-allied elite, symbolic and actual children were used to promote a vision of Cuban nationhood that had little in common with the one articulated by the island's nineteenth-century nationalist heroes. Whereas Martí had once drawn on the symbol of the child in calling for the establishment of an independent, egalitarian, and multiracial republic, by the mid-twentieth century, this initially liberatory politics of childhood had become implicated in a radically different nation-making project, one that helped generate and police the raced and classed inequalities defining prerevolutionary society.

At the same time, as poor Cuban youth continued to work, hustle, and beg for a living throughout the 1950s, the injustices of a two-tiered educational system and the problem of street children continued to provoke public outcry. They also contributed to a growing sense of shame and frustration among more progressive Cubans. Haunted by the specter of Martí's love for children, they increasingly feared that the suffering of tens of thousands of Cuban boys and girls reflected poorly on them both individually and collectively and undermined the republic's moral legitimacy. A renewed commitment to their hero's vision of the foundational relationship between childhood and the nation once again began to provide focus and urgency to progressive Cubans' demands for meaningful political and social change.

After 1952, when former army sergeant Fulgencio Batista staged the coup that extended his government and suspended constitutional freedoms, Cubans chafed under a dictatorship that dealt the death blow to their already diminished faith in the republic and increased their desire for national moral renewal. Economic stagnation and the appalling rates of poverty in the countryside, most visibly manifested in the suffering of campesinos and the swollen bellies of their gastroenteritis-infected children, contributed in no small part to the anti-Batista insurgency that began the following year with Fidel Castro's assault on Santiago's Moncada barracks. Drawing inspiration from the utopian nation-making project of the "generation of the 1930s," the youthful revolutionaries who became known as the M-26-7 were aided by a vigorous student underground that organized strikes and encouraged civil disobedience in the nation's capital.

As resistance to the U.S.-sponsored dictatorship grew, Cuban school-children were caught between opposing political camps that struggled to control the content of their education and their loyalties. The classroom became a place of conflict and confusion, as children attempted to reconcile laudatory representations of the United States in their textbooks with increasingly vocal critiques of North American support for Batista and continuing U.S. hegemony over their island. Washington's support for the violent and repressive regime also dismayed parents, and even elite families began to question their blind loyalty to all things northern. They began to reassess the North American lifestyle and values they had worked so hard to transmit to their children.

Anti-American sentiment, always under the surface of Cuban emulation of the United States, grew concurrently with a new appreciation for local cultural forms. Nationalist writer José Pardo Llada condemned Cubans' eagerness to *extranjerizarse*, or imitate foreign ways, seeing the North American gangster, cowboy, and detective comic books so popular with the island's children as a betrayal of national identity. Artist María Luísa Ríos criticized snow-covered northern representations of Christmas and called on parents to incorporate local motifs into holiday decorations. Journalists urged Cubans to patronize local businesses and choose clothing, furniture, and household goods suitable to life in the tropics. Privileged families were urged not to take their annual holiday trips to Miami and New York but rather, in the words of the popular song "Conozca a Cuba," to "see Cuba first, and foreign countries later."

Cubans began to examine the role language played in shaping and expressing—or rather, obscuring—their children's sense of national identity. Havana's elite private schools, it was charged, stressed English literacy so much that many graduating students could not write in their home language. The popular usage of English slang expressions was criticized. While the Cuban Congress debated a bill to prohibit the use of foreign languages in business names and advertisements, more and more Cuban parents began to teach children the correct Spanish words for ice cream, hot dogs, and hamburgers.[50] The new emphasis on teaching children to speak and write "correct" Spanish, unadulterated by imported phrases, was a reversal of a century-old trend, and a powerful reflection of the cultural transformations already in process on the eve of the 1959 Revolution.

During the last years of the Batista regime, as during the Machadato, nationalist sentiment reached a fever pitch at the same time as violence and repression became a constant part of life. Newspapers were filled with graphic images of the bloody and fly-infested corpses of rebels and escaped prisoners. Concerned parents tried to shelter their children from these images, and many spoke of Batista and Castro only when they were out of earshot. The threats to children were very real. Bombings of schools and theaters were weekly, if not daily, occurrences. Countless innocent bystanders, including many children, were killed and maimed in the late 1950s.

These dangers did not stop young Cubans from forming their own political opinions. Angered by the glaring inequalities of prerevolutionary life, growing numbers of poor and working-class Cuban adolescents from the cities and countryside joined the youth cadres of the M-26-7 and other underground anti-Batista groups. As early as 1955, Fidel Castro addressed the aspirations of these underprivileged young people by promising that "a revolutionary government would undertake the integral reform of the educational system" and open new paths to social mobility for the poor of all ages.[51]

It is perhaps to be expected that Castro's promises of increased educational opportunities won him many supporters among the nation's campesinos and urban laborers. But the youngest resistance fighters were often not poor, black, or from peasant families. Middle- and upper-class youth were also aware of the extreme inequalities of republican-era Cuba, and many were angered by the repression and corruption of their government. Inspired by Martí's vision of democratic and egalitarian nationhood, more and more privileged young people joined the anti-Batista struggle, seeking to topple the dictator and establish the moral republic that would bridge the socioeconomic and cultural gaps separating them from the rest of the island's children.

The youth of the underground resistance movement were active both in the countryside and in the nation's cities, contributing significantly to the Revolution's eventual triumph. Batista's secret police eventually killed more than 20,000 of Castro's supporters, making no exceptions for the movement's younger members. Teresa Caruso, a resident of Havana during the 1950s, witnessed the violent repression of the prerevolutionary years firsthand, recalling that "every sunrise revealed dozens of corpses. . . . The most barbaric methods of torture, not excluding castration, were daily incidents in the police stations where the groans of a whole generation of youths were heard as they were tortured for information or for having aided the revolutionary movement."[52]

Batista's indiscriminate use of violence and terror did not deter these young revolutionaries, many of them teenagers from the capital's elite families, with parents who also participated in revolutionary activities. Progressive Catholic youth groups, increasingly active since the early

1940s, also played an important role in supporting the insurgency. Unlike many senior clergy who retained closer links to the conservative Church in Franco's Spain, Catholic students found common cause with other young people calling for the reform of their nation in accordance with the tenets of Christian social justice.[53] Tapping into the spiritual and moral imperatives of the time, the Jesuit-educated Castro would lead to the brink of a Revolution Cubans of all ages inspired by unfulfilled dreams of independence and social justice—and by a vision of the future that placed children at the heart of an ongoing quest for national self-determination.

DURING THE REPUBLICAN PERIOD lasting from 1902 to 1958, Cubans from different social classes, races, and political allegiances followed José Martí's lead in identifying childhood as a central site from which to launch a range of struggles for national sovereignty, democracy, and multiracial social justice. At the same time, however, North American politicians, entrepreneurs, and missionaries pressed Cuban children into the service of their competing interests, supported by local elites who believed that Cubans' racial inferiority and political immaturity left them ill-equipped for self-rule and that U.S. control of Cuba was crucial to Cuba's own national destiny.

Throughout this period of mediated sovereignty and uneven modernization, U.S.-allied Cuban elites and a growing middle class also relied on children to justify their wealth and privilege in a society characterized by the persistence of raced, classed, and gendered inequality. This betrayal of José Martí's vision and government indifference to widespread suffering among the island's youngest citizens provoked the resurgence of an originally liberatory politics of childhood and united progressive Cubans of all ages in a moral crusade to overthrow the Batista dictatorship and renew their republic. The overlapping and conflicting goals of all these actors, expressed through symbols and discourses of childhood and imposed on the bodies and minds of actual children, served to dramatically articulate the unfinished nature of the Cuban struggle for independence and propelled the island toward a second nationalist revolution.

It thus came as no surprise when, after his triumphant arrival in Havana in January 1959, Fidel Castro declared that the Revolution had been fought on behalf of the island's children. More surprising to the many Cubans who had supported the overthrow of the Batista dictatorship would be the unexpected direction that the Revolution would take, and the starring role that children would play in shaping the nation's destiny in the tumultuous years to come.

2

¿La Revolución— es para los niños?

The Politics of Childhood and the Origins of Dissent in Revolutionary Cuba

When the Batistato, as the Batista regime was known, fell on New Year's Day 1959, 500 members of the nation's military and political elite immediately fled the country. Otherwise, the news provoked an immense outpouring of joy.[1] Cubans of all races and social classes, in rural and urban areas, cheered Batista's flight and danced in the streets. One week later, progressive middle-class professionals and workers, Catholic students and campesinos, parents and children poured into Havana's wide thoroughfares to throw flowers to the bearded revolutionaries who marched in victorious procession through the capital. The hated tyrant had been ousted, and many Cubans believed that the youthful liberators of the M-26-7 had redeemed their nation. An ebullient media, freed from the censorship and terror of the Batista years, joined in unanimous celebration of the triumphant Revolution that would cleanse their republic of corruption and finally establish the long-desired moral republic, guaranteeing freedom, progress, and prosperity for all.

Many children, perhaps too young to understand the historical significance of the event, were nonetheless powerfully moved by the outpouring of happiness. Román de la Campa recalls returning to Havana after a Miami holiday on the same day that Castro arrived in the city: "The festive atmosphere at the port was unforgettable. . . . On the way home we saw people of all ages and social classes jumping with joy in the streets as if it were New Year's Eve."[2]

From the first days following the Revolution, however, euphoria and revolutionary fervor were accompanied by an outpouring of darker emotions, the product of almost sixty years of frustrated national aspirations, emotions exacerbated by the humiliation and fear of the recent dictatorship. Personal and political hostilities, class envy, and the rage of the marginalized and dispossessed combined to give rise to rioting and looting in the shadows of celebration. Gastón Vásquez, the adolescent son of a Spanish merchant, watched as a crowd smashed the windows of his father's shoe store in Centro Habana and stole the inventory before similarly vandalizing other stores on the street. Initially supporters of the Revolution, Vásquez's family had even bought M-26-7 bonds to support the anti-Batista insurgency; within a few years, the teenager and several of his relatives would join forces with others, both on and off the island, to conspire against the Castro government.[3]

Children's recollections of the first weeks of 1959 provide vivid evidence of the complex and often contradictory responses to the Revolution's triumph, responses provoked by the persistent tension between competing nation-making projects within the broadly based moral crusade that sought to remake the republic. On New Year's Day, Cubans of all races, classes, and political affiliations put aside differences and self-doubt to celebrate the rebirth of their nation. They invited insurgent leaders to form a broadly based provisional government that would bring back democracy and introduce the reforms that would eradicate government corruption and remake their society according to José Martí's egalitarian vision. However, this fragile consensus was soon threatened by disagreements over the Revolution's policies, by concern about the ideological composition of the government, and especially by opposition to the increasingly authoritarian leadership of Fidel Castro.

Within the first volatile year of the Revolution, as the nation passed from a brief celebratory moment into a more contentious period, symbolic and actual children played an important role in official and media efforts to articulate the Revolution's nature and goals, maintain consensus, and shore up the popularity of the frequently reorganized government. However, even as individuals and groups who had taken little interest in the events leading to Batista's fall became passionate Castroites, many of Castro's earliest supporters on the island and in the United States became increasingly disenchanted.[4] As a result, the revolutionary leadership began to rely more heavily on an evolving politics of childhood, disseminating child-centered messages through the strategic manipulation of an enthusiastic media and a growing number of increasingly staged public rallies and demonstrations. Children and discursive representations of childhood would thus quickly become central to the revolutionary government's efforts to both manage a changing relationship with the United States and mobilize a broader pool of citizens, young and old, in support of its initiatives.

As dissent became more vocal during the summer of 1959, Castro began to build on earlier claims that children were the primary beneficiaries of the Revolution's largesse in order to reframe them as political actors in their own right. Bypassing the institutions of family, Church, and school that had traditionally mediated interactions between the state and the island's young people, Castro pursued an ever more intense relationship with the nation's children, encouraging them to express their support for his Revolution and defy its detractors. In so doing, he disrupted traditional social norms that required children to show deference and obedience to adults even as he upheld children's unquestioning loyalty to him as a model of political behavior for Cubans of all ages.

This increasingly authoritarian refashioning of Martí's democratically inspired politics of childhood facilitated Castro's rapid evolution into an autocratic and paternalistic leader who exercised an unprecedented emotional hold over the masses. Children came to play a prominent role in a normative discourse that framed those who disagreed with the trajectory of the Revolution as not only indifferent to the destiny of the island's young people but corrupt, reactionary, and even traitorous, tainted by association with the failed republic that had preceded it. Symbolic and actual children thus contributed powerfully to the narrowing of political freedoms on the island, precluding the possibility of a democratic alternative to Castro's leadership by the end of 1959.

A NATION REBORN: CHILDREN, REVOLUTIONARY NATIONALISM, AND THE MORAL REPUBLIC

In his first interview after descending from the Sierra Maestra, Fidel Castro spoke to journalists Carlos Castañeda of *Bohemia* magazine and Jules Dubois of the *Chicago Tribune* about the nature, structure, and goals of the provisional government. The Cuban Revolution, he insisted, was not communist. It would safeguard private property, guarantee civil liberties, and ensure that democratic elections were held within four months. Nor would the leader of the Rebel Army assume the role of head of state, a position that had already been filled by President Manuel Urrutia.[5] Finally, Castro gave assurances of Cuba's continued desire for friendship with the United States. Making note of the image of La Virgen de la Caridad on a medallion around Castro's neck, Castañeda approvingly interpreted this as a sign of Castro's Christian faith and goodwill toward the Catholic Church, and especially toward those progressive clergy who had supported him since his imprisonment after the failed Moncada attack in 1953. Following this interview, *Bohemia*—Cuba's most widely read news weekly, which enjoyed a level of credibility surpassing that of most periodicals because of its resistance to Batista-era censorship—published three sold-out editions of 1 million copies each in homage to Fidel Castro and the M-26-7. The magazine and its chief editor, Miguel Angel de Quevedo, quickly joined the ranks of the Revolution's most fervent media allies.[6]

Slightly more than a month later, however, Prime Minister José Miró Cardona and his cabinet resigned without explanation, giving the lie to Castro's statement that he would play no role in the nation's governance. On February 16, *Revolución*—the official newsmagazine of the M-26-7—happily announced Castro's swearing in as prime minister. "Now," the article concluded with satisfaction, "the government, the Revolution, and the people will take the same path."[7]

Though Castro's ascension to the office of prime minister betrayed his previously stated political commitments, many Cubans welcomed his more visible political role. The new government's popularity did not rest exclusively on Castro's popularity, however. Perhaps more important at this early moment, the Revolution's legitimacy derived from its successful ousting of the detested Batista regime, its proclaimed respect for constitutional and electoral processes, and its promise of moderate economic and social reforms in line with Martí's vision of the moral republic and the platforms of Christian social democratic parties throughout Latin America.[8] These principles formed the basis for consensus among the broad coalition of individuals and groups who were represented in the Urrutia government and had participated in the anti-Batista movement, including members of the M-26-7, the Directorio Revolucionario Estudiantil, and the Federación Estudiantil Universitaria, as well as Catholic youth groups like the Agrupación Católica Universitaria and individuals of all ages and social classes who participated in the civic resistance.

Castro turned to children early and often to shore up his popularity and the provisional government's legitimacy, framing himself as the embodiment of José Martí's values and seeking to establish the Revolution as the fulfillment of the nineteenth century independence struggle. Stat ing in February that "the *mambises* initiated the war for independence that we have completed on January 1, 1959," Castro framed the Revolution as the realization of the island's long-deferred dreams of national autonomy.[9] In doing so, he offered the Cuban people the opportunity to cast off their legacy of self-doubt and invited them to participate in a collective coming-of-age celebration—one that had been delayed for more than sixty years by Cuba's dependency on the United States.

Castro frequently returned to this central theme in the island's nationalist tradition, stating that throughout the first half of the twentieth century, the United States had deprived the nation "of the prerogative to govern itself . . . like a little child to whom they said: 'We will give you permission to do just this, and if you do more we will punish you.' The Platt Amendment was imposed and we either behaved ourselves—behaved ourselves in the manner convenient to the foreign country—or we would lose our sovereignty."[10] Drawing on turn-of-the-century representations of Cuba as a child under the care of a benevolent North American father figure, Castro turned these notions on their head to proclaim the island's newfound sense of adulthood and to reject the island's infantilizing relationship with the United States. This early deployment of Martí's liberatory politics of childhood provided Castro and his government with a powerful source of legitimacy and gave the Revolution a moral imperative that spoke to Cubans of all races and classes across the island.

The provisional government further strengthened its legitimacy by demonstrating its determination to establish Martí's moral republic, targeting the island's youngest citizens as recipients of its earliest social justice initiatives. Even before the Revolution's triumph, rebel soldiers had begun constructing clinics in the poorest and most remote regions of the island. Prenatal and pediatric medicine was given top priority; in the first few months of 1959, the new government began to construct Maternal Homes for women who lived in underpopulated rural zones and previously had no access to hospital care. Programs were quickly established to send pregnant women to these homes several weeks before giving birth, where they were provided with comfortable accommodations, nutritionally balanced meals, and prenatal medical assistance. Expectant mothers also attended orientations where they received instruction about birthing techniques and infant care. These initial efforts quickly contributed to falling infant mortality rates in poor and rural communities.

The new government also drew on Martí's legacy in making the expansion of literacy and primary education to all parts of the island one of its first priorities. Rebel soldiers and community members worked with the government to hastily put together makeshift schools and to repair and renovate existing school buildings, as well as to adapt nonacademic facilities to the Cuban population's pressing educational needs. Nationalized or abandoned properties, including the mansions and summer homes of elite Cubans who had followed Batista into exile, were quickly refitted as public schools. An ambitious program to house, clothe, feed, and educate child beggars was undertaken in Camagüey province, while in Havana, the Ministry of Social Welfare designated two luxurious estates appropriated from Batista supporters to be used as boarding schools for 400 street children.[11] Sixty-nine military forts and installations were soon converted into schools across the island, among these the Moncada army barracks in Santiago de Cuba.[12]

Successful efforts to expand health care and educational services to all the island's children earned the support of many of the island's clergy and some of its religious hierarchy. On January 3, 1959, Enrique Pérez Serantes, archbishop of Santiago de Cuba, issued a pastoral message titled *Vida nueva*, in which he proclaimed that the Revolution had brought new life to the island. In his letter, Pérez Serantes, long a Castro supporter, sang the new prime minister's praises and reiterated Church support for the provisional government's plans to restore democracy and undertake a program of Christian social reform in benefit of the island's neediest citizens. Many other Catholic intellectuals and priests, including Father Ignacio Biaín, editor of the island's widely disseminated Catholic magazine *La Quincena*, offered statements, bulletins, and homilies in which they voiced their support for the Revolution and their conviction that it was inspired by Christian precepts.[13]

The Church also supported early economic reforms that benefited many Cuban children. In January 1959, rents and electricity and telephone rates were lowered between 30 and 50 percent. Pharmaceutical prices were reduced, as were postal charges. The minimum wage was increased, and taxes on middle- and working-class households were reduced. At the same time, new laws eliminated loopholes through which many wealthy Cubans evaded paying taxes. These reductions in rents and the cost of other essential goods and services, combined with wage increases, increased the purchasing power of poor, working-, and middle-class families and made possible improvements in the nutrition, health, and general standard of living of many children. Many boys and girls also made their first trips to Woolworth's and other department stores in the early months of revolutionary prosperity and took home longed-for store-bought toys and games—a visible manifestation of the Revolution's commitment to constructing a moral republic "for the children."

Revolutionary policy initiatives were accompanied by a public relations campaign that also relied heavily on child-centered discourses and images to contrast its own virtues with all things associated with the corrupt Batista regime. The M-26-7 publication *Revolución*, together with the pro-Revolution *Bohemia*, took the lead in using Cuban understandings and practices of childhood to justify the violence of the anti-Batista insurgency and the military trials and public executions of the dictator's police and military collaborators—a source of concern and embarrassment even for many of the Revolution's supporters—by detailing their crimes in newspaper articles and documentaries shown in movie theaters. These texts enumerated the former regime's neglect of children and the torture and murder of its opponents, many of them adolescents.[14]

One of the most visceral attacks on the Batistato appeared in an article the socialist newspaper *Hoy* printed claiming that one of Batista's senators had sacrificed a child in a ritual of African witchcraft. The newspaper accused Francisco Jímenez Hernández, a wealthy farmer resident in the sugar mill town of Jagueyal, of the February 1956 murder of three-year-old Emilito Tápanes. Arguing that the child's death revealed the former regime's indifference and cruelty toward children—and perhaps impugning Batista's own mixed-race origins—editorial commentary asserted that "the tyranny not only committed political crimes. . . . What was always suspected has now been proven. Let it be known: the child was sacrificed in a ritual of witchcraft."

The article accused Jímenez of having participated in multiple human sacrifices; indeed, Emilito Tápanes's murder was allegedly part of a second attempt to cure the senator's gravely ill brother through a ritual that involved feeding him the toddler's intestines and bathing the brother in the child's blood. The author claimed that the Batista supporter had used his wealth and connections to the former dictator's corrupt police force to avoid imprisonment for almost three years, but now, he concluded with satisfaction, the senator would finally face revolutionary justice.[15] *Hoy's* coverage of Jímenez's arrest, so at odds with its usually dry political and economic analysis, was not only sensationalist; it was also strangely self-contradictory, evoking the ghosts of a race- and class-inflected moral panic dating back to the turn of the century to drive home the Revolution's decisive break with the island's past. It nonetheless contrasted in a visceral way the alleged degeneracy of the Batista regime with the new government's commitment to protecting the island's children.

In the first months of 1959, political cartoons also reminded Cubans that attacks by Batista-era military and police caused the deaths of many innocent children, even as they featured frequent photos of rebel leaders and soldiers embracing their own smiling sons and daughters. One such cartoon depicted two prerevolutionary air force pilots on a bombing run over a peaceful seaside village. The caption quoted one pilot directing the other to "Drop the grenade now, now! I see a woman and child over there!"[16] Photographs, film images, and political cartoons like this one sought to shore up the Revolution's still-plentiful reserves of legitimacy by keeping memories of the Batistato's terror and oppression fresh in the population's minds, even as it publicized its own efforts on behalf of the nation's youngest citizens. This child-centered discourse sought to remind Cubans why the Revolution had been fought and why it deserved their unconditional support.

CHILDREN AND THE BREAKDOWN OF
REVOLUTIONARY CONSENSUS

In spite of efforts to maintain the popular momentum of the first few months of 1959, for many Cubans, revolutionary euphoria was already beginning to fade. Concerns about the direction of reform were rising both on and off the island—as were questions about the Revolution's ideological underpinnings. To that end, when Castro visited the United States in April 1959, he appeared on *Meet the Press* to reassure North American viewers that his government was not communist. The elections he had originally promised within four months had been postponed, he explained, because the Cuban people did not desire them; in accordance with their wishes, they would now be held within the next four years.

Castro also downplayed the increasingly anti-U.S. tenor of his speeches, reassuring viewers that the Revolution was committed to friendship between the two nations. Nonetheless, Cuba would not accept further aid from the United States. While continuing to desire the goodwill of its northern neighbor, he claimed, his government did not wish to enter into any agreement that might curtail its autonomy. Castro's statements sought to mollify North Americans' pervasive fear of communism even as he boldly articulated one of the key sources of the Revolution's legitimacy— the extent to which it had come to signify a collective coming of age for Cubans and a rejection of the nation's historically infantilizing relationship with the United States. Returning to Cuba in May, Castro appeared on local television to reemphasize the nationalist message of his *Meet the Press* interview. He insisted again that neither he nor the Revolution was communist, characterizing it as not red but "verde olivo," the olive green of the Rebel Army uniform.[17]

These nationalist messages, though widely popular, did not satisfy everyone. A growing sector of the population was distressed by Castro's assertions that the provisional government's legitimacy lay in neither elections nor U.S. recognition, as it had throughout the republican era, but rather in the popular support the Revolution inspired among the people, especially the working classes and rural poor. Still, many Cubans remained enthusiastic about the Revolution and its redistributive programs, including the Agrarian Reform Law of May 1959, which nationalized all properties of more than 150 *caballerías*.[18] Even the Catholic Church issued statements of cautious support for the agrarian reform, which it understood as consistent with the tenets of Christian social justice and an important step in the creation of a moral republic. Members of the Catholic student group Agrupación Católica Universitaria nonetheless warned that the concentration of power in the National Institute for Agrarian Reform represented a potential threat to private property rights.[19] Though criticism of revolutionary policies remained muted, political differences that had initially been subordinated to the moral imperative of the Revolution were beginning to reemerge.

By late in the summer of 1959, as unease and discontent continued to grow, child-centered discourses and media images increasingly provided Castro with a means to justify the postponement of elections and the mounting impositions of the Revolution's economic and social programs. Even as Castro began to consolidate power in his own hands by denying a meaningful political role to other members of the original anti-Batista coalition, he issued increasingly insistent calls for broad-based support of the Revolution, insisting that any discomfort or disagreement with revolutionary policies should be subordinated to the greater good—especially in matters related to children.

Media messages reminded people that the dictator and his elite supporters had presided over a cruel and corrupt regime that preyed most viciously on the young, while Castro repeatedly stated that anyone who criticized the Revolution did not care about Cuban boys and girls. He urged the well-to-do to consider the needs of the nation's children and argued that social justice, not modern consumer goods, was the true measure of civilization. In doing so, he once again cast himself and the Revolution as the inheritors of Martí's utopian nationalist vision. Castro reiterated the moral paradigm Martí had established for evaluating a nation's position in the modern world: "And if we measure the level of civilization of a country by the number of children afflicted with parasites? And if we measure the real level by the rate of illiteracy and the rate of infant mortality in the country? Any country that is thinking of the luxury of radios, refrigerators, televisions, etc., with thousands of children affected with tuberculosis . . . is a barbaric country."[20]

It was not enough, Castro argued, that civilization be measured by the standard of living enjoyed by the nation's elite. A just society could not allow a small group to "drive around in Cadillacs while in Manzanillo 150 children died annually of gastroenteritis." The *patria*, or homeland, should be one in which all, rich and poor, shared in the benefits of nationality. Once again echoing Martí, Castro explicitly privileged children in this moral definition of *patria*. The Revolution would not allow even one child to go hungry, uneducated, or without medical care in his or her homeland.

Although efforts to feed, clothe, and provide health care to the island's needy children enjoyed broad-based support, more and more people began to object to the revolutionary government's growing intervention in previously unregulated spheres. Unresolved debates over the role of private education in an egalitarian, multiracial republic resurfaced with the passing of the Educational Reform Act in the fall of 1959. Though most Cubans supported the extension of educational resources to children across the island, many Catholic and middle- and upper-class parents were alarmed by Laws 76 and 367, which established that private schools would be regulated according to the same standards as public schools. The laws further stipulated that private schools would be subject to regular inspections by state officials and that they would be required to use the same texts, authorized by the Ministry of Education, as those used in public schools.[21]

As a result of these early educational reforms, the Church—until then a cautious supporter of the Revolution—joined those expressing anxiety that Castro was impinging on freedoms guaranteed by the 1940 Constitution and undercutting the authority of parents, priests, and religious in their traditional role as arbiters of Cuban children's education and moral formation. Early efforts to regulate the island's private schools heightened fears that the Revolution was being overtaken by growing representation of the Partido Socialista Popular (PSP, which had been known as the Partido Comunista Cubano in previous decades and reassumed that name in 1965) in the provisional government. A substantive anticommunist critique thus first entered the revolutionary public sphere through debates over education and childrearing—an unsurprising occurrence, considering that the anti–private school movement of the 1930s and 1940s had been spearheaded by Juan Marinello and other prominent Communist leaders.

At the same time, the curricula and learning environment in Cuban public schools also became increasingly politicized. In order to staff the growing number of primary schools being constructed across the island, new teachers from working-class or rural communities—many of them recent graduates of the first revolutionary schools established in the countryside—had been hastily trained and put in charge of their own classrooms. These new teachers embraced the ideologically charged content of freshly printed textbooks and dedicated themselves to nurturing a revolutionary *conciencia* in their pupils, organizing them to attend rallies and marches and to participate in voluntary work brigades and neighborhood campaigns. For many Cuban parents, these educational initiatives and the corresponding politicization of curricula and after-school activities confirmed their concern about the Revolution's radicalizing tendencies.

Similar fears had already begun to emerge within the provisional government, many of whose members opposed the increasingly radical direction of revolutionary reforms. Though the members of the diverse anti-Batista coalition had originally set aside their differences in order to forge a shared nation-making project, by July, the unresolved contradictions among their competing political goals reached a crisis point. Once again framing himself as the heir to Martí's utopian vision, Castro attributed the impasse to "moral differences" with President Urrutia, a respected moderate, and offered publicly to resign as prime minister. After the Cuban people took to the streets to demonstrate their continued support for Castro's leadership, the provisional government refused to accept his resignation. Instead, they charged President Urrutia with attempting to obstruct the process of reform and compelled him to step down, replacing him with a longtime member of the PSP, Osvaldo Dorticós Torrado.[22]

As the summer came to an end, the fragile consensus that held together an increasingly divided provisional government continued to break down. Then, in October, Huber Matos—a senior officer in the Rebel Army and high-ranking official in Camagüey's provincial government—resigned from revolutionary service. Matos wrote his close friend and comrade-in-arms, Fidel Castro, denouncing the communist turn taken by the Revolution and asking Castro to fulfill the promises made in the M-26-7's 1956 manifesto. He was promptly arrested. Several additional members of the provisional government resigned their cabinet posts, protesting both Matos's detention and the placing of PSP members in positions of power within the government, especially since the PSP had withheld support for the anti-Batista insurgency until the last days of 1958.[23]

Matos's arrest and the mass resignations of cabinet ministers sent shock waves throughout Cuban society and reached as far as the United States. Denying allegations of favoritism in the newly reorganized government, Fidel Castro again insisted that neither he nor the Revolution was communist and reiterated his desire for peaceful relations with the

U.S. government. Turning to the figure of the child to negotiate a tense moment in U.S.-Cuba relations and to reassure the island's U.S.-aligned middle and upper classes, the revolutionary media rereleased a series of articles about Cuban leaders traveling to New York City in the months immediately following the triumph of the Revolution, accompanied by photographs of them interacting with local children.

Sentimental images of kindly revolutionaries playing with trusting and affectionate North American boys and girls sought to make visible the Revolution's benevolent intentions and the humanist values that united the two nations.[24] Through them, an emotionally resonant politics of childhood that had historically expressed Cuban resistance to U.S. hegemony was adapted to reassure North Americans and Cuban moderates that friendship between the neighboring countries was still possible. At the same time, the photographs subtly subverted the asymmetrical relationship between the two by recasting the Cuban delegates as loving father figures to vulnerable North American children.

These same contradictions were present in a bewildering mélange of pro- and anti-U.S. media messages during the last months of 1959. In November, a series of articles in *Bohemia* explained a wave of juvenile delinquency on the island by attributing it to "the influence of what is happening in other countries." Without directly naming the United States, the commentary appeared in the same issue as a lengthy photo essay about juvenile delinquency among Puerto Rican youth in New York City, explaining that their social maladjustment was an inevitable product of the hardship and racial discrimination they faced in New York's ghettoes. Other articles that appeared that month, ostensibly discussing similar problems on the island and expressing approval for the creation of police-directed "youth patrols," similarly framed Cubans—and especially their children—as innocent victims of the United States. They reflected a tradition of anti-U.S. and anti-imperialist rhetoric that had long played a complex but important role in Cuban politics.

By the fall of 1959, nationalist sentiments were more explicitly articulated through the child-centered discourses so central to the Revolution's self-definition.[25] Anti-U.S. messages were, nonetheless, still in the minority. In the second half of the year, revolutionary media focused on the moral, rather than political, values that inspired the reorganized government's policies and emphasized its commitment to fulfilling the aspirations of all sectors of Cuban society. They did so through frequent coverage of the Revolution's activities on behalf of all the island's children, regardless of their race or social status. To reach out to the government's popular base,

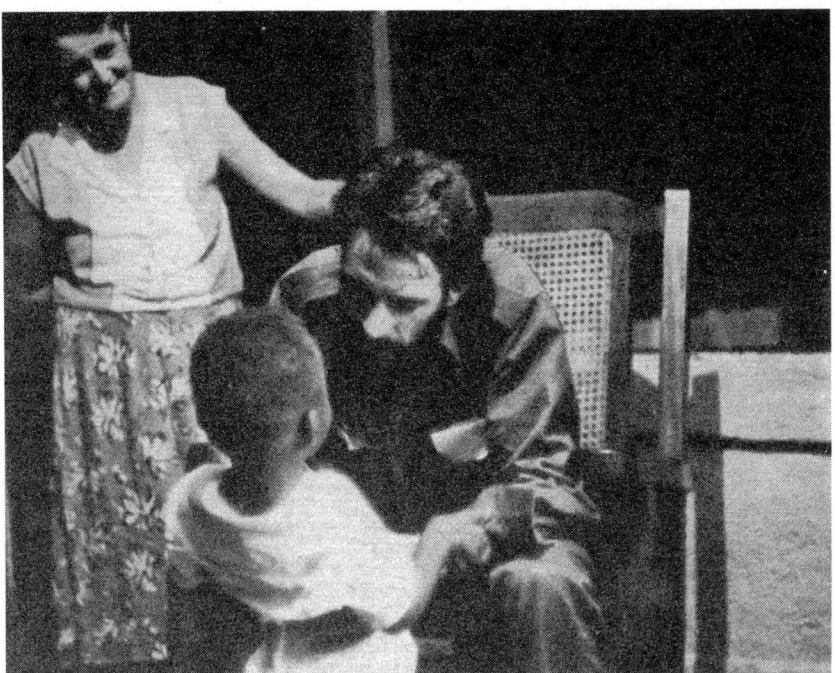

Images of rebel soldiers visiting campesino families, including this one of a barbudo leader holding a black child, strengthened the Revolution's claims of identification with the island's poorest and most vulnerable citizens. From Bohemia, November 8, 1959. *Courtesy of the Cuban Heritage Collection, University of Miami Libraries, Coral Gables, Florida.*

sympathetic journalists and editors prepared stories about Fidel and Raúl Castro, Ernesto "Che" Guevara, and Camilo Cienfuegos visiting campesino families in the countryside and published images of the rebel leaders playing with black and mulatto children.

Images like these reminded poor, rural, and black Cubans of the Revolution's commitment to improving the lives of their sons and daughters, solidifying its popularity among the groups whose marginalization revolutionaries were working hard to redress. Images of rural poverty, featuring dirty children with blonde hair and European features, sought to anticipate and disarm racially motivated complaints that revolutionary services were being unfairly directed toward improving the lives of struggling Afro-Cuban families, whom many elites continued to view as a drain on society. These images of white children sought to evoke an emotional response from privileged urban Cubans by exposing them to the poverty and abysmal living conditions of the island's youngest and neediest citizens.

The images also provided moral justification for an agrarian reform policy that relied on the appropriation of privately owned midsized and large farms.

The reorganized government similarly deployed white children to elicit support for policies directed at urban Cubans and the middle classes. Advertisements in *Bohemia* invited readers to purchase savings bonds that would fund the construction of single-family residences across the island; individuals who bought the "Ahorro y Vivienda" bonds would be entered in a lottery, through which the provisional government would give away ten houses every week. The ads featured a fair, sundress-clad girl about three years old. Riding a tricycle on a sidewalk in front of one of the small lottery homes, the toddler waved to her mother, also wearing a sundress, as she worked in a flower garden. The girl's father, returning home from work at a white-collar job, approached the neatly appointed bungalow, suit jacket tossed jauntily over one shoulder.

The advertisement depicted a street full of similar houses, in front of which other white housewives worked in identical flower beds. It was designed to appeal to Havana's aspirational lower middle and middle classes, whose hopes for the future were still heavily influenced by North American images transmitted to Cuba through movies, television, and popular magazines. This ad campaign demonstrated that the revolutionary government had not yet begun to reshape many Cubans' Hollywood-influenced dreams of middle-class family life in a prosperous, modern nation; in doing so, it sought to reassure U.S.-aligned Cubans of the Revolution's reformist nature and to mobilize support for the government's initiatives. That this was the main purpose of the ad campaign was made clear by the accompanying captions, which used morally and emotionally resonant language to urge Cubans to buy government bonds and thus "make their happiness" by "cooperating, in a clean and honest way, with one of the most generous works of the Revolution—the construction of private homes for you and all Cubans!"[26]

CASTRO AND THE CHILDREN: MOBILIZATION, DISSENT, AND GENERATIONAL CONFLICT

During the last few months of 1959, the Revolution's broadly based popularity continued to rest on media discourses that reminded Cubans of the myriad ways their children benefited from the Revolution's commitment to creating an egalitarian, multiracial society. A significant minority of Cubans nonetheless insisted that schools, health care, and new homes

During 1959, the revolutionary media disseminated family-centered images like this one that spoke to the desires of Cuba's aspirational urban lower middle classes. From *Bohemia, November 8, 1959. Courtesy of the Cuban Heritage Collection, University of Miami Libraries, Coral Gables, Florida.*

represented only a partial fulfillment of their national aspirations. They called public attention to the ways the Revolution was diverging from Martí's vision of the moral republic, which had also emphasized the democratic values of individual liberty and representative government.

As these critiques became more frequent and more forceful, Castro turned to the symbolic figure of the child, and increasingly the bodies and minds of actual children, to shore up the Revolution's legitimacy and recruit from a broader pool of potential supporters. He also began to mobilize children as part of efforts to suppress dissent, simultaneously recasting Cuban boys and girls as political actors in their own right and framing their unquestioning devotion to him as a model for adult political behavior. In strategically using children to consolidate his own power, Castro began to diverge from Martí's original politics of childhood in ways that both threatened traditional Cuban understandings and practices of childhood and contributed to the narrowing of political freedoms on the island.

By the autumn of 1959, the pro-Castro media had begun to develop earlier depictions of children as the primary beneficiaries of the Revolution in order to reframe them as competent political actors capable of great contributions to the nation's past, present, and future. Newspaper and magazine articles celebrated children's honesty, courage, selflessness, and patriotism, reflecting the romantic notions of childhood that infused Martí's writing, ideas with which the Revolution sought to associate itself.

In November 1959, when an aviation accident killed five people in Jagüey Grande, *Bohemia* published the news under a photo of the youngest victim, fourteen-year-old Leonel Barrios Castillo. The article made only cursory mention of the other four deaths and focused instead on Barrios Castillo, a boy "of extraordinary intelligence and the character of a man," who had supported the anti-Batista insurgency by participating in Rebel Army activities in his home district. The article lamented the lost boy but celebrated the fact that his premature death had "turned him into an example of love toward the new Cuba" and concluded that he would "always live in our memories."[27]

Much more than the requisite coverage of a fatal plane crash, the article's morally resonant tone transformed Leonel Barrios Castillo, a "boy-man-martyr," into a powerful unifying nationalist symbol. It demanded an affective response from adult readers by drawing an association between Cubans' love for children and their love of *patria*—the "new Cuba" that the Revolution was struggling to bring to life. It also offered an inspiring example to Cuban young people of their importance to the revolutionary nation-making project. The article thus reflects the pro-Castro media's self-conscious manipulation of child-centered texts and images to elicit emotional outpourings of support for the Revolution.

But not everyone was convinced by sentimental stories. As discontent continued to mount, the revolutionary media increased the frequency with which it resorted to child-centered messages in formulating ever more explicit demands of support for the Revolution. On November 1, *Bohemia* published a photograph of a recent progovernment march. It featured two preteen boys clad in makeshift Rebel Army uniforms. One carried a Cuban flag and the other a rifle; his left hand waved a placard bearing an image of Fidel Castro. Demonstrating the fusion of spiritual, moral, and political values that inspired early revolutionary fervor, he also wore a rosary around his neck. The photograph's caption read: "Not even the children failed to show up for their appointment with the government of the Revolution. These two little guys march in military attire, carrying, together with the flag, Fidel's portrait. Thus the people showed that they were not afraid; that they were there in full ranks because that was their government and that was their cause."[28]

The photograph and accompanying text reflected the growing visibility of children in mass political demonstrations. While it is true that children increasingly swelled the ranks at prorevolutionary events, both government officials in their speeches and the media attributed symbolic significance to their presence beyond all proportion to their actual numbers. This revealed the extent to which the government and the progovernment media sought to benefit from the deliberate conflation of the Revolution, Fidel, and the nation with idealized notions of youthful virtue and promise. Encouraging children to see themselves as legitimate political actors in their own right, the text and image also targeted adults, reinforcing the notion that supporting the Revolution was right and good—a course of action chosen by the island's youngest and purest citizens. Media images of children rallying to support Castro thus sought to motivate or shame adults into assuming their political duties to the Revolution, implying that those who did not express a similarly childlike confidence in their leader were lacking in virtue and commitment to the *patria*.

Inspired by popular slogans proclaiming, "Children Are the Revolution," many young people leapt to the opportunity to defend Castro against dissenters. Their new political prominence encouraged many children to transgress widely held expectations of deference to adults. Thirteen-year-old Juan Alberto Fernández Puntonel, from Cienfuegos, wrote an emboldened

Two boys march in a revolutionary procession. One wears a rosary while carrying an image of Fidel Castro, demonstrating that Catholicism and Fidelismo were not initially seen as mutually exclusive. From Bohemia, *November 1, 1959. Courtesy of the Cuban Heritage Collection, University of Miami Libraries, Coral Gables, Florida.*

letter to *Bohemia* journalist Augustín Tamargo, demanding an explanation for his recent critique of a government initiative. "Do you sincerely believe," he asked, "that the revolutionary government, the only one that has governed honorably in Cuba and the only one in the world in which it is the people who decide the policies that must be followed for the well-being and prosperity of the Nation, could be a government to be condemned, even in the least?"

The adolescent boy adopted a peremptory tone that would almost certainly have been perceived as impudent in prerevolutionary days. However, rather than take offense, the chastened journalist published the entire letter in a self-critiquing column. In language that conflated the boy's revolutionary fervor with both the virtue of childhood and Martí's romantic nationalism, Tamargo called his adolescent critic "the flower of patriotic love, the rose of Martí, next to his heart," and offered him up as "a symbol of the new Cuban generation, that perhaps might not beat out their antecedents in spirit of sacrifice but that we will always have to envy for the beautiful future, heavy with promises, that History seems to have reserved for them."[29]

The column not only legitimized young people's newfound political agency; it also celebrated their right to form their own opinions (as long as they were pro-Revolution) and their prerogative to challenge adults who held different ideas. Sentimental rhetoric aside, Tamargo's reaction to the young boy's letter indicated a rising intolerance for dissenting voices in the last months of 1959. The boy's indignation that a journalist would presume to critique the Revolution both reflected and reinforced the narrowing of political freedoms on the island after the resignation and arrest of Huber Matos in October.

As Fidel Castro further consolidated his control of the reorganized provisional government, he focused especially on his ever closer relationship with the island's children. Embracing his new role as father of the nation, he chose more and more often to address children directly in emotionally resonant speeches at school openings and other mass events. He praised their participation in revolutionary campaigns and rallies and exhorted them to study, march in defense of the Revolution, and perform volunteer work in their neighborhoods, encouraging even the nation's youngest citizens to view themselves as essential to Cuba's future.

News coverage of the September 14 conversion of the Columbia Fort prison into a *ciudad escolar*, or "school city," was dominated by descriptions of the intense emotional bond between Castro and the children. *Bohemia* asserted that the massive rally which celebrated the school's opening "had two protagonists: childhood and Fidel Castro." Ignoring the other adults present, parents and revolutionary officials alike, the magazine declared that "thousands of children, reunited in the central plaza, had a heart-to-heart dialogue with the representative of the Revolution." In his speech to the students, Castro once again stressed the political agency of children and reminded them, "You are the ones who will have to make the true revolution, and you will do it by studying."

The article concluded by holding up the adoration expressed by Castro's youthful supporters as a model for the correct political attitude of all Cubans: "That afternoon, Fidel Castro didn't lower himself to the level of the childlike mind; rather, the children's spirits lifted themselves up to him. The children responded to him as his best audience. The Revolution stopped being the exclusive concern of adults and enveloped all ages. . . . Even a child could understand and feel it."[30]

On November 15, Castro attended another youth rally in Havana. Standing above them in a military jeep, he addressed a crowd of cheering adolescents and children. "People who want to understand what is happening in Cuba today should keep this in mind: this is a Revolution of young people, and young Cubans are the ones who give substance and meaning to the social transformations of the moment." The speech once again sought to associate the Revolution with youthful virtue; however, foreshadowing the more radical turn the nation would soon take, it also suggested that the Revolution was aligned first and foremost with their aspirations for the future and that anyone who challenged its direction placed him- or herself at odds with the nation's young people.

ON DECEMBER 11, 1959, amid preparations for the Christmas season, Huber Matos was found guilty of treason and sedition and sentenced to twenty years in prison. His swift transformation from rebel soldier and high-ranking government official to political prisoner signaled the end of moderate coalition rule in revolutionary Cuba.[31] Though the reorganized government continued to enjoy widespread popularity, many former supporters reached the conclusion that the price they had paid for long-desired reforms was unacceptably high. Fidel Castro was displaying an ever more undemocratic temperament and moving the nation in unexpectedly radical directions. Though a few held out hope that Castro intended to restore the 1940 Constitution and hold elections at some point in the future, their hopes grew dimmer as the days passed. Moreover, as U.S. leaders became convinced of the Revolution's communist tendencies, the possibility for productive bilateral relationships between the two nations diminished.

By the end of the year, however, the reorganized government had successfully harnessed the powerful symbolism of the child to shore up its legitimacy and had begun to use actual children to silence its opponents. A constant stream of newspaper and magazine articles reminded Cubans that education and health-care initiatives and urban and agrarian reforms had directly benefited the island's poor, working-class, and rural children, linking their well-being to the survival of the Revolution. Moreover, incessant media coverage of the nation's youngest citizens marching at pro-Castro rallies offered a compelling response to the voices of dissent that arose in response to Castro's increasingly authoritarian leadership, framing the rebel leader as the only legitimate heir of Martí's legacy and the Revolution as the only movement capable of realizing Martí's vision of the moral republic.

The rapidly evolving politics of childhood that infused Castro's speeches with moral and emotional resonance further strengthened the bond between the rebel leader and Cuban children, contributing to the consolidation of his personal power even as it narrowed the possibilities for public debate about the Revolution's future trajectory. Diverging markedly from Martí's vision of the relationship between children and the nation by the end of 1959, revolutionary discourses of childhood had already begun to undercut the traditional authority of parents, the Church, and religious educators and to reflect a nascent Marxist-Leninist conception of the dialectical relationship between generational conflict and political and social change.

More important, however, discourses that conflated the virtue of children with Fidel Castro, the Revolution, and ultimately the Cuban nation facilitated an alarming new trend in the nation's public life: the categorical refusal to accept dissenting voices as an inevitable expression of the diverse political goals and unreconciled nation-making projects of a still-divided citizenry. In the two years to come, they would play a key role in reducing a pluralistic debate about the island's future to a stark dichotomy in which children faced off against their elders, the moral against the immoral, the revolutionary against the counterrevolutionary, and the national against the antinational.

3
CHILDHOOD AND CIVIL SOCIETY IN REVOLUTIONARY CUBA

By mid-1959, Fidel Castro had successfully deployed an evolving politics of childhood to limit Cubans' access to political decision making. At the same time, the Revolution launched a similarly child-centered campaign to appropriate the resources and moral capital still residing in the island's fractious but nonetheless vibrant civil society—and then destroy it.[1]

Though progressive civic actors, the Catholic Church, and the non-state-sponsored media initially supported revolutionary reform efforts, they espoused distinct visions of the nation's future and encouraged public debates that drew attention to the increasingly antidemocratic nature of Castro's leadership. They also promoted competing social justice projects that clashed with what Andrés Suárez called the "administrative character" of an increasingly top-down Revolution, threatening its efforts to frame itself as exclusively equipped to construct Martí's moral republic.[2] As a result, beginning in the last months of 1959 and accelerating in the new year, the Castro government and revolutionary media sought to deploy symbolic and actual children to deemphasize, discredit, and eventually suppress Cuban civil society.

Rejecting the Church and the middle classes as agents of social change, even while appropriating key aspects of their Christian worldview and social justice aspirations, Castro and his allies increasingly recruited children to their struggle to establish the revolutionary state as the only legitimate source of national redemption. As the role of Catholic youth and urban professionals in the Revolution's triumph and initial reforms began to be delegitimized, the working classes, and especially their children, were simultaneously constructed as the true protagonists and benefactors of the revolutionary process. Expressions of dissent on the island were more and more attributed to putative class and generational differences and framed as a threat to the well-being of children, the Revolution, and the nation.

By the last months of 1959, a discourse that had previously framed the "humanist" Revolution as the protector of all the nation's children became increasingly bifurcated and combative. Sentimental celebrations of the virtue and promise of the Revolution's young supporters took pride of place in revolutionary speeches, newspapers, and magazines increasingly concerned with justifying the persecution of the Catholic Church and affiliated organizations, physical attacks on the non-state-sponsored media, and Fidel Castro's increasingly personalistic exercise of state power. Representations of childhood thus played a powerful role in establishing in the discursive realm the ideological prerequisites for a process of radicalization that took material form in an ambitious agrarian reform law, the politicization of education, and the nationalization of foreign and domestic banks and industries by the summer of 1960.[3] At the same time, Castro's radicalizing politics of childhood also laid the groundwork for a massive middle-class exodus from the island; it would also spur on the emergence of a Counterrevolution, organized around its own politics of childhood, that far exceeded earlier Batistiano efforts to topple the regime.

CHILDHOOD AND STATE–CIVIL SOCIETY
COMPETITION IN EARLY REVOLUTIONARY CUBA

Cuba's urban middle class, inspired by the legacy of charismatic Catholic student leaders like José Antonio Echevarría, provided some of the earliest and most committed members of the anti-Batista insurgency. Progressive civic organizations and private citizens also stood behind the Revolution's early social reforms and economic interventions. They responded enthusiastically to public appeals framed in the morally and emotionally resonant discourses of childhood that provided the revolutionary government with so much of its legitimacy. Eager to play a role in building Martí's moral republic, they made possible massive social spending by supporting the confiscation of properties seized from Batistianos, by volunteering to pay back taxes they had withheld from the dictator, and by making direct donations to fund initiatives like the May 1959 Agrarian Reform. The Instituto Nacional de Reforma Agraria alone benefited from more than $8 million worth of private donations for the purchase of farm machinery and supplies for a new class of small farmers.[4] However, progressive Cubans also continued to sponsor their own social justice projects, many of which provided education, health care, and other aid to needy children.

Many of their programs enjoyed the support of U.S.-affiliated industry leaders and professionals.

Throughout most of 1959, the conservative newspaper *Diario de la Marina* and the English-language *Havana Post* carried positive coverage of the revolutionary government's ambitious clinic and school construction programs. They also published child-centered advertisements informing Cubans about these programs' aims and achievements, including a series commissioned by the revolutionary Ministry of Public Works that featured smiling children under the slogan "Revolution Means to Build." At the same time, the non-state-sponsored media ran prominent articles praising privately organized social justice projects that targeted disadvantaged boys and girls.[5]

On September 30, the *Diario de la Marina* carried an article highlighting civic organizations' commitment to reforming the island's health-care system. It drew attention to the urgent need for the expansion and professionalization of pediatric medicine in Cuba. This massive undertaking, the article argued, would require collaboration between the state and private organizations. It quoted a speech by Enrique Galán, newly appointed rector of the Cuban Society of Pediatric Medicine. Acknowledging the doctor's prorevolutionary sentiments, the *Diario* noted that Galán began his talk by "offering a tribute to the martyrs of the Revolution, who spilled their blood to reinstate the freedoms that had been torn from it by a despotic government," before moving into an analysis of the state of pediatric medicine on the island.

Stating that "social-medical assistance to the poor child is, without doubt, the greatest responsibility of our Society and its members," Galán deplored the current insufficiency of services and asserted a role for professional medical associations in improving the health of needy Cuban children. "We have the responsibility to declare publicly that in Cuba we lack no less than 3,000 hospital beds for poor children. . . . At the present moment there are only around 400 available in Havana. Shockingly, in the five capitals of the other provinces, the number of available beds doesn't reach 300. We must collaborate, at least in an advisory capacity, with the official organisms to ensure that closed hospitals be put into immediate service . . . that already existing ones be turned into true hospitals, and that the necessary additional ones be created according to the [population] density of each province or municipality." Galán went on to discuss the need for a national children's health insurance plan, which he felt could be equally well-administered by the government or a "private entity," to ensure equal access to medical care for all young people. He concluded with a rhetorical flourish reminiscent of the moralizing child-centered discourses so frequent in revolutionary speeches and publications: "To the Cuban child, to that child who lacks shoes, malnourished and belly distended with internal parasites, we must give immediate attention." He also took a moment to praise the Revolution's most radical initiative yet, arguing that "nothing can triumph unless we cultivate the first fruit of our agrarian reform, which is a healthy and well-fed citizen."[6]

In disseminating the remarks of the nation's leading authority on pediatric medicine, the Catholic and probusiness *Diario de la Marina* made no attempt to hide Galán's revolutionary sympathies or his desire to collaborate with the provisional government's well-publicized efforts to extend health care across the island. Their coverage of his speech nonetheless emphasized that the Revolution had yet to meet its goal of providing medical services to all Cubans. Moreover, it highlighted the doctor's argument for the continuing relevance of civic and private initiatives in the reform of the health-care system. As such, both Galán's speech and the *Diario's* coverage—ostensibly offered in a spirit of revolutionary collaboration—represented a threat to the Revolution's efforts to depict itself as the exclusive caretaker of the nation's needy children. As such, it offered an implied challenge to one of the key tenets on which the new government's legitimacy was founded.

Similar tensions existed between the revolutionary campaign of educational reform and competing civic and private sector school-building projects. Mining and sugar companies, prominent wealthy citizens, the Catholic Church, and various Protestant missionary organizations had long been active in augmenting the republic's inadequate educational system; in spite of newly passed legislation mandating stricter state regulation of the nation's public and private schools, they expected to continue exercising this function within a Revolution that had not yet explicitly ruled out a leading role for industry, civic organizations, or private citizens in its reform efforts. The independent media concurred, devoting significant editorial attention to non-state-sponsored educational initiatives.

On September 20, 1959, the *Havana Post* reported on a benefit party held by local sugar magnate Julio Lobo. The CEO of the Galban Lobo firm had gathered leading Cuban industrialists at his Vedado home to celebrate the inauguration of a Patronato pro Escuela Rural Cubana, a fund to build rural schools across the island. Speaking to reporters in attendance at the party, Lobo alluded to Martí's special concern for the education of rural children as well as to revolutionary discourses linking the nation's destiny with the expansion of educational opportunities for its young people.[7] "The education of the rural children has always preoccupied me, as it has so many other businessmen of our country," Lobo declared, "mainly because we understand that the future of our country rests on the development and preparation of those children who will become the men and women who will better its standard of life and permit its development on a large scale of agriculture and industry."

Recognizing the widespread need for new educational facilities across the Cuban countryside, Lobo emphasized that the ambitious goals of the Patronato could not be funded or overseen by any one individual or group. He stated that the first phase of the project would involve a vigorous publicity campaign to promulgate the idea and to "knock on the door of every merchant, industry, and private home" to raise funds, and he called on all citizens to support his firm's initiative.[8] In doing so, he asserted the important role to be played by Cuba's capitalist class in educational reform and declared his intention to collaborate with the Revolution in the building of a modern and moral republic.

The Galban Lobo firm also took out full-page advertisements, featuring photographs of solemn-faced *guajiro* (rural) children in *yarey* hats, in the probusiness *Diario de la Marina*. Headlined "A Call to the Economic Classes for the Expansion of the Cuban Rural School System," the ads announced that Galban Lobo "feels the patriotic obligation to cooperate in the development of the rural schools" and invited "all corporations, industries, and businesses of Cuba, as well as citizens of sufficient resources" to take part in their "new civic crusade" on behalf of "the Cuban child, foundation of the new generation."[9] In calling on businesspeople and well-off individuals to support his Patronato pro Escuela Rural Cubana, Julio Lobo was reaching out to a progressive middle class that still believed civic organizations could take the lead in promoting social justice in revolutionary Cuba.

On September 24, the *Havana Post* reported at length on the inauguration of a new school, built by the Moa Bay Mining Company, in a remote corner of Oriente Province. The opening ceremony was attended by Mirta Terrero, secretary of the Department of Education; the mayor of Moa; and representatives of the Revolutionary Armed Forces and the mining company. The article noted approvingly that the corporate-funded school would fulfill the dreams of students from both Moa and the neighboring village of Los Mangos, where "a large number of children of school age have been unable to attend school because of the lack of facilities"; it also noted that the mining company had made substantial contributions for the construction of a Catholic church in the town and had funded construction of a post office/communications building and an aqueduct and sewage disposal system.[10]

The presence of military officers and government officials at this September 1959 inauguration indicates that the Revolution was still willing to collaborate with industry to meet what the *Post* called the island's ongoing "school problem." However, the Moa Bay School opening did not appear in *Revolución*, the official organ of the M-26-7, or even in the prorevolutionary weekly *Bohemia*. Instead, these publications featured articles emphasizing the decisive action of the Revolution to extend education and health care to all the island's children, deemphasizing or leaving unacknowledged civic, industrial, or private social justice initiatives.

The tension between state-sponsored and civic responses to the island's continuing educational crisis was especially prominent in coverage of Catholic schooling and child welfare programs. On September 17, the *Diario de la Marina* published a two-page editorial titled "A Great Work of Catholic Social Action: The Don Bosco Salesian School of Guanabacoa." Featuring a series of photographs of uniformed boys working, studying, and playing under the supervision of attentive Brothers, the article traced the Salesians' history of educational outreach and social work among the city's poor and orphaned youth. Making clear that the project both predated the Revolution and sought to continue its mission without support from the revolutionary government, the *Diario* praised the school for both its long-standing commitment to poor Cuban children and its service to the *patria*, noting that "during thirty-three years it has forged thousands of useful men for the nation, in a silent, determined, and constant effort that has benefited hundreds of orphans and destitute children."

Framing the progressive Salesians as faithful servants of God and of Martí's moral republic, the *Diario* also recognized "the cooperation and the generosity of the people and a group of benefactors who have given the Salesians indispensable economic assistance." Thanks to their support, the Colegio Don Bosco boasted a current enrollment of 950 students, most of whom lived in the school's "ample and hygienic" dormitories. These students enjoyed a "well-seasoned diet" and free medical and dental care. However, the *Diario* reminded readers, the school's ability to provide poor Cuban children with the necessary "civic, religious, and scientific formation" to prepare them for life as "future citizens" depended not only on wealthy benefactors but also on the nation's private citizens and small business owners. It urged readers to send donations to the Brothers in Guanabacoa, thereby preventing "this grand work of love toward our fellow man" from disappearing.[11]

Though it is impossible to speculate on the intentions—reformist or reactionary, altruist or self-interested, or perhaps a combination of both—underlying non-state-sponsored school-building projects, they clearly conflicted with the Revolution's promotion of its own efforts. By encouraging Cubans to donate funds for the continuation of civic educational initiatives, the independent media directed attention and resources away from the Revolution's school-building programs and toward competing social justice projects. Moreover, coverage of the opening of new privately funded schools and fundraising campaigns to support existing ones reminded the public of organizations and individuals whose commitment to the care and education of Cuban children predated the Revolution; in doing so, they provided such groups with the visibility and prestige to challenge the Castro government's right to unilaterally restructure education on the island.

The *Diario de la Marina* argued this point in a series of editorials opposing the new Educational Reform Act, insisting that the act had been created and promulgated in an undemocratic manner and would unleash unwarranted state intervention in the island's schools. Its critique went no further, expressing concern over an overreaching piece of legislation without questioning the provisional government's preeminent role in establishing educational policy for the nation. Recognizing the right of the Revolution to "enter with a pickaxe to demolish those educational edifices, institutions, and methods that it considers ineffective or antiquated," the *Diario* nonetheless feared that the Educational Reform Act would have deep repercussions in the arena of private education: "We understand— as do many educators—that such an important question should be aired publicly and not behind closed doors. Why now, when roundtables and forums are so in fashion, aren't the problems of education being discussed in a worthy, serene, competent manner, among those who because of their capacity, knowledge, and experience, deserve to be heard?"

These sentiments, the article continued, were shared by Felipe Donate, head of the Cuban Teachers Professional Association, and a group of "distinguished educators" who had organized under his leadership to call for a greater voice for teachers in the process of educational reform. Emphasizing that the resolution of these issues was of utmost importance in shaping the nation's destiny, the text concluded that "the education of our children is too delicate a matter for such far-reaching and resonant innovation to be introduced without mediation and wide discussion."[12] In providing sympathetic coverage to the activities of professional educators' groups, the *Diario* joined with Cuban teachers in demanding that the provisional government guarantee civic organizations and private citizens a continuing role in the formulation and implementation of the nation's educational policy. Together, teachers and the independent media challenged the Revolution's claims to being the sole legitimate dispenser of education to Cuban children.

The revolutionary leadership answered this challenge by asserting its exclusive right to administer educational reform on the island. Supportive media emphasized coverage of government initiatives and deemphasized the ongoing role of individuals and community organizers in the establishment of many of the Revolution's new schools. In October, *Bohemia* published a petition Mario González de Chávez Clavero had organized to raise awareness about the need for a school on the Finca Santa Rita in the municipality of Quemado de Güines. A few weeks later, local resident Salvador Rodríguez wrote the magazine that he had donated land for the school and described the quick progress that had been made toward its construction, overseen by a locally constituted committee of parents and neighbors. A good revolutionary, he nonetheless stressed in his letter the government's involvement—by all accounts minimal—in the efforts to build the school, concluding with an expression of "many thanks to the Revolutionary Government!"

The accompanying editorial acknowledged the efforts of local residents but reminded *Bohemia* readers that the school was a product of the government's benevolence rather than the residents' initiative. While expressing satisfaction that the children of an underserved region would now enjoy improved educational opportunities, the article portrayed the community not as a model of successful civic organizing but as the beneficiary of Fidel Castro's generosity. Driving home this interpretation, a picture of children and parents gathered on the site of the Finca Santa Rita School appeared under the bold headline "School Granted."[13] This selective version of events at Finca Santa Rita reaffirmed the top-down approach to social justice initiatives and the curtailing of individual and civic engagement that had begun to define the Revolution after the reorganization of the provisional government in the summer of 1959.

Already concerned with the upsurge in education-related civic organizing, the provisional government's leaders were shaken by a storm of Catholic activism similarly seeking to influence the trajectory of the Revolution. The progressive youth of the Agrupación Católica Universitaria and Juventud Obrera Católica, organizations with years of experience advocating for the island's working classes and rural poor, had offered their support as volunteers in some of the Revolution's earliest efforts to ameliorate the worst inequities of Cuban society.[14] However, by the summer of 1959, progressive Catholics had been excluded from visible roles in these projects.

At the same time, they began to suspect that the Educational Reform Act's regulation of private education was the first step toward curtailing the autonomy of Catholic schools and restricting faith-based associations. Young people thus organized to assert their intertwined Catholic and patriotic identities and to remind Fidel Castro of his promise to respect the religious values that had inspired their support for the Revolution.

On the fourth Sunday of September, Havana's youth celebrated the twenty-third annual Cuban Catholic Youth Day. They paid homage to the nation by making floral offerings at monuments to Antonio Maceo and José Martí before participating in a midday open-air mass in the capital's Plaza Cívica. The *Diario de la Marina* reported approvingly that this event, though a Havana tradition since 1936, "reached a new resonance this year because of the large crowds that attended" and "manifested the apogee of Cuban Catholicism, reaffirming in our nation's new generation the spiritual ideals that come down to these: God and the Homeland."[15]

In spite of—or perhaps in defiance of—official efforts to conflate the Revolution, the nation, and the island's virtuous young people in the public consciousness, the article made no reference to revolutionary precepts or values. Instead, the *Diario* presented images of Cuban youth offering honors to the heroes of the independence struggle and participating in Catholic rituals as a competing model of patriotism and morality. Moreover, Catholic children and adolescents were pictured fulfilling their duties to the *patria* under the supervision of Catholic priests, drawing inspiration and guidance not from Fidel Castro but from the nation's religious leaders.

Catholic youth activism also interfered with the provisional government's unceasing efforts to mobilize youth to rally and march in support of the Revolution. In November 1959, the 25,000 members of Juventud Católica organized their own mass demonstration in honor of Cuba's national patron, the Virgin of Charity, and participated in the island's first National Catholic Congress. At least 1 million Catholics of all ages attended the Congress *misa* and activities in Havana's Plaza Cívica, the very location where many of Fidel Castro's own rallies were held. The massive turnout challenged Castro's boasted ability to attract previously unprecedented crowds, and their chants of "¡Caridad, Caridad, Caridad!" invoked Cuba's patron saint as an equally powerful national symbol. Catholic youth thus rejected the idea that Fidel Castro was the sole embodiment of the revolutionary nation and demonstrated their adherence to a competing faith-based vision of the moral republic, insisting on remaining active and autonomous participants in its construction.[16]

Mass demonstrations by Catholic students, workers, and professionals, as well as social justice messages issued by clergy, raised the stakes in the competition between the Revolution and faith-based activism for pride of place at the vanguard of social reform on the island. They produced a dramatic increase in religious participation, especially among youth, as churches became highly politicized sites of alternative expressions of national and moral consciousness.[17] In the weeks following the National Catholic Congress—the first and last to be held in revolutionary Cuba—Castro and his allies turned to children to counter the upsurge in this increasingly politicized form of civic activism.

By recruiting boys and girls to the Revolution's own campaigns, the revolutionary government sought to divert bodies, resources, and enthusiasm away from community and Church-based associations and direct them toward state-led organizations and programs. Moralizing representations of children in official speeches, publications, and advertisements also sought to motivate adults to avoid non-state-sponsored groups and activities and to commit their voluntary energies exclusively to the Revolution. Images of selfless and compliant child volunteers provided a powerful model for Cubans of all ages, embodying Cubans' appropriate role as supporters of top-down revolutionary initiatives rather than as civic leaders or individual actors.

In an effort characteristic of these early attempts to mobilize children, the Ministry of Agriculture launched a campaign in the autumn of 1959 to repopulate the island with fruit trees. Advertisements focused on young people as potential participants; they pictured children replanting trees, declaring, "You too can help!"[18] In order to facilitate youth involvement, the ads provided detailed instructions on how to save, wash, and dry seeds and instructed children to turn them in at neighborhood schools.

Advertisements like these encouraged children to see themselves as crucial to the campaign's success even as they pressured recalcitrant adults to assume responsibilities to the Revolution that the island's best and brightest had enthusiastically embraced. There were, however, limits to the expression of that enthusiasm. Participation in revolutionary initiatives, while encouraged and increasingly expected, would nonetheless take place within state-enforced parameters. Even as children began to explore their newfound agency within revolutionary social campaigns, government officials and the media disseminated new discourses that deemphasized previous understandings of the Revolution as driven by the combined efforts of diverse individuals and organizations and reframed it as a top-down movement directed by and embodied in the person of Fidel Castro.

¡Cuba necesita repoblarse de FRUTALES!

¡Usted también puede ayudar!

Esa es la noble tarea que debemos afrontar los cubanos de hoy: repoblar a la patria de árboles frutales. Para eso es imprescindible recobrar y recolectar todas las semillas posibles, para nutrir nuestros viveros.

¡Coopere Ud. también! Reúna todas las semillas que usted pueda y llévelas a la estación de policía o a la escuela más cercana, o al "Banco de la Semilla", Edificio Atlantic, 23 y 12, Vedado. Allí las recogerán las Delegaciones Municipales de Agricultura para remitirlas al Ministerio.

¡No defraude a Cuba en esta generosa campaña! ¡Cada semilla que usted bota... es un árbol que pudo haber sido!

COMO CONSERVAR LAS SEMILLAS:
1- Quíteles toda la masa o pulpa que puedan tener adherida, y lávelas.
2- Séquelas cuidadosamente para quitarles toda la humedad.
3- Empaquételas, ya bien secas, en una caja, preferiblemente de cartón.

DEPARTAMENTO DE REPOBLACIÓN FORESTAL
Ministerio de AGRICULTURA
El futuro de Cuba está en la tierra.

This advertisement for a tree-planting campaign featured an idealized image of a youthful volunteer, both to mobilize other children in support of revolutionary initiatives and to motivate—or perhaps shame—adults into participating. From Bohemia, November 8, 1959. Courtesy of the Cuban Heritage Collection, University of Miami Libraries, Coral Gables, Florida.

These discourses portrayed Castro as a generous paternal figure and the island's citizens as devoted children whose compliance with their father's will, rather than their own initiative, would guarantee access to the Revolution's resources. The discourses disregarded the fact that few of the state's early redistributive efforts would have succeeded without the support of Cuba's middle class and activist Catholics. And they did not convince many Cubans, who persisted in viewing civil society as a legitimate and effective space in which to contribute to the building of the moral republic. As late as December 1959, progressive Catholic and middle-class social justice projects continued to compete with state agencies in providing clothing, food, and medical care to the urban and rural poor of all ages, contradicting the government's claims that it alone held the power to produce meaningful social change.

Church-affiliated leaders had also demonstrated their ability to compete with Castro as organizers of the island's children and young people, disrupting efforts to link youthful activism, virtue, and nationalism exclusively with the Revolution. An increasingly politicized civil society, with its spiritually derived values and alternative vision of the nation's future, was thus quickly becoming the most serious threat to the legitimacy of the Revolution and an obstacle to the consolidation of power in its leader's hands.

NAVIDADES EN CUBA LIBRE: CHILDHOOD, FIDELISMO, AND THE DISCREDITING OF CIVIL SOCIETY

Christmas, a holiday long associated with children, offered a timely opportunity to appropriate the spiritual and moral capital of Catholic and middle-class activists while simultaneously discrediting their social justice projects. At the same time, government officials and their media allies used evocative seasonal discourses and imagery to more firmly locate Fidel Castro and the revolutionary state within a cherished Christian moral paradigm. Conscious of the symbolic importance of the holiday season in a family-oriented and at least nominally faithful nation, the government began planning as early as September 1959 for the spirit-filled celebration of "Navidades en Cuba Libre," or "Christmas in Free Cuba." Throughout the autumn of 1959 and especially during the month of December, the state-sponsored media portrayed the Revolution, rather than the birth of Jesus, as the source of holiday joy, and drove home new images of Fidel Castro as the benevolent father and giver of gifts to Cubans of all ages.

In November, the Casa de las Américas, under the direction of the Revolution's most prominent female leader, Haydée Santamaría, staged a nationwide children's competition around the theme "Christmas on the American Continent." *Bohemia* magazine announced that children under the ages of fourteen were invited to submit drawings, compositions, and songs expressing their understanding of "the most excellent of the Christian world's celebrations." Building on excitement generated by the holiday, *Bohemia* further linked the Revolution to popular notions of Martían nationalism, proclaiming: "The Revolution, unlike authoritarian regimes, cannot view the child as simply a receptacle of adult ideas but rather [must see children] as having their own sense of life; in this grand opportunity it will stimulate the creative initiative of Cuba's young scholars, in whom it sees, as Martí did, the hope of the world."[19]

Simultaneously, the Ministry of Education launched a nationwide effort to mark the first Christmas of the revolutionary era as the most patriotic and joyful the island had ever experienced. Work began immediately to organize Cubans to volunteer their time, effort, and resources to prepare for the advent season. Homes and businesses across the island were adorned with Christmas trees, colorful paper chains, and decorations, and brigades of children were mobilized to go house to house to collect donations to decorate the streets of their barrios. Competitions were arranged and medals awarded to neighborhoods with the best decorations. On Nochebuena, dances were held in the streets in towns and cities across the island; revolutionary Santa Clauses sporting black beards, in honor of Fidel and the M-26-7's rebels, distributed gifts. Children stayed up all night, visiting the homes of family members and neighborhood friends.

While most families celebrated in ways similar to Christmases past, the revolutionary media offered an alternative explanation for these expressions of seasonal joy. According to Justina Alvarez, women's columnist for the socialist newspaper *Hoy*, the preparation and celebration of the island's first revolutionary Christmas, a work carried on by Cubans of all ages, was proof that the Revolution "advances forward, forward, carried on the shoulders of the men, women, and children of the nation."[20] *Bohemia* concurred, announcing that this year the island would experience "a distinctly Cuban Christmas, an unforgettable holiday season in Free Cuba, now that the era of oppression that kept us for seven long years under a reproachable tyranny has happily passed."[21]

The magazine also ran child-centered cartoons explicitly framing the Revolution's accomplishments and Fidel's benevolence as the sole reasons for holiday happiness. One such cartoon, appearing in an official advertisement, bore the slogan "This Is How a Cuban Christmas Tree Is Made." It featured children clamoring to hang schoolhouses, desks, and books on its branches. The caption read, "Schools are planted, and then lit up with thousands of teachers; the shadow of the prison is erased; classrooms are filled with light, with books, desks, pencils. . . . And when there is education for all children, there is freedom and justice for all men. . . . The people take to their feet and hang their laughter on this tree, because now they have a reason to sing to the world: Happy Holidays!"[22]

Through cartoons, advertisements, and media coverage, the Revolution and its allies thus sought to transform Cubans' understanding of the holiday season, replacing their traditional Catholic-influenced paradigm with a new model that emphasized Castro's benevolence and primacy as giver to the people of all good gifts—in the form of redistributive programs and public works. In doing so, they sought to harness for the Revolution's own

Cartoon of children decorating a "revolutionary" Christmas tree, laden with the gifts the Cuban people had received from the Revolution: schools, agrarian reform, etc. From Bohemia, *December 20, 1959. Courtesy of the Cuban Heritage Collection, University of Miami Libraries, Coral Gables, Florida.*

purposes the moral and emotional resonance of the Christian worldview that inspired middle-class civic activism on the island.

Christmas Day, however, would not be the apogee of celebration. In keeping with the nationalist tenor of the island's first revolutionary holiday season, state-allied media and businesses were discouraged from promoting North American–influenced customs and products and urged to focus reporting and advertising on the more "Spanish" Epiphany, celebrated by children throughout Latin America as El Día de los Reyes, or Three Kings' Day, on January 6. Government-sponsored Three Kings' Day activities provided a powerful opportunity to deploy the politics of childhood in support of revolutionary nationalism and in opposition to U.S. cultural hegemony on the island. More important, they were a compelling showcase for displays of the Revolution's spiritual and moral sensibilities and Fidel Castro's paternal benevolence, manifested through their concern for the happiness of the island's needy children.

In preparation for the arrival of Los Reyes, the Ministry of Social Welfare had launched Operation Toys for Poor Children in early December. After conducting a hasty census to determine the age and gender of the island's poorest children, the ministry launched a public-private campaign to gather donations of "drums, skates, dolls, and go-karts" from unions, revolutionary organizations, and private citizens. The toys would be distributed to children's homes in disadvantaged neighborhoods across the island on January 6.

Though Operation Toys depended on collaboration between the state and civil society, revolutionary officials and media depicted the project as an initiative of the revolutionary government and emphasized its exclusive leadership of the campaign. To that end, the headline on the front page of the January 3 edition of *Hoy* announced that "All the Children of Cuba Will Have Toys on This 'Night of the Kings'"; the subtitle read, "The People Multiply by Five the Social Welfare Budget for Toys," and noted that the mother of recently deceased rebel hero Camilo Cienfuegos would distribute toys "in his name" at a revolutionary children's party. This was being done so that "all the children of Cuba may laugh happily on this first Three Kings' Day of revolutionary Cuba."

The state-sponsored media also used Operation Toys as an opportunity to criticize similar prerevolutionary projects. In a veiled attack on Catholic groups that had long distributed Christmas and Kings' Day gifts to children, the article insisted that the Revolution had taken on this function in order to eliminate the previous custom, whereby Cubans of limited means had been forced to join "long humiliating lines of humble people begging for a toy for their poor child."[23] According to this logic, Catholic expressions of care and compassion for children, originating in a civil society tainted by association with the corrupt former republic, served only to enforce the injustice of the prerevolutionary status quo. In contrast, state-sponsored charity—though similarly dependent on community and private donations—was framed as the embodiment of the Revolution's unique spiritual and moral imperative, expressed through its determination to spread holiday joy among all the island's boys and girls.

Special efforts were made to prepare for Three Kings' Day celebrations in rural zones, where officials of the National Institute for Agrarian Reform (INRA) had participated heavily in the census taking and collection of donations; many urban *municipios* had covered their own costs for the program, allowing the entirety of the ministry's budget to be dedicated to gathering and transporting toys to the countryside. Throughout the last days of December and into the New Year, cargo loads of gifts were transported to the countryside by truck and train, and by January 3, the Revolutionary Air Force also began airlifting toys to the regions hardest to reach. Acknowledging that "almost all sectors of society, workers, students, professionals, and the middle class, have offered their support," revolutionary media nonetheless made clear that the leadership of Operation Toys remained the exclusive prerogative of the Castro government. The participation of civic actors in the campaign was described as strictly auxiliary, while photographs of military aircraft loaded with toys vividly reinforced the benevolence of a revolutionary state so committed to children that it was willing to deploy the defenders of the *patria* to secure their happiness.

However, as Three Kings' Day approached, it became evident to planners that the state's resources were insufficient to the task. The government turned once again to civil society to save the imperiled Operation Toys. On January 5, Minister for Social Welfare Raquel Pérez issued a call to Cubans to increase their donations, since, she said, there were still parts of the country where the demand for toys had not been met. The nation's Customs Office also turned over two truckloads of holiday gifts ordered from abroad to the ministry for "Revolutionary Resolution." Anticipating the charge that the government had confiscated toys purchased by Cuban parents for their own children, *Hoy* insisted that the "resolved" gifts had either been abandoned, or the date for reclamation had expired.[24] Those children whose holiday toys were diverted to the countryside thus became participants—albeit perhaps unwillingly—in the public-private collaboration that underwrote Operation Toys for Poor Children.

On January 6, children across the island were visited not by *los magos* Melchior, Caspar, and Balthazar but by gift-bearing representatives of the Revolution, clad in olive green. With the assistance of the Banco de Seguros Sociales de Cuba and the Revolutionary Air Force, 25,000 toys were distributed in the most isolated regions of Oriente, including the zones of Songo, La Maya, Sierra Cristal, Calabazas de Sagua, Concepción, and Mayarí, as well as Isla de Pinos and Ciénaga de Zapata. More than twenty military-helicopter loads of toys were distributed to 5,000 children through the region.[25]

Hoy's political cartoonists drove home the message of Operation Toy: the Revolution was both uniquely concerned with and exclusively equipped to offer gifts to the Cuban people. Cartoons like those that had appeared in *Bohemia* during Christmas week similarly appropriated the Catholic imagery of the Epiphany and applied it to Fidel Castro and his government, depicting grateful *guajiros* clutching gifts from "El Rey Barbudo"—a reference to Fidel's beard—while others dressed the Three Kings in cloaks labeled "Instituto de Ahorro y Vivienda" and showed the *reyes* distributing houses to the people.[26]

An explicit example of the effort to appropriate the morally and emotionally resonant discourses of the Christian holiday season appeared on the front page of the January 5 edition of the socialist newspaper *Hoy*. The headline "A Child Asks 'Rey Mago Fidel' to Provide Arms to 'Defend Cuba'" called readers' attention to a letter from eleven-year-old Enriquito Enríquez Estorino, addressed to "Mister 'Rey Mago' Fidel, Dear Commander." The letter read:

> I was going to write to the three Reyes Magos as in previous years, but since you are bearded just as they are, and the reason for the great benefits that have been given to our *patria* and, in particular, to Cuban children, bringing us happiness and tranquility and a world of hopes, I . . . direct this letter to you so that on Three Kings' Day (after fulfilling my responsibilities with my family and with my Cuba by collecting pennies and by belonging to the juvenile patrol) you might give me a weapon so that I can defend this Revolution as my father does. My dear "Rey Mago Fidel," I am still small, but I have enough courage to help the cause of my people and defend my little brothers from the threats of the war criminals. Send me gifts, Fidel, and count on me as you can count on all the children of Cuba.[27]

The letter reinforced the revolutionary campaign to frame Castro and his gifts to the nation as the source of seasonal joy, demonstrating how successful it had been in embedding the rebel leader in the island's Christian-influenced holiday discourses and imagery, and by extension in its spiritual and moral paradigm. The letter also offered a model for patriotic citizens of all ages desiring to fulfill their duties to the homeland through Fidel-worship, support for the state's top-down social initiatives, and even—revealed in the jarring image of an armed eleven-year-old boy battling Batistiano attackers—through the armed defense of the Revolution. Enriquito Enríquez's letter, likely written as a school assignment, thus contributed to official efforts to appeal to Cubans' Christian-inflected values and sensibilities, even as it anticipated the radicalization of revolutionary policy and an increasingly combative politics of childhood in which, by the early months of 1961, the figure of the child *miliciano* would play a powerful role.

LA REVOLUCIÓN EN EL CAMPO: COMPETITION BETWEEN THE STATE AND CIVIL SOCIETY IN THE COUNTRYSIDE

As the holiday season came to a close, the revolutionary government intensified efforts to divert moral capital away from the Catholic Church and the urban middle class by launching a campaign to revitalize the Cuban *campo*. One of the first efforts was a program to regularize common-law marriages, prevalent among the island's working classes and rural poor, thereby legitimizing the children produced by those unions. This program unfavorably contrasted the prerevolutionary Church's reduced presence in the countryside—many rural parishes had lacked a full-time priest and thus had limited access to the family-strengthening sacraments of marriage and baptism—with the Revolution's commitment to rural households.

In January 1960, the revolutionary government began to celebrate collective marriage ceremonies in the countryside. In Fomento, a village in Las Villas province, sixty couples were married that month, responding to official exhortations that they regularize their relationship and the status of their offspring by having themselves and their children entered in the new Civil Register. In the same month, forty-six couples were married in similar fashion in Camagüey.[28] Programs to regularize marriages and register children, while reinforcing the conservative and Catholic-inspired family values of the republican era, were seen as a transitional step toward legislation that would legitimize children born to unwed parents without requiring them to participate in marriage ceremonies.

Fidel Castro's special interest in this program may have originated in the wounds of his own childhood: he was born the illegitimate son of an eastern landowner and his domestic servant lover, whose marriage when he was an adolescent allowed for Castro's legitimization and his baptism, prerequisites to his enrollment in a Catholic secondary school.[29] Regardless of its inspiration, the campaign to formalize common-law couples and recognize their children would undercut the Church's traditional role as arbiter of family life and reduce the role of Catholic charities and schools—many of which dispensed services in line with religiously defined notions of morality—in the lives of needy children.

The state-sponsored media provided in-depth coverage of other revolutionary efforts to furnish badly needed services to the countryside, and especially to rural children. The Pancho Pérez Tobacco Cooperative, funded by INRA with grants from the Ministry of Public Works and constructed by students, members of the Rebel Army, and civilian volunteers, received in-depth coverage early in January 1960. The tobacco cooperative would provide rural *tabaqueros* with reinforced concrete houses equipped with electricity, glass windows, modern bathrooms, and washing machines. A six-classroom school, complete with a full-service kitchen, dining area, and carpentry workshop, had also been built. A journalist reporting on the construction of the cooperative exulted that its young students would receive a better education than had ever been possible in the country-side. They would also enjoy the use of a theater, two swimming pools, and a baseball diamond. "Sports will be done there," the reporter mar-veled. "Imagine! The peasants of our earth, doing sports!" Neglecting to thank the local volunteers who had actually built the facilities, he stressed the Revolution's generosity to rural communities and concluded by evok-ing God's favor on the government's efforts to revitalize the countryside. "Blessed be Agrarian Reform!"[30]

The Revolution's ambitions to build up to 10,000 new schools across the countryside, and especially its program to convert military forts and prisons into educational centers, took pride of place in the campaign to discredit non-state-sponsored social justice projects and deny civic actors a meaningful role in the establishment of the moral republic.[31] Television coverage and photographs of Fidel Castro attending rural school open-ings drove home the message that the new schools were not the product of public-private collaboration and local efforts but rather the singular gift of the Revolution, an expression of Fidel Castro's deep concern for the well-being of all Cubans—for all of them were his children.

In January, Castro presided at a ceremony inaugurating a new edu-cational center in the newly converted Moncada barracks in Santiago de Cuba, where he spoke to hundreds of flag-waving schoolchildren set to begin studying at the school. Official pronouncements and the revolution-ary press hailed the transformation of this and many military forts into rural schools as evidence of the Revolution's humanist values and rein-forced the image of Castro as a loving paternal figure to Cuban children.[32] They described the youthful Fidel-worship that animated rural school openings, deeming it a fitting response to the rebel leader's generosity and commenting approvingly that children "fought to get close to Fidel Castro, holding out their hands and lifting up their arms to him. And the Prime Minister let the young ones take his hand, and he smiled at them with the tenderness of a father . . . and those that were able to touch him and even those that couldn't, went home to bed with great satisfaction. Fidel had given them classrooms, teachers, workshops! They could be happy!"[33]

At the same time, the state-sponsored media struggled to explain the repeated occasions on which rural Cubans, unwilling to wait for the Revolution's official representatives to reach their communities, organized to build and run their own schools. These schools were belatedly recognized and claimed by the Revolution as part of its program of rural educational reform.[34] Official silence on grassroots rural school-building projects further contributed to suppressing public knowledge of civic activism in the *campo* and reinforced the increasingly hegemonic notion of the Revolution as the sole source of reform in the countryside.

In February 1960, the revolutionary government continued its well-publicized campaign of rural revitalization, dramatically improving children's access to adequate housing, education, sanitation, and recreation. At the same time, media representations of these initiatives facilitated the Revolution's ongoing efforts to appropriate the spiritual and moral capital of a progressive Catholic-influenced middle class and discredit the autonomous social justice projects that competed with its own programs. This process of appropriation and delegitimization would lay the groundwork for what came next—the suppression of non-state-sponsored activism and the almost total destruction of the institutions of a still vibrant civil society.

THE POLITICS OF CHILDHOOD AND THE SUPPRESSION OF CIVIL SOCIETY

By the end of 1959, the tolerance of individual and community-led activism, even—perhaps especially—efforts that proclaimed social justice commitments claimed by the Revolution, was coming to an end. Beginning early in the New Year, Castro made clear that opportunities to participate in constructing the moral republic would be limited to the Revolution's supporters and that these would consist solely of voluntary work in the state's top-down reform campaigns. Cubans who wished to defend the Revolution could also join armed workplace, university, or youth patrols; attend mass rallies in support of Castro and his initiatives; and join together at demonstrations to denounce his enemies. Through these activities and these alone, citizens of all ages could exercise their citizenship in the revolutionary nation.

At the same time, extrarevolutionary actors began to fall increasingly under attack—a process that had originated in the summer of 1959 with the University of Havana's loss of its constitutionally guaranteed autonomy and the purging of as many as two-thirds of the university's professors who had protested the curtailment of academic freedom.[35] By January 1960, the most important remaining institutions of civil society, the non-state-sponsored media and the Catholic Church and affiliated organizations, represented the most serious threat to the Revolution's increasingly hegemonic influence over public life.

Initial efforts to repress the Cuban media dated back to November 1959, when *Prensa Libre*, *El Avance*, and *Diario de la Marina*—the three major dailies known for their criticism of revolutionary policy—each published stories questioning the resignation of Huber Matos. However, beginning shortly after the New Year, the Castro government and its allies launched a coordinated attack on the independent press, issuing a series of increasingly indiscriminate accusations of media conspiracy against the Revolution. Nonrevolutionary newspapers, magazines, and journals were subjected to harassment and intimidation by revolutionary militias and PSP-dominated typographic unions, who demanded that these publications accept editorial oversight by "the people." Access to increasingly scarce supplies of paper and ink, newly subject to rationing, became dependent on publications' willingness to subject their content to revision, or to print a qualifying *coletilla* that offered a revolutionary counter to arguments at odds with the official interpretation of events.

Publications that refused to accept the imposition of the *coletilla* fell victim to more aggressive sanctions. One of the first newspapers to suffer physical attack was the conservative *Diario de la Marina*. First established in 1832, the *Diario* had initially offered its cautious support for the Revolution; however, by the end of 1959, the newspaper's criticism of the new government's policies, its stubbornly pro-U.S. stance and insistence on publishing articles in support of Church and privately funded social justice initiatives, had marked it as a "reactionary" publication. On May 12, 1960, a group of armed *milicianos* broke into the *Diario*'s offices, vandalized the premises and machinery, and forced the printers to publish a revolutionary tract. The next day, chief editor José Ignacio Rivero sought asylum in the Peruvian embassy.[36] When a *Prensa Libre* journalist wrote about the suppression of *Diario de la Marina* and the threat this represented to freedom of the press in Cuba, that publication was seized by the government.

In the first half of 1960, children began to be deployed in attacks on independent publications accused of fomenting opposition to the Revolution.

Young boys and girls were regular participants in public acts of denunciation of what was increasingly referred to as the "counterrevolutionary press." In January, residents of Bejucal gathered to stage a symbolic burial of non-state-sponsored newspapers and magazines, including *Diario de la Marina, Crisol,* and *Prensa Libre,* as well as U.S. publications, including the *Miami Herald* and *Life* magazine. Under the leadership of journalist Rubén Chaviano Gavillán, chair of the local branch of the Directorio Revolucionario, children and adults shouting, "Paredón! Paredón! [To the firing squad!]," congregated in Maceo-Gómez Park. They marched across town in procession behind a coffin representing the "counterrevolutionary press," staging a symbolic burial of the coffin as a demonstration of their anger at public critiques of the Revolution.

Coverage of the Bejucal press burial in *Hoy* noted approvingly that "the entire town joined in" with enthusiasm, to the extent that "even the children were able to demonstrate their repudiation of the nation's *vendepatria* [sellers-out of the nation] press and of the mercenary magazines and newspapers" of the United States. Photographs accompanying the text featured children gathered around a sign reading, "May the Reactionary Press Rest in Peace." Utilizing language similar to that found in descriptions of other media burials in *Bohemia* and *Revolución, Hoy* interpreted the participation of presumably virtuous children in the mock burial as evidence of the moral correctness of this denunciatory act, as well as proof that the entire nation supported the Revolution and condemned dissenters.[37]

Mock burials and burnings of both domestic and foreign publications, organized by representatives of the revolutionary government, continued across the country into late in the summer of 1960. At the same time, more and more non-state-sponsored publications fell under attack by armed mobs and militias, vulnerable to charges that their critique of the government's policies and initiatives was proof of their membership in a reactionary and morally bankrupt elite. Dissenters of any kind, regardless of their actual political sympathies, were categorically defined as enemies of the Revolution, the people, and especially the children on whose behalf the Revolution had been fought. According to this official perspective, it was therefore fitting and even necessary that children be active participants in the mass demonstrations against the rapidly disappearing independent press.

The irony, not lost on the disaffected journalists who left the country in 1960 for exile in Spain, the United States, and other Latin American nations, was that many of them—including *Bohemia*'s fervent *fidelista* chief editor Miguel de Quevedo and journalist Carlos Castañeda—had initially participated in media efforts to represent children as both the symbol and main beneficiaries of the Revolution. By reinforcing a powerful discursive link between children's well-being and the survival of the Revolution, members of the island's non-state-sponsored press had unwittingly contributed to the rapidly radicalizing politics of childhood that created the ideological conditions for their own suppression.

Once the independent media had been submitted to revolutionary discipline, the Castro government turned its militias and mobs on the Catholic Church—the most vigorous opponent to the increasingly authoritarian Revolution and its last competitor for control of the hearts and minds of the island's children. Throughout the winter and spring of 1960, Sunday masses across the island were interrupted by violent attacks led by groups shouting denigrations and pro-Revolution slogans. These confrontations were especially frequent in wealthy congregations like Havana's Jesús de Miramar Church, but they also took place in middle- and working-class congregations like those of Artemisa, Bauta, and Sagua la Grande and at the cathedral in Habana Vieja.[38]

Then, in August 1960, Cuba's five archbishops issued a joint pastoral declaration to be read at all the nation's parishes. Reiterating the Church's commitment to "profound social reforms based on justice and charity," the bishops nonetheless cited papal encyclicals rejecting Marxist materialism as antithetical to Christian morality and affirmed the right of Catholics to express their opposition to communist doctrine, arguing that freedom of speech should not be suppressed "in the name of a poorly understood sense of civic unity."[39] Following this barely veiled critique of the Revolution, the island's parishes were subject to an even more violent series of denunciations and attacks. Church services and meetings of Catholic organizations like Juventud Obrera Católica became regular sites of protest and clashes with revolutionary mobs, and dozens of parishioners were arrested.

Priests and powerful bishops nonetheless continued to exercise their right of public address and circulated printed material criticizing the heavy hand of the Revolution and the betrayal of its promise to respect freedom of religion. In light of the almost total suppression of the independent media and subsequent absence of other venues for the expression of dissent, the Catholic leaders' influence over the rapidly shrinking Cuban civil society continued to grow. Juventud Obrera Católica and Acción Católica, left-leaning Catholic student groups that maintained strong Afro-Cuban and working-class memberships, also raised their voices to protest Castro's authoritarian rule and the state's persecution of faith-based groups. In doing so, they gave lie to class-based explanations of increasing opposition to the Revolution and disrupted the binaries between young and old, poor and privileged, rural and urban, black and white, reactionary and revolutionary, nation and antinational that underwrote its radicalization.[40]

Progressive Catholic organizations continued to circulate widely read monthly newspapers as late as October 1960, when their publication was prohibited. That same month, Monsignor Eduardo Boza Masvidal published an open letter titled "Is the Social Revolution Being Realized in Cuba a Christian One?," condemning revolutionary efforts to marginalize the Revolution's original Catholic and middle-class supporters. In the letter, Boza Masvidal answered his own question in the negative. Critiquing Castro for stirring up class antagonism in order to justify his policies, the archbishop warned that "pitting the poor against the rich . . . is not to reestablish justice but rather carries injustice to the opposite extreme. The Christian thing would be . . . to create well-being mutually and [opportunities for them to] love one another as brothers." He also criticized the Revolution's "lack of respect toward the natural right of property" and toward the family, as well as its systematic attack on the United States and growing friendship with Russia and other socialist nations.[41]

Enraged, Castro fired back in a series of speeches accusing the Cuban clergy—many of them transplanted Spaniards—of fascist and pro-Franco sympathies, charging them with practicing "selective Christianity" and asserting that revolutionaries who sacrificed themselves on behalf of others and gave to the poor were the "true Christians."[42] If the island's Catholic leaders were truly Christian, he challenged—ignoring their history of faith-based charity and social justice work—they should "leave their temples" and go to the countryside to volunteer in the Revolution's program to help the sick, build houses, and promote agrarian reform. In a bewildering jab at middle-class Cuban housewives, he challenged them to demonstrate their Christian credentials by dedicating themselves to knitting and embroidering nightgowns for children who had no clothing. Dismissing privileged Catholic Cubans as "Pharisees," insincere and self-interested servants of a foreign power, Castro irrevocably established the Revolution as the authoritative example of "what it means to be a Christian" and counterposed it to Church-affiliated organizations and individuals, whom he accused of going "to the doors of the temples [to] conspire against the homeland." With these angry words, he made clear that the remnants of a discredited Catholic-influenced civil society had no place within his increasingly narrow vision of the revolutionary nation.[43]

THE CUBAN REVOLUTION'S DRASTIC SHIFT to the left, usually traced to the beginning of 1960, actually had roots in a discursive realm of contestation and radicalization dating back to at least the middle of 1959. By Christmas of that year, civic activism in support of a socially transformative but anticommunist and democratic nation-making project had begun to threaten the Revolution's efforts to frame itself as the sole inheritor of Martí's vision of the moral republic. In response, the Castro government launched a child-centered campaign to discredit non-state-sponsored reform initiatives and represent Castro as the sole dispenser of gifts to Cubans of all ages.

The suppression of Cuban civil society was accomplished through the promulgation of a morally and emotionally resonant child-centered discourse that helped divert the spiritual and moral capital of familiar nationalist symbols and discourses, religious beliefs and practices, and cultural traditions, away from a once vibrant civil society and into the service of the revolutionary government. Flesh-and-blood children were also deployed to denounce the Revolution's critics among the non-state-sponsored media and counter Catholic claims to a leadership role in the construction of the moral republic. They helped establish the Revolution as not only a political and social process but an exclusive moral paradigm—one that focused more and more narrowly on the interests of the poor and the working classes, and had less and less room in it for selfish and "bourgeois" calls for the safeguarding of electoral democracy, property rights, and the cherished civic freedoms of speech, association, and religion. Children thus contributed to the narrowing range of ideas and actors eligible for inclusion in the category of "revolutionary," culminating in Fidel Castro's claims that the Revolution, not the values of Catholic social justice, represented the radical fulfillment of Christianity.

An increasingly combative politics of childhood played a powerful role in key trends characterizing this period: the destruction of Cuba's civil institutions and silencing of public debate over the Revolution's consolidation in the hands of a supreme leader, the deterioration of Cuba's relationship with the United States, and the nascent alliance with the Soviet Union. However, the elimination of the last remaining spaces for peaceful efforts to influence the nation's trajectory also compelled many Cubans to join an emerging Counterrevolution. Given the prominence of children in this process, it is unsurprising that counterrevolutionaries would use their own variant of the politics of childhood in order to articulate their opposition to the Castro government and express their alternative vision for the island's future. As a result, the battle between revolutionary and counterrevolutionary nation-making projects was destined to play itself out through a struggle for control of the meanings attributed to childhood—and for control over the bodies and minds of flesh-and-blood Cuban children.

4
CHILDREN, RADICALIZATION, AND THE CUBAN COUNTERREVOLUTION

Between 1960 and 1961, childhood emerged as one of the primary sites of struggle in which the forces of Revolution and an emerging Counterrevolution battled to determine Cuba's destiny. As the Castro government implemented increasingly radical economic and social policies, officials and the state-sponsored media relied heavily on representations of children to explain the Revolution's sharp turn to the left and pursuit of a new strategic relationship with the Soviet Union. At the same time, Fidel Castro sought to consolidate his position as supreme leader and father of the Cuban nation by operationalizing new understandings and practices of childhood, establishing exclusive government control over the education and ideological formation of children, and forging ever closer linkages between himself, young people, and the revolutionary state. In response, middle-class parents, clergy, and private school educators joined together to resist the radicalization of a Revolution they had once supported. In doing so, they created a conservative and Catholic-inflected variant of the politics of childhood in which the protection of middle-class notions of childhood, the safeguarding of the republican institutions of the patriarchal family and the private school, and the defense of the traditional authority of the Church became central to their quest to reassert José Martí's vision of the moral republic.

During these tumultuous two years, competing discourses of childhood became increasingly salient as pro- and anti-Castro actors alike pressed the symbolic figure of the child into the service of mutually antagonistic nation-making projects. As a wave of political violence swept the island, Cuban children found themselves more and more frequently drawn into "adult" struggles, directly impacting the dialectical relationship between radicalization and Counterrevolution even as their own day-to-day lives were transformed by the upheaval in their society. As the politics of childhood spilled over from the discursive realm and into the streets, pro- and counterrevolutionary forces not only fought "for the children," battling on behalf of the child-centered values and customs that underlay their competing visions of the island's future, but also fought *through* flesh-and-blood children to wrest control of the nation from the hands of their enemies.

After the defeat of the U.S.-backed exile invasion at Playa Girón, Cuban young people would assume an even more prominent role in the newly declared socialist Revolution, even as tens of thousands of middle-class refugees fled the island to protect their sons and daughters from communist indoctrination. As a virulently anti-Castro exile community began to emerge in southern Florida, the politics of Cuban childhood that had first emerged during the island's turn-of-the-century war of independence would assume an even more important role in the struggle to make or remake the Cuban nation.

CHILDREN, THE UNITED STATES, THE U.S.S.R., AND THE RADICALIZATION OF THE REVOLUTION

By the beginning of the Revolution's second year, as U.S. hostility to the Revolution increased, child-centered images and discourses were more and more frequently employed to assert a North American threat to the island's independence. They also played an important role in gradually introducing Cuban citizens, many of whom remained committed to a democratic and reformist vision of the Revolution, to the need for a new strategic relationship with the socialist world.[1] Even as the expanding presence of Partido Socialista Popular (PSP) members in the highest circles of the Castro government revealed the Revolution's shift to the left, positive stories about children in socialist nations—already common in the socialist newspaper *Noticias de Hoy*—began to appear in revolutionary speeches and publications, providing further evidence of the government's political reorientation and introducing Cubans to favorable images of the Soviet Union.

As the PSP's official publication, *Hoy* made no secret of its admiration for the U.S.S.R.; its pages were punctuated with photo-essays and stories about children in socialist nations, emphasizing their happiness and well-being and contrasting their improved life chances with the fate of young people in capitalist societies. *Hoy* increasingly linked the well-being of socialist children and the benefits to Cuban children of Castro's prochild initiatives in health care and education, drawing parallels between Soviet efforts on behalf of children and the revolutionary process taking place in Cuba.

By the beginning of the Revolution's second year, the state-sponsored media had begun to refer to Cuba's membership in a shared anti-imperialist, if not yet openly socialist, international project. Messages reinforcing this shift in international alignment often appeared in letters written by children. As the Revolution embarked on a search for new allies and markets among countries not allied with the United States, messages from young people in socialist nations began to take prominence. On January 1, 1960, *Hoy* celebrated the first anniversary of Batista's flight by publishing a letter from the Committee of Youth Organizations in the U.S.S.R., directed to "socialist youth" in Havana. Written in broken Spanish—perhaps left unedited to emphasize its authenticity and foreign origin—the letter offered greetings and congratulations, in the name of "millions of boys and girls from the Soviet Union" to the "glorious Cuban youth . . . on the first anniversary of the Revolution's triumph."

Alluding to international socialism's sympathy for the island's new government, the letter stated that the children of the U.S.S.R. joined the Cuban people in commemorating this happy day, wishing them "great success in the construction of the fatherland [and] the solution of the fundamental economic challenges before the Cuban people." The letter concluded by offering its best wishes for the "strengthening of Cuban independence," calling for the continued "defense of the Cuban Revolution against the attacks of its enemies."[2] These encouraging words referred not only to continuing attacks on the island from Batistianos in Florida but also to ongoing economic attempts by the United States to force the Revolution to moderate its path—and alluded to the important role children might play in resisting U.S. imperialism and constructing the revolutionary nation.

Publishing the letter on the front page of its first 1960 edition, *Hoy* employed a discursive strategy already familiar to readers of the revolutionary media: the construct of virtuous Cuban children as *voceros*, or political prophets, whose intuitive understanding of essential truths uniquely equipped them to speak on behalf of their nation. These were qualities, presumably, that Soviet children shared with Cuba's youngest citizens, providing the basis for their sense of identification with the island's youth and a model for solidarity between the two nations. Moreover, the virtue of Soviet youth both reinforced the fundamental legitimacy of the socialist project and allowed them to intuit its animating presence within the

Cuban Revolution, providing advance validation for Cuba's soon to be formalized relations with the U.S.S.R.

In February 1960, as hostility between Cuba and the United States continued to grow, Cuba established its first official diplomatic contact with the Soviet Union. Deputy Premier Anastas Mikoyan arrived on the island—ostensibly to open a Soviet exhibition at Havana's Palacio de Bellas Artes, an event that drew Cubans of all ages. The exhibition included displays of Soviet-made consumer goods, books, tools, and machinery. It also included a series of documentary films and cartoons aimed at children, shown free of charge in the Teatro de Bellas Artes. Coverage in *Hoy* concentrated on images of Cuban children marveling at Soviet-made cameras and playing pianos imported from the U.S.S.R., as evidence that the island's citizens, so long "deceived by the lying, self-interested propaganda of reaction and imperialism" were awestruck by the overwhelming quantity and quality of Soviet-made goods on display.[3] The newspaper thus used images of children to construct the U.S.S.R. as a favorable alternative to continued trade with the imperialist United States.

Echoing this sentiment, celebrated Afro-Cuban poet Nicolás Guillén wrote that Mikoyan's visit and the exhibition's success were proof of the Cuban people's desire for closer ties with the U.S.S.R. Cuba's young people, Guillén argued, were especially enthralled by the Soviet Union, evidenced by "the crowds of children—in the end, children of the new era—wonderstruck by the Soviet scientific advancements, and especially by the 'Sputniks.'" Cuban children's delight in these Soviet innovations, the poet argued, reflected these young citizens' intuitive understanding that the U.S.S.R. represented an exciting alternative model for Cuban development. Moreover, the children's enthusiasm reflected "a sharp rise in Soviet prestige," offering a welcome challenge to the predominant influence of the United States on the island.[4] *Hoy*'s emphasis on child-centered images and discourses provided a morally resonant apologetics for the U.S.S.R.'s socialist nation-making project, encouraging noncommunist Cubans to identify previously unexplored affinities between Marxism-Leninism and Martí's vision of the moral republic, even as it deepened ties between the Revolution, the island's "old guard" communists, and its Moscow patrons. The newspaper thus provided a model for state-sponsored media seeking to strategically deploy Cuban children in the service of the Revolution's campaign to forge new ties with the Soviet Union.

The island's independent media were less enthusiastic. Though none dared to openly criticize Fidel Castro's decision to receive Mikoyan, a number of these journalists interpreted the Soviet premier's visit as welcome evidence of Cuba's newly restored national sovereignty, without any discussion of a possible alliance with the U.S.S.R. A few went so far as to publish anticommunist editorials featuring photographs of the bleak living conditions in the Soviet Union. More serious than this mild display of media dissent, however, was the reaction of Havana students to Mikoyan's visit. Enraged that the Soviet leader had placed a hammer and sickle–shaped wreath before the statue of José Martí in the city's Parque Central, more than 100 white, black, and mulatto high school and university students took to the streets in protest. They staged a procession, headed by a neatly dressed preadolescent boy and girl, who replaced the offending flower arrangement with another shaped like a Cuban flag adorned with a banner that read, "To you, our Apostle—to make amends for the visit of the assassin Mikoyan." These Cuban young people sought to assert the primacy of Martí's vision of a moral republic free of imperial oversight—by the United States or any other nation—over the potential benefit of a strategic relationship with the U.S.S.R. For doing so, they were beaten by militia members, arrested, and accused of counterrevolutionary conspiracy. The only periodical to publish pictures of the detained, bruised, and bandaged youth was *Prensa Libre*; the state-sponsored media, aware that the student protest represented a serious threat to the image of political consensus that justified the Revolution's increasingly authoritarian leadership, largely preferred to ignore the incident.[5]

Despite these displays of popular aversion to a formal alliance with the U.S.S.R., Castro's determination to align the island with the Soviet Union prevailed. Before the end of Mikoyan's short visit, the deputy premier signed a trade agreement to purchase 5 million tons of Cuban sugar and extended a $100 million credit and promise of technical assistance to the Castro government. In April, Cuba and the Soviet Union resumed official diplomatic relations, suspended since Batista's 1952 coup. As the island's ties to the U.S.S.R. deepened, Fidel Castro deployed a rapidly evolving politics of childhood to help shift the Revolution to the left. In line with Marxist-Leninist perspectives on the role of young people in a communist society, Castro more and more frequently stressed the need to reinterpret the child as an autonomous political actor, capable of rendering and expected to render specific individual service to the Revolution. The future of the nation, Castro emphasized, was in the hands of the new generation of schoolchildren, who would be acclaimed by history for their efforts on its behalf. They would be the "admiration of the children of the future" because they would be "the ones who will finish the work of the Revolution."[6] Castro encouraged the children to think of themselves as the inheritors of a great patriotic obligation that they could fulfill through study and service to the revolutionary government.

Children were increasingly called on to fulfill political functions: to demonstrate their love for and loyalty to Fidel Castro by joining mass organizations and initiatives, marching in parades, and participating in ever more militant rallies. Then, in January 1960, the government decreed that all Cuban students would learn to bear arms.[7] During the following summer, Castro established a new militia, composed of young people between the ages of twelve and seventeen, to guard confiscated properties from former owners and to ensure high production levels among workers. Christened the Asociación de Jóvenes Rebeldes (AJR), or Association of Rebel Youth, the new organization included former members of the PSP youth group and individuals selected on the basis of their commitment to volunteer labor in cooperatives, factories, and other work sites.

The presence of armed AJR *milicianos* in public spaces represented a startling shift in the social balance of power between children and adults; many of the gun-toting "Young Rebels" were barely adolescents.[8] It also signaled the growing political importance of young people in revolutionary society as well as the growing prominence of Cuban communists within the Revolution. As the Castro government continued to pursue a new relationship with the U.S.S.R., the Revolution's refashioning of children's lives challenged middle-class understandings of childhood as a time of dependence, innocence, and play. It also disrupted relations within the patriarchal Cuban family and threatened the traditional authority of the clergy. These changes seemed to mirror Soviet notions of childhood, inflaming anticommunist anxieties at exactly the moment when the Revolution launched a radical program to nationalize much of the island's industry and private property.

In June, when U.S. refineries in Cuba refused to process petroleum supplied by the Soviet Union, Castro responded by taking possession of them as well, provoking outrage in Washington. Castro's action threatened not only U.S. economic interests on the island but, perhaps equally important, the very notions of Cuban immaturity and dependence and U.S. wisdom and benevolence that had structured interactions between the two countries since 1898. Thereafter seeking to remind Cubans of their appropriate role in their long-standing parent-child relationship with the United States, Congressman Mendel Rivers (D-SC) denounced "the bearded pipsqueak of the Antilles" for acting against U.S. wishes in "a country that was conceived by America, delivered by America, nurtured by America, educated by America, and made a self-governing nation by America." This childish ingratitude, Rivers warned, would not go unpunished.[9]

In the face of ongoing attacks from Florida-based exiles, and fearing the growing possibility of U.S. military intervention on the island, Castro increased efforts to mobilize Cubans, including children as young as thirteen, into civilian militia units, and he sought military aid from the U.S.S.R. Russian and Czech weapons flowed into the island throughout the final months of 1960, providing Cuba with the modern weapons that the Revolutionary Armed Forces and militias lacked and that, thanks to the new U.S. embargo, NATO nations had been unwilling to furnish.

The Revolution thus celebrated its second Christmas in a context of unprecedented hostility between Cuba and the United States and increasingly close ties to the socialist world. News coverage of the holiday season, while still focused on children, accordingly deemphasized many of the "bourgeois" and Catholic images around which the first revolutionary Christmas celebrations had been organized. Havana department stores advertised a selection of toys, prices "newly regulated by the Ministry of Commerce," that reflected the militant tenor of the times. La Nueva Isla department store offered an extensive collection of "all the toys your child could wish for," including a militia costume for girls ages two to eight for $6.99; olive green nylon "militia packs" for boys aged three to ten for $4.95; and a militia field campaign tent for $6.50.[10]

Cubans enjoyed a holiday season rich in militant allusions to the people's ability to repel North American attacks on their finally independent homeland. The revolutionary media's coverage of state-sponsored holiday celebrations even more dramatically reflected the anti-U.S. fervor of the moment. The January 6, 1961, edition of *Revolución* featured a photograph of a pigtailed toddler playing with her Three Kings' Day gifts, counterposed against smaller images of adults manning antiaircraft guns along Havana's boardwalk; the headline proclaimed, "The children with their toys and their parents with the weapons of the fatherland." A caption informed readers that "while men and women, fathers and mothers, organized to fight against the imperialist invader, the children have their special day. Because even under threat of bullets, the Revolution doesn't forget them."[11] A later retrospective of the holiday season included photos of children filling the streets of the city, greeting the costumed kings and receiving gifts from *milicianos*. Above their beribboned and lovingly combed heads, a banner proclaimed, "There is nothing more important than a child: Fidel Castro." One of the photos mocked U.S. attempts to intimidate Cubans into abandoning their Revolution, asking, "When will the invasion arrive? Ha ha ha!"[12]

Cuban bravado in the face of U.S. hostility increased Fidel Castro's popularity and attracted attention from socialist nations. Children in these places, and perhaps especially in the Soviet Union, where journalists and teachers offered the defiant rebel leader to young people as a role model, were encouraged to reach out to Cuba with messages of solidarity. In February 1961, representatives of the socialist Pioneers troupe at School 221 in Leningrad sent Castro a letter expressing their admiration for the Revolution, for its leader, and for his special concern for children. The letter began: "Dear Comrade Fidel: We students from Leningrad send warm greetings to you. . . . We are filled with enthusiasm by your firmness and faith toward freedom and join our voices to yours to cry out with the Cubans, '¡Cuba, Sí! ¡Yanquis, No!'" The Pioneers praised the revolutionary leader for his "courage, decisiveness, perseverance, and self-abnegation, which are an example for all Soviet children." They also sent Castro a Pioneer's neckerchief and invited him to be an honorary member of their troupe.[13]

Writing to Castro was undoubtedly an officially approved endeavor for these Leningrad children, one that had necessarily received the full support and assistance of Soviet teachers and their school's Party representatives. As such the letter represents a small but symbolically powerful contribution to the accelerating process of alliance-building in which Cuba and the U.S.S.R. were engaged. The letter, published in its entirety in *Hoy*, further reinforced the association of children's presumed virtue with both the radicalizing Revolution and its new socialist allies, working to confer legitimacy on the ever closer ties Cuba was developing with the Soviet Union.

EL AÑO DE LA EDUCACIÓN: THE IDEOLOGICAL EDUCATION OF CUBAN CHILDREN

The spheres of childhood and education figured prominently in efforts to counter opposition and to demonstrate Cuba's anti-imperialist credentials to the socialist bloc. On December 31, 1960, Fidel Castro joined 10,000 teachers and 1,000 foreign guests at the Ciudad Libertad school city, where they had gathered for dinner, dancing, and celebrations to welcome 1961, the Year of Education. In the year to come, Castro told his audience, the Revolution would dramatically increase the pace of school construction and teacher training, expand early childhood education through the creation of 300 *círculos infantiles*, and embark on a massive literacy campaign, at the end of which he promised no illiterate person would be found in Cuba.[14] In support of this goal, the school year would be cut short by two months, and teachers and students from sixth grade and above would be mobilized as volunteer literacy instructors. Echoing the profoundly militant tenor of the holiday season, Castro concluded that "in the same way that we have organized the National Militias, so will we organize the Army of Education."

Castro made clear that the goals of the Year of Education were not strictly limited to improving access to learning for Cubans; they would also serve the Revolution's broader political agenda, including its defense against international detractors and a growing Counterrevolution. Identifying childhood as a key site for struggle between pro- and anti-Castro Cubans, the government began to insist on teachers' obligation to take charge of the correct ideological formation of the island's children. A new mass teacher's organization was founded, the Frente Revolucionario de Profesores Secundarios; seeing themselves as pioneers in the integration of teachers at all educational levels into the service of the Revolution, the Frente's members vowed to use the island's classrooms to promulgate official revolutionary doctrine and promote new laws and initiatives.[15]

The organization's first public act took place on February 6, when more than 8,000 secondary school teachers responded to a call to attend a meeting at Havana's Palacio de los Trabajadores theater. Education Minister Armando Hart addressed the crowd first. He asserted that educators were the people most obligated to understand the Revolution, since their work with future generations held the key to "the correct development of the social form" of the nation.[16] Teachers had an urgent obligation to defend the Revolution and to oppose the efforts of reactionary Catholic educators, who sought to create disorder and to "poison" children with "ideas contrary to those their parents defend, contrary to all those who were working to create a society founded in virtue, in efficiency, in work."

"The counterrevolution has selected teachers and education in order to realize its criminal work," he declared, "inaugurating in these days a new era of counterrevolutionary agitation that wants to have its headquarters in the schools of our country." However, he continued, the Revolution's supporters would fight back. Just as rebel soldiers had gone to the trenches in combat for the Revolution, teachers would now be called on "to occupy, in the schools, together with the students, the trenches and the positions of combat in the Revolution, and you will have to occupy them because you must defend the Revolution."[17]

Teachers thus found themselves compelled, whether by conviction or by circumstance, to participate in the initiatives of the Year of Education. Their first task was to strengthen ideological content in school curricula. New textbooks, pictures, and slogans encouraged Cuban children to imagine their lives as infused with revolutionary meaning and instructed them in the Revolution's history, values, and initiatives. An essential component of ideological education was the strengthening of reverence for Fidel Castro and the justification of his increasingly authoritarian leadership. While Fidel-worship was partly a spontaneous phenomenon, by 1961 it would become institutionalized in new public school curricula and methodologies that consistently linked the leader and his agenda to the well-being of the island's children—and by extension to the well-being of the nation.

Teachers encouraged children to express their devotion to Fidel Castro in essay, poetry, and letter-writing assignments that were frequently published in the state-sponsored media. A special issue of *Bohemia*, dedicated to children, featured a number of these compositions, including a letter from a nine-year-old girl named Albita. In an expression of girlish hero worship, she asked the *comandante-en-jefe* to send her a photo, "dedicated to me in your own handwriting," as a Three Kings' Day gift. Demonstrating an understanding of politics reinforced by ideologically derived curricula, she also warned Castro to "keep your shirt closed so that you won't get shot by one of those bad people who set bombs and who don't like the Revolution. I know this will make you feel very hot, but it's better that you should be hot than die."[18] Encouraging children to identify emotionally with Fidel Castro, teachers contributed to the ideological formation of young people and encouraged them to invest their hopes and dreams for the future in the Revolution's supreme leader.

Children from impoverished rural families—*becados*, or scholarship students, who traveled from the countryside to attend new boarding schools—were targets of some of the Year of Education's most comprehensive ideological education initiatives. Boarding schools, in many cases staffed by hastily trained and inexperienced teachers, were run with militaristic discipline. They relied heavily on rote learning, memorization, and drills that encouraged uniformity of thought and expression. Moreover, *becados* were required to live at school. While consolidating children from isolated areas in larger central schools was a practical strategy, it also had an ideological purpose: children were deliberately removed from their homes in order to increase the state's ability to engineer a revolutionary learning environment and "to replace old ideas with new ones in the absence of parental influence."[19]

Scholarship programs served both pragmatic and political purposes: the Revolution founded programs that offered educational services, housing, food, and clothing to the island's neediest children even while dramatically expanding the state's capacity for social control of the young. The efficacy of this approach to the ideological education of poor and rural students would be confirmed by the revolutionary fervor of many former *becados*, many of whom graduated from accelerated sixth-grade equivalency programs and immediately entered crash teacher-training programs. Aspiring teachers, most of them from campesino families and ranging in age from thirteen to fifteen—though some were as young as eleven—entered programs like the one established in 1960 at the Minas del Frío School in the Sierra Maestra. In line with the militaristic tenor of many of the Revolution's new educational programs, teacher training also involved a combination of ideological formation and physical conditioning, seen as necessary for teachers who would go to rural and mountainous areas. Climbing mountains, sleeping in tents and lean-tos, and withstanding cold and rain was also envisioned as a way for students to vicariously relive the hardships experienced by rebel soldiers and thus to build identification with their revolutionary project.

Graduates from the Minas del Frío training program were quickly put into service as teachers in new schools across the Cuban countryside, where they were charged with the intellectual and ideological formation of other children.[20] Placing adolescents in charge of their own classrooms helped meet the enormous demand for education in the island's rural communities; however, the minimal age gap between student and teacher during this period of the Revolution's radicalization also blurred the lines between child and adult, making the rite of passage to adulthood as much about the child's relationship to the state—and the authority conferred by his or her assumption of duties to the Revolution—as it was about any developmental milestone.

Through the training and deployment of children to meet social needs traditionally filled by adults, revolutionary leaders contributed to a process of cultural change in which a new "coming of age" rite, represented by full incorporation into revolutionary citizenship and service, thus began to supersede traditional practices demarcating childhood from adulthood. While many rural children carried heavy responsibilities on family farms, worked for wages, and married in their early teens, new expectations that children would assume revolutionary commitments as independent political actors clashed with customs of paternal authority, deference, and family loyalty prevalent among Cuban campesinos. At the same time, Cuban youth, especially young blacks and teenaged girls, understood efforts to incorporate them into revolutionary projects as an official endorsement of their desire for greater autonomy and respect within their families and in society.

The early deployment of poor and rural adolescents as primary school teachers foreshadowed the massive mobilization of middle-class youth in the Campaña de Alfabetización, or Literacy Campaign. Launched in January 1961, the campaign sought to raise the educational level of the nation at the same time as it provided ideological training for citizens of all ages. However, in the Literacy Campaign as in all programs of the Year of Education, children were a key focus. As the Castro government pursued strategic ties with the Soviet Union, the campaign sought to inculcate privileged young literacy instructors and their pupils in the Revolution's increasingly leftist ideology. Moreover, as fears of a U.S.-backed invasion grew, planners of the campaign also produced morally and emotionally charged discourses and images of youthful literacy volunteers for public consumption, drawing on representations of middle-class children to shore up public support for the Revolution.

Politicized middle-class adolescents were put to work mobilizing Cuban children to participate in the Literacy Campaign. On February 26, Aldo Alvarez, director of the National Executive Commission of the Rebel Youth, gave a presentation, "Cuban Youth and the Year of Education," on the Televisión-Revolución program "People's University." He spoke to the task that had been placed in the hands of the Rebel Youth: the recruitment of 100,000 young literacy volunteers. Thousands of Cuban children had already volunteered for the program, he said. Indeed, a pilot brigade of youth literacy instructors, comprised of 236 volunteers of both sexes, had left Havana that day, charged with establishing guidelines for the work of literacy education. They had been designated the first troops of the "Conrado Benítez Literacy Army."[21]

To further motivate young people to participate in the campaign, a "Semana de la Juventud" would be celebrated across the island from April 22 to April 28, and a grand party for children and youth would be held on opening day on Havana's Prado. A number of scholarships would also be made available for Cuban young people to study in Havana schools as well as to pursue technical training in the Soviet Union. Young literacy workers also enjoyed the support, moral and material, of socialist youth around the world. The World Federation of Youth pledged to donate 1 million pencils and other scholastic supplies to the campaign, and the Soviet Youth promised to pay for the construction of a school in the Sierra del Escambray, in the counterrevolutionary stronghold.

In a now familiar discursive move, Alvarez conflated youthful enthusiasm for the literacy campaign, support for the Revolution, and love for the nation, contrasting Cuban young people's support for the campaign with the "counterrevolutionary" attitude of the administrators of "numerous private schools." Schools controlled by the "falangist clergy," he stated, had "repeatedly refused to cooperate in the literacy crusade," insisting that "they couldn't interrupt classes for this patriotic work." He also noted that some private schools were demanding that parents pay tuition for students who had volunteered to spend up to eight months out of class to participate in the campaign.

However, resistance to the Literacy Campaign was not limited to private school teachers and clergy; even during this preliminary stage, many parents expressed reservations about allowing their children to participate. Responding to fears that the revolutionary government was trying to separate children from their parents by sending them to do volunteer service away from home, Alvarez insisted that the parents of the literacy *brigadistas* had not only authorized their participation; many of them had also revealed their own revolutionary zeal by volunteering to serve as literacy instructors themselves. He also stressed that every youth volunteer needed to be at least thirteen years old—though in practice many were as young as ten—and must have completed the sixth grade.[22]

Alvarez's comments alluded to an unspoken reality: since most rural and working-class children did not have a sixth-grade education, the overwhelming majority of young literacy volunteers were from middle- and upper-class homes. Though many of their families opposed their involvement in the Literacy Campaign, the government nonetheless prioritized the mobilization of middle-class youth, seeking through them to advance both the educational and ideological goals that had inspired the Year of Education. These well-educated children had great practical value, not only as literacy volunteers but also as healthy, well-groomed middle-class youth who would travel across the island, embodying exactly the kind of image the Revolution sought to project. If they could be convinced to participate, these enthusiastic and well-mannered young people would powerfully reinforce the associations that the media had worked so hard to establish between the Revolution and the virtues of youth.

Of equal importance were the political dividends to be gained by removing middle-class youth from potentially counterrevolutionary homes and exposing them to positive interpretations of the Revolution. Reflecting on the intertwined educational and political goals of the literacy campaign, a representative of the Federación de Mujeres Cubanas, or Federation of Cuban Women, stated that the literacy campaign "constituted . . . a vital learning opportunity for the literacy instructors themselves, many of them young people and even children." To that end, campaign posters encouraged privileged white children to imagine what their lives would have been like if they had been born poor or black and urged them to take up their pencils and books to continue the fight to establish José Martí's long-awaited racially egalitarian republic. One such poster featured an image of Mariana Grajales, the Afro-Cuban mother of independence hero General Antonio Maceo, embracing a young white literacy volunteer; with her free hand, the elderly lady pointed to a remote mountain village, urging the child to wage war against poverty and racial inequality by teaching the *guajiros* to read.[23]

Pedagogical materials used by *alfabetizadores* similarly contained a strong ideological component designed to raise the revolutionary consciousness of youthful literacy volunteers and their students. For example, the widely used literacy manual *Alfabeticemos* contained a series of short lessons titled "Fidel Is Our Leader," "Nationalization," "The Revolution Turns Prisons into Schools," "Imperialism," and "Friends and Enemies." Another encouraged volunteers and pupils alike to associate José Martí with Fidel Castro by including illustrations of the Apostle embracing the *comandante-en-jefe*. Another text, titled "Estudio, trabajo y fusil," defined the ideal revolutionary youth as equally dedicated to "study, work, and rifle." Books and training manuals used in the Literacy Campaign thus encouraged youthful militancy and reinforced ideological conformity in both teacher and student.[24]

Revolutionary leaders sent youthful *alfabetizadores* to live, work, and study with Cuban campesino families, not only to increase the educational levels of rural populations but to expose the urban literacy volunteers to the difficult conditions outside the capital city. This exposure, it was hoped, would help privileged young Cubans develop a sense of solidarity with the less fortunate. In facing and overcoming hardship, children would also have the opportunity to demonstrate that they were "truly young revolutionaries, adaptable to the way of living in which they will need to pursue their activities in favor of the people."[25] For middle-class and Catholic children, raised to revere the long-suffering heroes of Cuban independence and to respect the Lenten traditions of fasting and repentance, participation in the Literacy Campaign offered a way to share in the suffering of the nation's rebel redeemers and to be reborn with them and with their island. However, calls for self-sacrificing young people to participate in the "battle" to eradicate illiteracy gave them pride of place at the center of a newly militaristic politics of childhood that diverged ever further from Martí's utopian vision, even as the state-sponsored media depicted the Literacy Campaign as the greatest expression yet of the Revolution's moral imperative.

Recognizing the symbolic power of young *alfabetizadores*, the revolutionary media published countless photographs and articles praising these child volunteers. One such image, of a boot-clad girl resting in a hammock, was accompanied by a caption that read, "Still just a 'squirt,' this young teacher, conscious of her patriotic duties, has renounced the diversions of adolescence to join the legions of rural educators. A genuine product of the Revolution."[26]

The symbolic figure of the youthful *alfabetizador*—not to mention his or her actual body—could also be deployed to fight the Revolution's enemies. Many young literacy volunteers worked in the Sierra Escambray, the second largest mountain stronghold on the island and the center of counterrevolutionary activity. Some fell victim to the violence that plagued the area. An unknown number of adolescent volunteers also fought with local militias and participated in intelligence-gathering activities. Their presence may additionally have inhibited the Escambray insurgency—a counterrevolutionary campaign that lasted more than four years and claimed thousands of peasants' lives, as well as those of army troops sent to repress the uprising—since youth wounded in counterrevolutionary attacks had enormous symbolic value for the Revolution.[27]

By celebrating children's participation in the Literacy Campaign, the revolutionary government reinforced the notion of children as political actors and institutionalized a new relationship between the child and the state. The correct place for children would no longer be the "private" sphere of family life; instead, they would be expected to assume an active role in the revolutionary nation-making project. However, not all Cubans celebrated this reenvisioning of childhood or saw children's activism as evidence of the Revolution's virtue. In fact, youth participation in the Literacy Campaign and the new understanding of the child's role in Cuban society that it reflected further alienated many Cuban middle-class parents from the revolutionary regime. Parents worried that illness or injury would befall their children while living in intimate proximity to peasant families in their small and unsanitary *bohíos*. They also worried that their daughters would be housed in coed dormitories under the care of state officials. Many feared that the increased opportunities for unsupervised contact with adolescents of the opposite sex might lead to loss of virginity or pregnancy.

The varied programs of the Year of Education, while well-received by a majority of Cubans, nonetheless threatened traditional age-based hierarchies and the raced, classed, and regionally inflected norms of patriarchal family life across the island, provoking resistance from campesino and urban middle-class parents alike. Early in 1961, efforts to further the goals of the Revolution by incorporating privileged children into the Literacy Campaign dramatically increased opposition to the Castro government and accelerated the exodus of those very young people from the island.

The Literacy Campaign thus launched an untold number of young people, including many of the 14,000 unaccompanied Pedro Pan children who would be sent into foster care in the United States, on a nation-making journey that coexisted in dynamic tension with the travels of young *alfabetizadores*. Just as the involvement of children in the Literacy Campaign consolidated the revolutionary nation-making project, the experiences of anti-Castro child refugees would contribute powerfully to the growth of the Counterrevolution on the island and to the discursive construction of the exile nation in southern Florida.

CHILDREN AND THE COUNTERREVOLUTION

By the summer of 1960, dispossessed of their property and businesses and disoriented by the rapid dissolution of the island's civil society, middle-class Cuban mothers and fathers grew increasingly alarmed by the disruption of family life. Catholic priests and private school teachers shared these fears and resented new educational laws that curtailed their traditional role in guiding children's thinking and activities. Gearing up for the 1960 academic year, anti-Castro and anticommunist parents, educators, and clergy forged a nascent alliance around a crucial set of counterrevolutionary goals: to defend traditional notions of childhood, family life, and education and safeguard them from state intervention as part of a broader resistance to the Revolution's turn to the left. As the school year progressed and hostilities between pro- and counterrevolutionary sectors increased, a significant number of children would join the anti-Castro alliance and be caught up in the political violence that overtook the island.

By September 1960, many private school educators found themselves at odds with the Revolution. Some used their positions of power in the classroom to criticize Fidel Castro, share their anticommunist political views with students, and discourage young people from participating in mass demonstrations of support for the government. Silvio González, director of the Jesuit-run Belén Technical School, warned the student body that he would not allow militia members, communists, or members of the revolutionary state's security apparatus to interfere with the orderly functioning of his school. Nor, *Verde Olivo* magazine reported the director as saying, would he tolerate the presence of "perturbing elements" among the student body. Throughout the school year, González repeatedly interrupted classes to submit students to "counterrevolutionary talks" and even threatened to expel students who expressed support for the Revolution.[28]

Student-led opposition movements also sprang up in many of the island's Catholic middle and high schools, often organized with teachers' blessings. A student strike was organized for November 14, 1960, both to protest government intervention into the scholastic lives of the nation's children and to pay homage to Porfirio Ramírez, a Catholic student leader who had been executed by firing squad on October 14 after being found guilty of counterrevolutionary activities in the Sierra Escambray. Responding to charges that the student strike had been organized by religious teachers in private schools, Catholic clergy insisted that the movement had been organized by students acting in accordance with their own political and spiritual convictions.

The Church nonetheless threw its support behind the strike. On November 13, it declared a day of mourning for Porfirio Ramírez, and Catholic parishes across the island read a pastoral letter, titled "Rome or Moscow," by Archbishop Enrique Pérez Serantes. In the letter, Pérez Serantes signaled his estrangement from Fidel Castro and derided communism as appealing to the bitter and maladjusted, to those who lacked "substantial values," and labeled it a "mortal virus" to which young students were particularly vulnerable.[29] Adopting a familiar motif from the revolutionary politics of childhood, he framed innocent Cuban children as victims of a cruel and morally bankrupt state. The villain in his speech was not Batista, however, but the rebel leader who had overthrown the dictatorship.

Anti-Castro exiles, including former Catholic student leaders, also contributed to the emergence of a counterrevolutionary politics of childhood. Echoing the state-sponsored media's extravagant rhetorical flourishes, they condemned the persecution of the Church and private school educators and issued sensationalist exposés of communist designs on the island's innocent boys and girls. However, even as they decried the Revolution's assault on the Cuban family, the counterrevolutionaries, by indoctrinating and militarizing children, also used young people in their operations, introducing them to anti-Castro ideas and benefiting from their involvement in acts of resistance and sabotage.

Anti-Castro exiles lent their support to youthful dissenters via the CIA-sponsored Radio Swan, appealing to an idealized collective memory of youth activism during the republic to urge students to take action against the revolutionary government.[30] On October 26, 1960, a former leader of the Agrupación Católica Universitaria broadcast a message to Cuban students, telling them that it was their duty to join the strike in order to "show the world that Porfirio Ramírez wasn't alone." The following day another message was broadcast: "Attention Cuban student. Join the strike on November 14 against the communist traitors who govern our fatherland. Remember that you are indebted to the great martyr Porfirio Ramírez."[31]

Counterrevolutionaries on and off the island increasingly deployed their conservative and Catholic-inflected variant of Martí's politics of childhood, using morally and emotionally resonant discourses to incite panic and social upheaval and promote opposition to Fidel Castro. They issued bulletins warning that the revolutionary government intended to nationalize all private schools and turn priests, nuns, and teachers into state employees. They also stated that classes in religious education would soon be prohibited and that all schools would be forced to use communist textbooks.

Radio Swan continued to stoke the fears of Cuban parents during October 1960, broadcasting reports of a new *patria potestad* law that would grant custody of their sons and daughters to the state (the Spanish legal term *patria potestad* is commonly translated as "parental authority"). The reports stated that "the communists in power" intended to win over the hearts and minds of Cuban children, first by "supplanting God with Fidel" and then by teaching them that love toward their mothers, brothers, or any relative were feelings that they should suppress. Similar broadcasts, directed specifically toward mothers, sought to exploit maternal affections and women's presumed protective instincts toward their children. They stated that an imminent revolutionary decree would remove boys and girls from their homes on their fifth birthday and install them in centers for communist indoctrination. They would come back home as "materialist monsters" when they were released from state custody at age eighteen. Depriving Cuban women of the love of their children and of their right to raise them as they saw fit, Fidel Castro intended to become "the supreme mother of Cuba."

Counterrevolutionary propaganda relied on an idealized notion of Cuban motherhood that measured feminine virtue in terms of a woman's dedication to her children and by her willingness to sacrifice herself to protect them from harm. On October 27, Radio Swan broadcast the following message: "Cuban mother, the government will take away your child and indoctrinate him with communist values. They will tell him that Che isn't an adventurer but rather a good and brave man who helped liberate the fatherland; that Fidel is the father of the nation. . . . Cuban mother, they can take away your clothing, your food, and even kill you, but nobody can take away your right to raise your child; remember that there is no animal more savage than the one that defends her cub. Offer your life to a just cause like ours, before surrendering your child to the beasts." These alarming messages continued through the autumn of 1960, exhorting Cuban mothers to fight the Revolution's designs on their young and to refuse to allow their children to be removed from their care. Strengthening the nascent alliance between middle-class parents and Catholic clergy and educators, united in defense of the traditional patriarchal family and the *patria*, Radio Swan nonetheless echoed the paternalistic rhetoric of the revolutionary media. Reminding Cuban women and children of their supporting role in an equally male-dominated Counterrevolution, exile propagandists urged mothers to oppose Castro by obediently following the instructions of their priests and taking their children to Church to ensure their correct doctrinal formation.[32]

At the same time that the first *patria potestad* rumors were being publicized through Radio Swan, other frightening child-centered rumors began to circulate. Since many middle-class Cubans had emigrated from Spain or were children of immigrants, the stories drew on their intimate knowledge of the Spanish Civil War, recalling the republican government's removal of young boys and girls from battle zones and relocation of them to Russia. Terrifying tales of communist violations of mothers, the murder of infants, and the forced indoctrination of children spread like wildfire. Children were also exposed to these rumors by their parents and teachers. Sonia Almazán del Olmo remembered the terrifying stories told by missionary priests at the American Dominican School in Cienfuegos: "They gathered us in the school patio and they began to talk to us . . . about the missionaries who'd come from Russia, about how they [the communists] used bayonets to open the bellies of pregnant mothers and take out the babies, and about how they took children away from their homes to indoctrinate them . . . about how they took them to camps because it was the State that educated them."[33]

Stories of young people being forced to spy on their parents and to report on them to the Revolution also began to circulate—exacerbated by the recent creation of Comités de Defensa Infantil (CDI), children's branches of the recently formed neighborhood vigilance groups known as the Comités de Defensa de la Revolución (CDR). So, too, did the rumor that the government was taking custody of children whose parents had been jailed for counterrevolutionary activities and sending them to the U.S.S.R. as an additional reprisal for the parents' crimes.[34] Stories of resistance in defense of children also appeared. Among these was the apocryphal tale of fifty mothers in the town of Bayamo who had signed a pact to kill their children before surrendering them to Castro.

The fears produced by child-centered propaganda, intended to provoke resistance and destabilize the Castro regime, succeeded primarily in creating panic among Cuban middle-class families and provoking an early wave of youthful emigration from Cuba to the United States. However, parents, teachers, and clergy who remained on the island also began to take action against the Revolution. They launched a campaign to resist what they understood as a conspiracy to remove boys and girls from their families and place them in the custody of the revolutionary state. They also organized to defend parents' rights and private religious education and to oppose the communist indoctrination of Cuban children.

At the beginning of November 1960, the Church-sponsored National Confederation of Parents' Associations held its third annual congress. Participants resolved to petition the government to guarantee that Christian education would be provided in all the nation's schools. In their final declaration, delegates addressed the *patria potestad* rumors, affirming that the freedom of choice in education was "an inalienable right" and that its exercise constituted "the most sacred of a parent's duties." The congress also reaffirmed that the Church, as "spiritual mother of all Christians," had an essential part in educating children, whereas the state should be limited to playing a supportive role.[35]

Middle-class parents' fears reached a new high in December, when the government announced the establishment of a nationwide Ficha Escolar Acumulativa, or cumulative scholastic record, that would also gather family data on each public and private school student and document "all activities inside and outside school."[36] Many saw the government-administered *ficha* as yet another step toward state control of children's lives. Some feared that it had been put into place as a means of identifying the island's brightest young people, in order to send them to Russia for technical and ideological training. Others suspected that the scholastic record would be used to ensure children's and even parents' loyalty to the Revolution by distributing rewards and punishments, such as access to higher education and even jobs, in accordance with students' records of ideological conformity.[37]

By the end of 1960, as relations between the Church and state deteriorated into hostility, a politics of childhood that had manifested itself mainly in the discursive realm began to spill out into the streets. As growing numbers of Cuban children joined revolutionary mass organizations and youth militias, dissenting young people, many of them members of Catholic youth organizations and themselves former supporters of the Revolution, became involved in counterrevolutionary activities. Youth resistance spread into high schools like Colegio Belén and La Salle in Havana, as well as into middle schools and Church-sponsored youth groups. On February 28, 1961, the Nobel Academy in the Havana neighborhood of La Víbora was partially destroyed by a dynamite bomb that blew up the school's bathrooms, knocked down the walls of two classrooms, and caused multiple injuries to students. Among the eight students seriously wounded, sixteen-year-old María Eugenia Echániz and seventeen-year-old Olga Valdés Díaz required surgery to extract shrapnel from their faces, necks, and arms; despite the best efforts of the surgical team, the younger girl lost her left eye.

Two Nobel Academy students, Roberto del Castillo Fernández, sixteen years old, and Adrián Sánchez del Castillo, eighteen years old, were later charged with the attack. The state-sponsored media claimed that both boys were members of a counterrevolutionary students' group that met at Sacred Heart Catholic Church in La Víbora and had previously caused disturbances at the school, tearing pictures of revolutionary figures from classroom walls, attacking pro-Castro students with bottles, and provoking a brawl with classmates who supported the Revolution. Extensive coverage of the school bombings appeared in all of the major revolutionary newspapers and magazines.[38]

Condemning the attacks on March 4, Fidel Castro again charged Catholic teachers with aiding the Counterrevolution, accusing them of assisting those who "want to bloody our country" and "murder children." He warned them that the nation would stand against this alliance between the Church and counterrevolutionaries, because "the people know that it could be their child who is killed by a bomb, or who loses his or her arms or who is blinded."[39] To further guarantee the safety of schoolchildren and to prevent their exposure to counterrevolutionary propaganda, he decreed that the Association of Rebel Youth establish delegations in almost all schools, public and private, by the end of February. AJR *milicianos* were charged with monitoring the attitudes and behaviors of students and the revolutionary commitment of teachers.[40]

By the end of March, Castro's addresses to children had drawn sharply antagonistic lines between prorevolutionary young people and those who were unsure of or opposed to the radical transformation of their society. In a decisive departure from his previous Martí-inspired claim that the Revolution was "for the children," the rebel leader now made clear that his concern and largesse only extended to some of the island's young people—those who had demonstrated their loyalty to him and his increasingly radical vision for the nation. Cubans were embroiled in a war between classes, he argued, and the nation's youngest citizens were deeply implicated in its outcome.

At a speech given to the AJR's First Student Plenary, Castro explained to his young followers why political divisions among Cuban children and youth were inevitable. During a social revolution, he stated, it was to be expected that students who came from the "rich classes" would be against the new regime. This was the unfortunate product of their elitist education and the influence of their reactionary and self-interested elders, who resented the Revolution's disruption of their comfortable lives. He lamented that many privileged young people could be saved "for the Revolution and for the fatherland," if it were not for the pernicious influence of the clergy, "the intellectual and spiritual accomplices of this exploiting class," whom he accused of "inculcating these young people with hatred for the Revolution, hatred for the fatherland, and fondness for special interests and foreign domination of our country."[41]

Castro's class-based explanation for the bitter political divisions among young people notwithstanding, the reality was more complex. Many of the incidents of confrontation and violence involving children took place among private school students—both supporters and detractors of the Revolution—from the middle and upper classes. On April 11, a group of students at Havana's prestigious La Salle High School gathered on the patio to demonstrate their support for the Revolution; when they were expelled, a group of students and parents gathered outside the school to demand justice for the young revolutionaries.[42]

Politicized middle-class children also participated in state-sponsored meetings and rallies that sometimes degenerated into fistfights. On March 10, a meeting was organized by the Federation of University Youth and the Association of Rebel Youth to promote the literacy campaign and the integration of middle and high school students into the Conrado Benítez Brigades. Held at the Children's Theater in Holguín, the meeting was disturbed by shouting matches between revolutionary students and dissenters from the local Lestonac and Marist Brothers Catholic High Schools.

José Antonio Tamargo, also a student at Marist Brothers High School, denounced the dissenters. Returning to the school later that afternoon, Tamargo was attacked and beaten by the students who had earlier interrupted the literacy campaign meeting.

Taking advantage of the opportunity to present Catholic school students as the violent pawns of a reactionary clergy, *Bohemia* reported the attack as an example of "Falangist provocation" against the literacy volunteers. Another article in *Verde Olivo* featured Tamargo's first-person testimony along with photographs of him lifting his pants to show the bruises left on his legs by his attackers.[43] The state-sponsored media glossed over the fact that the attack was the result of a confrontation between pro- and anti-Castro students who attended the same private schools. Incidents like this one suggest that politicized middle-class and Catholic students still held diverse opinions about the Revolution, and that, despite official protests to the contrary, their opinions were not predetermined by their class position in Cuban society.

As political differences polarized the nation and its young people, children were also caught in violent confrontations between counterrevolutionaries and revolutionary armed forces and militias. On October 10, 1960, in the Havana municipality of Madruga, counterrevolutionaries fired on a vehicle carrying Haydée Machado Reyes and members of her family. Machado Reyes was gravely wounded and her twenty-two-month-old son, Reinaldo Muñiz Machado, was killed. On October 30, during the hijacking of a Cuban airliner, twelve-year-old Argelio Hernández Rodríguez was gravely wounded. On Christmas Eve a bomb exploded in the Flogar department store in Havana. It injured fifteen people, including four children.

In the New Year, rumors of a U.S.-led exile invasion of Cuba were confirmed by the North American media, spurring both revolutionary and counterrevolutionary forces onward in their struggle for control of the nation's destiny. Bombs and gunfights wounded and claimed the lives of more children as armed insurgents scaled up their efforts to destabilize the Castro regime.[44] Fearful parents began to seek ways of removing their sons and daughters from the island before they were injured or killed—or imprisoned for their own counterrevolutionary activities. Anti-Castro families turned to the Church for assistance in sending their children to Miami, where they joined the growing numbers of unaccompanied minors being cared for by Catholic welfare workers and exile volunteers.[45] Those who remained held their children close, waiting for the U.S.-backed invasion they hoped would liberate them from a Revolution they no longer recognized and establish, once and for all, the longed-awaited moral republic.

"PIONEERS FOR SOCIALISM": CHILDREN AND THE SOCIALIST NATION-MAKING PROJECT

In January 1961, as preparations for an exile invasion of the island continued, the CIA-sponsored Radio Swan stepped up its broadcasts of child-centered propaganda messages into Cuba, urging Cubans to take up arms to protect democracy, their families, and their Catholic faith. At the same time, the U.S. media heightened their own efforts to discredit the Castro regime, drawing on historically grounded infantilizing discourses that described the Revolution's leader as irrational, prone to childish temper tantrums and fits of hysterical rage.[46] The stage was set for the invasion that Castro had warned Cubans to expect. The coming attack would serve as the Revolution's first major test, giving Castro's army and militias the chance to prove that they could defend the island against its former oppressor. It would also provide children with a dramatic opportunity to demonstrate their value to the revolutionary nation-making project.

On April 17, during the attempted Bay of Pigs invasion, 900 cadets from a military school were mobilized to repel the attack at Playa Larga. More than half of the adolescent cadets were reported killed before Castro's army took the beach the following day. Armed *milicianos* as young as thirteen were also pressed into the defense of the *patria*, participating in raids on suspected counterrevolutionary hideouts and the arrests of accused sympathizers. They were also charged with guarding prisoners' camps. On several occasions, overly zealous young *milicianos* fired on imprisoned civilians with their machine guns, wounding a number of prisoners and killing at least three young men.[47] During police crackdowns leading up to and following the invasion, the CDIs, neighborhood surveillance groups of boys and girls between the ages of five and twelve, were mobilized along with members of the adult CDRs to investigate and report suspected counterrevolutionary behavior occurring in children's communities and homes.[48]

By April 20, the invasion had been repelled, and most of the 1,200 surviving members of exile Brigade 2506 were taken prisoner. The island erupted in victory celebrations, overwhelmed with relief and nationalist pride. The Revolution had undergone a historically unprecedented rite of passage: it had defied the powerful colossus to the North and declared, once and for all, Cuba's right to chart its own future without U.S.

interference. Cuba had proven definitively that it was no longer the dependent child of the United States. Moreover, the victory at Playa Girón confirmed Fidel Castro as maximum leader and father of the revolutionary nation and validated his claim to have fulfilled the struggle for self-determination initiated by José Martí and the Mambí army before the turn of the century. Rather than bringing about the collapse of his regime, as counterrevolutionaries and their supporters had hoped, the attack increased his popularity and provided him with additional momentum needed to transform a once broadly based crusade for the establishment of Martí's moral republic into a new socialist nation-making project.

One week later, the United States declared a total embargo on the island. Defiant revolutionaries jeered at the gesture, confident that their defeat of the U.S.-sponsored invasion had secured their entry into the socialist bloc, safeguarding the practical survival of the Castro regime and precluding the possibility of future invasion from the north. Soviet premier Nikita Khrushchev's statement warning against further U.S. interference on the island was read repeatedly on television and the radio. The state-sponsored media issued harsh condemnations of the United States and the counterrevolutionary exile community and provided extensive coverage of accelerating developments in the Cuban-Soviet relationship.

This dramatic shift in international alignments rapidly impacted the lives of Cuban children. In primary schools across the island, anti-U.S. messages infused the teaching of reading and writing and provided a thematic focus for art classes. Students were issued hastily printed texts praising the U.S.S.R. and offering a Marxist-Leninist interpretation of Cuban history. Classrooms were decorated with Soviet flags and portraits of communist leaders from around the world. Students in kindergarten and the primary grades were taught to chant call-and-response communist slogans that reinforced associations between children, the paternalistic leader of the Revolution, and the *patria*. "Who is your father?" "Fidel!" "Who is your grandfather?" "Nikita!" "What are we?" "Good Socialists!" "What are we trying to be?" "Good Communists!"[49]

The recently reconstituted Pioneers, a children's auxiliary to the Cuban Communist Party that had been disbanded in the 1940s, adopted a new slogan: "Pioneers for Socialism, Always Prepared!" Pioneer leaders worked rapidly to convert the organization into a national association. A massive enrollment and public relations campaign was mounted, exhorting boys and girls aged six through fourteen to join the movement and introducing them to the Revolution's newly adopted socialist ideology. Pioneers were also encouraged to pressure their parents to commit themselves to the newly declared socialist nation-making project. Some mothers and fathers needed no such motivation. On April 29, Radio Havana announced that newborn babies "all over Cuba are being named Yuri," in tribute to Major Yuri Gagarin of the Soviet Air Force, who had become the first man to orbit the Earth on April 12.[50]

During preparations for the upcoming May Day holiday, the first to be celebrated "under the glorious banners of socialism," Cuba's ties to the U.S.S.R. and Fidel Castro's ever intensifying relationship with the island's children grew hand in hand. Cuban youth were praised for their participation in defeating the exile invasion and empowered with even greater responsibilities in the defense of the socialist Revolution. Juvenile patrols and members of the Rebel Youth continued to patrol city and village streets at night, investigating and arresting suspected counterrevolutionaries. On May 1, the nation would commemorate the defeat of the "North American mercenaries" in Havana with the greatest march in the nation's history, during which the "youth of Cuba would march side by side with Fidel Castro."[51] Similar ceremonies were planned in Santiago and Camagüey.

On the evening before May Day, trucks, buses, and trains poured into Havana, bringing workers, peasants, and students of all ages from the four eastern provinces to march in the parade. The next morning, children enthusiastically joined the daylong procession through the Plaza Cívica, while Fidel Castro, President Dorticós, and high officials of the Armed Forces watched from a stand erected at the foot of the José Martí monument in the plaza's center. At midnight, boys and girls marveled at fireworks and applauded the burning in effigy of U.S. president John F. Kennedy. Then, before a jubilant crowd of hundreds of thousands, Castro announced the promulgation of a new constitution that prohibited elections and proclaimed the Revolution socialist.[52]

In the months following the failed attack, tensions between the revolutionary government and the Church reached an all-time high. The involvement of three Catholic priests and many young members of Acción Católica and the Agrupación Católica Universitaria in the exile invasion confirmed Fidel Castro's belief that counterrevolutionary clergy still exercised control over a significant number of the island's children and youth.[53] The time had come to strike a definitive blow against the Church and private schools, whose pernicious influence on young people could no longer be allowed to impede the Revolution's march toward socialism. Declaring that "a new world required a new school," Castro decreed the nationalization of almost 200 Catholic schools and orphanages and ordered the expulsion of all foreign priests.[54] Protestant and secular private schools were also nationalized, concentrating control of the island's educational system exclusively in the hands of the revolutionary state.

After the declaration of the socialist Revolution, the number of children traveling alone to the United States skyrocketed. As the demand for visa waivers and airline tickets grew and the Castro regime cracked down on the exit of unaccompanied minors, the network of clergy, private school educators, and private citizens already committed to spiriting children out of Cuba expanded to include collaborators in the embassies of Holland, Belgium, Japan, Switzerland, and Spain. Staff members at several commercial air transport companies, most prominently Holland's KLM Airlines, also joined the underground network. As more parents from progressively lower social classes sought a way of escape for their sons and daughters, gardeners, kitchen employees, bartenders, and waiters began to help children flee the island, providing intelligence and hiding and transporting travel documents.[55] Middle-class children nonetheless constituted the majority of those removed from Cuba; most working-class families opted at this time to stay, a decision stemming either from their support for the Revolution or from the lack of resources needed to leave.

Those who remained on the island enrolled in the newly nationalized schools for the academic term beginning in September 1961. No longer faced with ideological competition from the Church or private schools, the regime increased efforts to remake the educational system. Children were proclaimed the Revolution's best hope for uprooting ideas associated with formerly exploitative class relations and for the creation of a new socialist consciousness. In the years to come, as Cuba drew ever closer to the U.S.S.R., the Castro regime would rely on an increasingly Marxist-Leninist inflected politics of childhood in the battle to transform Cuba's republican political, economic, and social structures; create a new socialist culture; and defeat a persistent counterrevolutionary movement on and off the island.

IN THE MONTHS leading up to and following the Bay of Pigs invasion, middle-class fears that a radicalizing Revolution would disrupt family life, assert state control over education, and submit children to Marxist-Leninist and atheistic indoctrination were confirmed. These concerns had first arisen during the summer of 1959, when the promulgation of new educational laws placed greater control over academic calendars, curricula, and instructional methods in the hands of the new revolutionary government. Subsequent interventions in family life and education and threats to traditional notions of childhood angered many Cubans as much as, and perhaps more than, agrarian or urban reform laws or even the postponement of elections. However, the dialectical relationship between parents' already activated fears for their children and the growing dispossession and persecution of a Catholic and anticommunist middle class would produce a profound opposition to the trajectory of the Revolution and give birth to a counterrevolutionary alliance between families, educators, and the Church by the start of the 1960 academic year.

In January 1961, the intertwined social and political goals that inspired the Year of Education propelled the expansion of literacy and primary schooling across the country; but they also led to the creation of ideological education programs and child-centered mass organizations that forged direct linkages between children and the state and reframed the former as autonomous political actors, answerable to the Revolution as much as, if not more than, to their parents. Changing understandings and practices of childhood thus undermined Cubans' cherished family values and lessened parents' authority over children while increasing Castro's power over Cubans of all ages, spurring counterrevolutionary resistance in a moment of otherwise widespread support for the Revolution. Taking place in a context of the nation's severing of diplomatic relations with the United States and the cementing of new ties to the Soviet Union, these polarizing processes of cultural change compelled Cubans to choose a side—for or against the Castro government—and thereby contributed to the Revolution's accelerating radicalization.

Cubans on both sides of this political divide were nonetheless united by a shared belief that children were central to their radically different visions of the island's future. As organized resistance began to emerge in the summer of 1960, both the Castro government and its opponents frequently used representations of children and child-centered discourses to articulate their competing ideologies, rally Cubans to their causes, and discredit each other, relying on strikingly similar assumptions, discursive frames, and motifs in the pursuit of violently opposed nation-making projects. As time passed, revolutionaries and counterrevolutionaries not only fought *for* children but also increasingly fought *through* flesh-and-blood children to make the Cuban nation, irrevocably transforming childhood into a site in which the radicalization of the Revolution could be promoted or contested.

During these two tumultuous and increasingly violent years, the island's children were drawn into "adult" political struggles, directly impacting the dialectical relationship between radicalization and Counterrevolution even as their daily reality was transformed by their new salience in public life. The centrality of young people to Cuba's national destiny, beginning with the turn-of-the-century independence struggle and continuing through the failure of two U.S.-aligned republics and the Revolution's sudden embrace of the Soviet Union, ensured that the subsequent middle-class exodus from the island would also be articulated in child-centered terms. As a virulently anti-Castro exile community began to emerge in southern Florida, the politics of Cuban childhood would assume an even more important role at the center of a Cold War contest for control of the nation's future.

5
OUR CUBAN VISITORS

Immigration, Race, and the Cold War Politics
of Childhood in Miami, 1959–1961

During the first months of 1960, as Fidel Castro pursued a strategic new relationship with the Soviet Union, relations between the United States and Cuba deteriorated from distrust to open hostility. As the U.S. government began to explore covert operations to depose the Castro regime, officials also began to focus on Cuban children as a means through which to encourage counterrevolutionary activity and the exodus of middle-class families from the island, thereby destabilizing the Revolution and furthering U.S. Cold War foreign policy goals.

However, the growing influx of impoverished refugees to Miami–Dade County provoked Anglo-Americans' distaste for working-class immigrants and exacerbated white Miamians' historically racialized distrust of Cubans. Seeking to overcome their vulnerability as foreigners in a less-than-friendly city, exile journalists and informants joined hands with the federal government, local and state agencies, and refugee advocates to saturate local Spanish- and English-language media with discourses and images of childhood that deemphasized Cubans' similarities to other Latina/os and emphasized their whiteness, middle-class family values, and commitment to the U.S. democratic-capitalist nation-making project.

Throughout 1960, anti-Castro Cubans would thus adapt the Counterrevolution's politics of childhood for use in a new context, seeking to ensure a favorable reception in Miami by emphasizing their emerging community's conformity with the racial, social, cultural, and political norms of Cold War America. Their efforts paid off in April 1961, when the failed Bay of Pigs invasion produced a nationwide outpouring of anticommunist sentiment and mainstream America began to embrace the exiles and their children as welcomed guests of the United States. However, that welcome was neither inevitable nor unconditional. As white Miamians struggled to demonstrate their patriotic commitment to the nation's foreign policy goals by opening their arms to anti-Castro refugees, they nonetheless clung to racially inflected notions of Cuban difference and inferiority that would come to define the limits of both the exilic politics of childhood and Anglo-American hospitality.

RACE AND CUBAN IMMIGRATION IN PRE–CIVIL RIGHTS ERA SOUTH FLORIDA

The first anti-Castro Cubans who fled the island for exile in Florida were indeed overwhelmingly white and middle-class. Many of them also spoke English and, having traveled often to the United States, were familiar with North American culture. However, it was not inevitable that white Miamians would recognize these privileged, light-skinned, and well-educated Cuban as their racial or cultural equals. In fact, nationwide anti-Latina/o prejudices and regionally specific historical notions of what constituted "Cuban" would predispose many of the city's residents toward a racialized distrust of refugees from the island.

Cuban immigration to southern Florida predated the 1959 Revolution by almost a century. During the island's protracted independence struggle, tens of thousands of Cubans fled imprisonment, social upheaval, and deprivation on the island. Many of these original political exiles and economic migrants resettled in New York, Tampa, and Key West.[1] In the 1860s, several Cuban cigar manufacturers also moved their factories to these three cities, spurring further immigration to the United States and giving birth to a number of mixed-race and working-class *tabaquero* communities. Cigar workers played an active role in the liberation of their homeland from Spain, especially in the 1890s, when José Martí visited southern Florida seeking recruits and financial support to launch the final battle against the Spanish colonial regime.

After independence was declared in 1902, a small population of Cubans chose to remain in Key West, Tampa, Jacksonville, and Ocala, otherwise known as "Martí City."[2] However, subsequent Cuban immigration was often short-term and cyclical, since working-class Cubans struggled to find a permanent place in southern Florida's deeply stratified social order. Southern planters and elites, traditionally antiunion, were often also anti-Cuban, hostile to the tradition of labor militancy among Key West and Tampa cigar workers. Adding to these suspicions, many cigar workers were Afro-Cubans that had assimilated within Florida's African American communities. "Cuban niggers" were barred from living in white neighborhoods, and their children were segregated into black schools. Between the 1930s and the 1950s, Afro-Cubans were also targeted by the Ku Klux Klan and fell victim to racialized threats, harassment, and violence.[3] During the same period, the FBI and CIA investigated Afro-Cuban communities that they suspected of harboring secret communist groups planning "anti-American" activities.[4] More than a few southern politicians voiced similar concerns about the possibility of Cuban-led communist cells in South Florida.[5]

South Floridians were also suspicious of light-skinned Cubans. They distrusted their Spanish cultural inheritance, which they saw as degenerate and antidemocratic, and rejected their identification with Roman Catholicism, viewing it as an alien religion inherently incompatible with American values.[6] Nor did they accept light-skinned Cuban immigrants as unequivocally white. All Cubans, regardless of color, were feared as potential carriers of African blood that might nonetheless pass for white, thereby circumventing the "one drop" rule that structured the South's racial order. Poverty and underemployment among light-skinned Cubans were exacerbated by racialized forms of discrimination, embodied in the "Cubans need not apply" signs posted in the windows of local businesses.[7]

During the first half of the twentieth century, a growing number of middle- and upper-class Cubans also arrived in Miami as students, tourists, investors, and temporary political exiles, relying on the availability of cheap and regular passage on steamships and airplanes. In-migration from the island decreased during World War I and throughout the 1920s, when anti-immigrant vigilante activities surged in South Florida, exacerbated by labor unrest in the Cuban-dominated cigar industry. However, when tensions abated by the end of the decade, Cuban immigration resumed. During the tumultuous 1930s and 1940s, when wealthy white elites fled political upheaval on the island, Miami's Cuban population grew to approximately 20,000.[8] This community expanded dramatically between 1952 and 1959, the years of Fulgencio Batista's dictatorship, to include as many as 50,000 emigrants.[9]

By then, northern whites had begun to settle in Miami, bringing with them a modicum of racial tolerance that distinguished the city from the rest of Florida and the South. However, even more liberal northerners lacked an appreciation for Cubans' distinctive identity. Most white Miamians assigned the city's relatively small number of Cuban immigrants to the amorphous ethnic category of "Latin" that also included Puerto Ricans, Mexicans, Central and South Americans, Spaniards—and even Italians, Greeks, and other "Mediterraneans." The 1950 Miami-Dade census, which reported 20,000 "Hispanics" living in the county, did not break down the category by national origin—though it has been estimated elsewhere that this population was divided roughly evenly between Cubans and as many as 10,000 Puerto Ricans, many of whom were migrant agricultural laborers.[10]

As late as 1959, Miami's small Spanish-speaking society reflected the tendency of the Anglo-American mainstream to characterize Cubans as part of a broader "Hispanic American" or "pan-American" community. Before the emergence of a distinct Cuban exile media in 1960, Miami's most widely circulated Spanish-language newspaper, *Diario las Américas*, was Nicaraguan-owned and -operated; in line with its editorial mission of promoting "better understanding between the Americas," the paper reported heavily on activities by pan-Americanist organizations like Miami's Alianza Interamericana and Casa de las Américas. It frequently described the Cubans, Puerto Ricans, Dominicans, and Peruvians who appeared in its social pages as "valued members of our Hispanic American colony in Miami" or "esteemed members of the Hispanic circles of this city," only occasionally mentioning their distinct national origins.[11]

By the 1950s, a handful of entertainers and athletes had nonetheless begun to make the Cuban communities in Miami and New York City more visible. Afro-Cuban musicians like Mario Bauza, Miguelito Valdés, and Arsenio Rodríguez, as well as boxers like Kid Chocolate and Kid Gavilán, were popular across the United States. A number of black Cubans also played for Major League Baseball teams. However, the popularity of Afro-Cuban artists and athletes did not necessarily translate into greater social acceptance for Miami's Cuban immigrants. Instead, it reinforced the tendency of white South Floridians to conflate Cubanness with Africanness, and to associate both with the characteristics of musicality, physical strength, and sensuality also common to stereotypical constructions of black Americans.[12]

Before 1959, the few European-origin Cubans who were well-known in the United States also contributed to the racialization of Miami's pre-revolutionary Cuban community. Desi Arnaz Jr., a Santiaguero of Spanish descent whose wealthy family had come to Miami during the political turmoil of the 1930s, achieved unprecedented fame when he took on the role of the lustful, hot-tempered *conguero* Ricky Ricardo on the hit 1950s television series *I Love Lucy*. However, Arnaz's television persona reinforced historically grounded and racially inflected stereotypes of Cubans as immature, emotionally volatile, and hypersexual. Moreover, the wild drumming, dancing, and nonsensical "African" chanting featured in his character's musical performances further reinforced linkages between Cubanness and blackness and subsumed Cubans of all phenotypes into the category of racial other.

Miami's more privileged prerevolutionary Cubans worked to distance themselves from race- and class-inflected notions of Cubanness derived from North American popular culture and local knowledge of southern Florida's *tabaquero* communities. Among these were a small number of wealthy republican-era exiles and immigrants who had reestablished themselves in the Miami business community. Many of these elite Cubans enjoyed the benefits of U.S. citizenship and carefully cultivated a white racial identity.[13] However, their social position remained contingent on their embrace of American culture and lifestyle. Elite immigrants thus struggled to balance pride in their heritage and their leading positions in Miami's pan-American *colonia* with the need to at least publicly embrace a North American identity, suppressing markers of difference that would activate Anglo-American prejudices against Latina/os or invite the association of Cubanness with blackness.

Precisely because the status of these most privileged immigrants depended on the suppression of their ethnicity, Miami Cubans failed to develop a clearly articulated collective identity before 1959. Differences in race, social class, and worldview also limited the development of strong community ties among Cubans in Miami–Dade County. They were nonetheless united, albeit loosely, by their varying experiences of discrimination in the United States.[14] Nowhere was this more obvious than in the patterns of Latina/o residential segregation that predated the arrival of anti-Castro Cubans in Miami.

By the 1950s, many of Miami–Dade County's Spanish-speaking people—including many light-skinned Cubans with middle-class incomes—had settled in a neighborhood already known as Little Havana. This economically depressed four-square-mile tract to the southwest of the Central Business District was bordered to the north by similarly blighted black neighborhoods. The extreme residential segregation of the *colonia latina* linked prerevolutionary Cuban immigrants to both other Latina/os and African Americans in Miami. After 1959, the massive influx of anti-Castro refugees into Little Havana would reinforce white Miamians' tendency to associate Cubanness with blackness and invite unfavorable associations between the early exiles and the city's poor ethnic immigrants and minorities.

CHILDREN, ANTI-CASTRO REFUGEES, AND U.S. FOREIGN POLICY, 1959–1961

On the eve of the Cuban Revolution, Miami–Dade County was mired in a serious economic recession and struggling to keep a lid on racial troubles. Though Miami was ill-equipped to absorb a sudden wave of Cuban immigration, political leaders in Washington, D.C., had their own reasons for encouraging a massive exodus of anti-Castro refugees from the island into the city.

With the conclusion of World War II in 1945, the United States found itself engaged in a struggle for global hegemony with the Soviet Union. By the beginning of the 1950s, the Cold War competition between the democratic-capitalist nation-making project and the communist one redefined North Americans' collective identity and dominated U.S. foreign policy decision-making processes. After 1959, the exigencies of Cold War foreign policy also delineated the parameters of U.S.-Cuban relations and contributed to the deterioration of historically intimate ties between the two nations.

As early as 1960—as in the years following the 1898 Spanish-Cuban-American War—the U.S. government sought to shape the island nation's destiny in accordance with its own economic and geopolitical goals by strategically intervening in the lives of Cuban children. U.S. leaders and intelligence agents identified the politics of childhood as a powerful site in which to contest the radicalization of the Cuban Revolution. They sought to stimulate emigration by exacerbating Cuban parents' already heightened anxieties about the safety and well-being of their children. By encouraging the flight of middle-class Cuban families, U.S. officials hoped to deprive the Revolution of the expertise of technicians and professionals and drive the island's economy and infrastructure to the breaking point. Moreover, they also sought to create a growing pool of refugee men for recruitment into covert anti-Castro programs.

Responding to increasing political repression, social upheaval, and economic deprivation—as well as to the moral panic provoked by the CIA-sponsored *patria potestad* rumor campaign—counterrevolutionaries increasingly took up arms against the Castro regime, even as Catholic and middle-class families prepared to flee or sent their unaccompanied children off the island. A small number of anti-Castro Cubans, resentful of the previous U.S. support for corrupt and antidemocratic Cuban presidents, chose to relocate to Spain and Latin America; however, the overwhelming majority sought refuge in the United States, where many families had at least one relative already living in New York or southern Florida.

Cubans fleeing the Revolution faced little difficulty entering the United States; many already possessed visas, and those who did not were able to easily acquire them from the U.S. embassy in Havana. Moreover, in light of White House concerns about the nature of Castro's leadership, already minimal visa requirements for Cubans were further relaxed as early as the last months of 1959. By 1960, immigrations and customs officials were also instructed to allow virtually unrestricted admission to those who had left the island, even those who lacked appropriate entry documents.

Although the Cuban Revolution had not yet been declared socialist, the island's developing ties with the U.S.S.R. meant that anti-Castro Cubans enjoyed preferential status among all Latin American entrants to the United States. While the Immigration Restriction Act (1924) and the McCarran-Walter Act (1952) made entry difficult for all and almost impossible for nonwhite people, entry from the Latin American nations, in line with the Monroe Doctrine's assertion of U.S. economic and geopolitical hegemony over the Western Hemisphere, remained theoretically unrestricted. However, in practice, the U.S. government had long selectively excluded undesirable immigrants from the region, as demonstrated in the sweeping repatriation of Mexican immigrants (including a number of naturalized U.S. citizens and their children) during the 1930s Depression and again during "Operation Wetback" in 1954.[15]

At the same time, an evolving refugee policy created preferential entrance categories for asylum seekers whose admittance was seen as advancing the U.S. position in the global Cold War. This meant that applicants fleeing communist nations qualified for special admission to the United States.[16] Accordingly, Dominicans fleeing the bloody but U.S.-aligned Trujillo dictatorship during the 1950s were denied refugee status and received no resettlement assistance, even as anti-Castro Cubans' opposition to a Revolution veering rapidly to the left uniquely positioned them to support U.S. Cold War foreign policy goals.[17] They thus joined refugees displaced by the U.S.S.R.'s absorption of the nations of Eastern and Central Europe, including Hungarian freedom fighters that had resisted their homeland's incorporation into the Soviet Union, as welcomed guests of the United States.

Once in the United States, Cuban refugees and especially their children earned a starring role in propaganda supporting the nation's Cold War policy goals. By March 1960, in line with President Eisenhower's approval of a CIA plan to overthrow the Castro regime, plans to establish a means for mass communication to Cubans on the island were initiated. In order that "a powerful propaganda offensive" could be launched in the name of the Counterrevolution, covert funding was provided for the establishment of a number of exile newspapers. Arrangements were made to resume publication of *El Avance*, a leading Cuban daily that had recently been nationalized, in Miami, as well as for the paper's clandestine introduction into Cuba and for distribution at a nominal cost throughout Latin America. Funding was also provided for exiles to purchase commercial time on Miami radio stations, and for prominent Cubans to embark on hemispheric anti-Castro speaking tours.[18]

From the beginning, these CIA-sponsored propaganda efforts sought to establish a "deeply moving tone and motivating force for the liberation of Cuba" by appealing to Cubans' patriotic and spiritual values, by evoking the symbolic figure of José Martí and the moral republic, and especially by deploying the child-centered representations that had played such a central role in their historic aspirations to nationhood. The Eisenhower administration also instructed the U.S. Information Agency (USIA) to focus on "exploiting" the propaganda value of Cuban refugee children to stir up anti-Castro sentiment in the United States and throughout Latin America.[19]

In collaboration with the federal government and the voluntary agencies charged with overseeing refugee settlement in Miami, the U.S. media also energetically disseminated child-centered stories and photographs that provided tangible evidence of Castro's turn toward communism. They worked hand in hand with exiles to frame the Revolution as a threat to Cuban children, seeking to discredit the Castro regime in the United States as well as in Cuba, Latin America, and around the world. To that end, in March 1960, *U.S. News and World Report* published a series of photographs of uniformed Cuban children, marching, practicing judo, and studying; the caption under one photo read, "In class Luís is mindful of Castro's warning: children who do not study are not good revolutionaries."

The *New York Times* drew an even less subtle comparison between the Revolution's designs on children and the methods of ideological education and social control employed in the Soviet Union. "The pattern of training," the *Times* asserted, "is similar to that used by many totalitarian governments. It includes indoctrination in schools, on radio and in the press; military training from seven years of age; a hate campaign, this time directed against the United States; the organization of work brigades for boys fourteen through eighteen; and meetings and fiestas, all with a political purpose."[20]

Cuban children were thus at the heart of much of the U.S. government's most evocative anticommunist messages. However, North American interest in the island's boys and girls was not strictly instrumental. Beginning in mid-1960, the need to safeguard the spiritual and physical well-being of Cuban children had prompted a multinational clandestine effort to spirit young boys and girls off the island; this program would later become known as Operation Pedro Pan. Well before the establishment of the official Cuban Children's Program, this same concern for Cuban children had also motivated Monsignor Bryan O. Walsh, director of Miami's Catholic Welfare Bureau, to organize a comprehensive volunteer effort to house, feed, and educate unaccompanied minors.[21] However, despite the enormous propaganda benefits that could be derived from publicizing anti-Castro parents' heartrending decisions to send their children alone into exile, both programs actually received minimal media attention until years later.

After President Kennedy established the federally funded Cuban Children's Program in January 1961, Monsignor Walsh and an extensive network of volunteers strove to keep these unaccompanied minors out of the news, even while benefiting from the waiver of immigration requirements for the children they transported off the island and unprecedented levels of funding for their care in the United States. By providing tacit support for efforts to maintain media silence about the Pedro Panes, the U.S. government temporarily subsumed foreign policy priorities to less instrumental considerations—in this case, to the goal of protecting children, widely considered to be particularly vulnerable to communist indoctrination. However, the informal agreement to limit public discussion of unaccompanied Cuban minors was not incompatible with long-term U.S. foreign policy objectives that rested on the shared belief of government officials, journalists, exiles, and their advocates in the importance of children to the democratic-capitalist nation-making project.[22]

The decision to limit media coverage of Operation Pedro Pan was nonetheless an exception to the norm. North American journalists continued to seek opportunities to write stories that described Castro's sinister designs on innocent Cuban children. However, during the last months of 1960, it became increasingly difficult to travel to and from Cuba. As a result, the USIA and the English-language media began increasingly to rely on exile leaders and informants to produce child-centered anti-Castro propaganda. Aware that their preferential immigration status depended on their classification as Cold War refugees, anti-Castro Cubans acted out of both conviction and necessity in framing themselves and their children as the latest victims of international communism. They eagerly shared their personal experiences, anecdotal information, and rumors with U.S. newspaper, magazine, television, and radio reporters, contributing to the ever increasing barrage of stories that described their flight from the island as a heroic effort to protect their sons and daughters from communist indoctrination and deprivation.

Refugees drew on the same morally and emotionally resonant discourses deployed by CIA-sponsored propagandists and the anti-Castro movement on the island to justify their decision to seek asylum in the United States. These discourses gave voice to their sense of betrayal by a Revolution many had once actively supported, and expressed their deeply held anticommunist values and sincere fears for their children and their nation. At the same time, exiles also sought to adapt the counterrevolutionary politics of childhood to a new context, strategically aligning their need for preferential immigration status and resettlement assistance with the hardening of Washington's opposition to the Castro regime.

In doing so, refugees hoped to secure the conditions of their immediate survival during what most hoped would be a short sojourn in Miami. However, as tens of thousands of anti-Castro Cubans arrived in the city, tensions between U.S. foreign policy goals and local priorities would provoke a racially inflected backlash that placed unexpected new demands on children in the struggle to safeguard the well-being of the growing exile community.

CHILDREN AND ANGLO-CUBAN
RELATIONS IN MIAMI, 1959–1960

In the first six months following the Cuban Revolution, approximately 26,500 Batista-aligned Cubans sought refuge in the United States. These elite Batistiano families received little attention from the U.S. government and media.[23] Minimal public interest in these first exiles reflected most Americans' lack of concern with a Revolution that was initially not understood as socialist. Moreover, Batista supporters maintained a low profile, settling in Miami's affluent neighborhoods and enrolling their children in local private and Catholic schools. Comfortably self-supporting, they represented neither an increase in competition for local jobs nor a drain on municipal social services, and they therefore went largely unnoticed by the national and local government and media and by English-speaking Miami residents.

As early as the summer of 1959, however, some of the Revolution's original leaders and their children began to join the Batistianos in the United States. They were accompanied by a growing number of former Castro supporters, drawn from the progressive urban middle classes that had formed the majority of the Rebel Army and the M-26-7.[24] As radicalization progressed at an ever more rapid pace, these refugees were joined by a growing number of unaccompanied minors, whose parents sent them off the island to protect them from revolutionary threats to their physical, intellectual, and spiritual well-being. Most chose to avoid New York City's higher cost of living and rising crime rates, opting instead for Miami, which was relatively safe, offered inexpensive housing, and had a familiar tropical climate. Even more important to an exile population that expected a quick return to their homeland, it was only a short ferry trip or flight from Cuba.

Many Cuban refugees settled in Little Havana among other Cuban and Latina/o families. Once a largely middle-class Anglo neighborhood that had developed following the First World War, by 1959 Little Havana was losing population as a result of suburbanization and economic downturn. Single-family homes and small apartment buildings were rapidly deteriorating and retail trade had seriously declined. However, rents were low, and the area's access to public transportation and proximity to social services and employment opportunities downtown were appealing to refugees. Catholic churches and schools, also located nearby, contributed to the popularity of the neighborhood among recently arrived Cubans.[25]

By June 1960, the number of Cuban refugees in Miami had risen to more than 60,000.[26] However, in spite of federal support for those fleeing the island and widespread anticommunist sentiment among North Americans, feelings toward newly arrived Cubans and their children were less than enthusiastic. Though this first wave of exiles was overwhelmingly urban, educated, and middle-class, and relatively familiar with U.S. culture and the English language, white Miamians, who made up more than 80 percent of the city's population, were not initially predisposed to welcome Cubans as their equals.[27] Their earliest perceptions of the refugees were shaped more by historically rooted notions of racial difference than by any presumed similarities between exiles' religious, cultural, or political values and those of middle-class Americans.

Carlos Eire, sent to the United States as a refugee when he was eleven years old, recalls the racialized discrimination that even exclusively

European-origin Cuban refugees encountered in Miami. "We Cubans tended to be viewed by the locals as nonwhite intruders, even if we had blond hair and blue eyes. The lower you went on the social scale, the stronger the biases . . . but prejudices against Hispanics permeated the entire culture." These prejudices were exacerbated by the persistent association between Cubanness and blackness that permeated U.S. history and popular culture. Eire was shocked by representations of Cuba as a primitive island peopled by African savages in the textbooks issued to him after he enrolled in a Miami elementary school. His geography text featured only one photograph of Cuba: a grass hut, its doorway crowded with half-naked and barefoot black children.

Local notions of Cubanness, reinforced by history textbooks that reinforced racialized and infantilizing representations of Cuba dating back to the Spanish-Cuban-American War, prompted Eire's classmates to ask how he felt about wearing shoes "for the first time" after arriving in Miami. White children also asked if the privileged boy's Havana home had been equipped with a toilet. Other questions directed at the blond, blue-eyed author, including "Why aren't you dark?" and "Why do all Cubans have big lips?" pointed explicitly to the racialized lens through which many mainstream Americans interpreted even the lightest-skinned refugees.[28] Children's questions echoed the concerns of their parents, many of whom feared that the growing population of racially suspect, Spanish-speaking, and Catholic Cubans threatened to remake the city's ethnic and cultural composition.

Suspicion turned to hostility as awareness of the refugee population began to grow. Problems between Anglo-Americans and Cuban refugees first emerged in Little Havana, where a general trend toward suburbanization had left the neighborhood with excessive vacancies and contributed to the deterioration of buildings and facilities. However, Cuban families who filled rental properties that might otherwise have remained empty were not necessarily welcomed. In fact, a study commissioned by Miami–Dade County mayor Chuck Hall determined that the settlement of refugees and their children in the central city had provoked tension between Cuban renters and Anglo-American property owners, exacerbating the movement of white residents out of the area and contributing to the already prevalent racial and ethnic residential segregation of Miami.

The study attributed the problems of coexistence to the "different social customs" of Cuban refugees. These differences included "tendencies to gregarious behavior, the inclination toward large families . . . and a general inability to smoothly fit into the customary neighborhood patterns." These undesirable ethnic differences were having a negative impact on the quality of life of white residents in what the study mistakenly categorized as a "purely native neighborhood"—ignoring the significant pre-1959 Latina/o population for which Little Havana had been named. Cubans who were unable or unwilling to adapt to North American ways were therefore responsible for white residents' decision to move out of the neighborhood, a trend that had led to the "colonization of some of these areas into self-imposed Cuban quarters."[29]

Outside Little Havana, Cubans faced more explicit forms of discrimination. Despite the Cubans' middle-class origins and presumptive whiteness, Anglo-American Miamians objected to the refugees, whom they insisted on viewing through the lens of racial and cultural difference. White Miami residents perceived Cubans as clannish and loud, and disliked hearing them speak Spanish in their midst. They also reacted with alarm to extended Cuban families and the collectives of nonrelated nuclear families who sometimes pooled scarce resources to share the rent on small apartments. These kinds of survival strategies encouraged local residents to associate Cubans with other poor people of color and undesirably ethnic immigrants. They thus sought to erect barriers to their presence. As a result, by 1960, rental signs on apartment buildings stating, "No Cubans, no pets, and no children," became common throughout the city.[30]

Given the suspicion with which southern Florida whites had historically regarded prerevolutionary working-class, politically progressive, and at least nominally Roman Catholic Cubans, this less than enthusiastic welcome was perhaps inevitable.[31] However, the preexisting racialized distrust of immigrants from the island was not the only factor affecting refugees' reception. The growing destitution of each successive group of new arrivals further reinforced associations between Cubans and other poor immigrants and people of color and awoke Miami residents' fears about their potential impact on municipal infrastructure, services, and public order.

In mid-1960, when Fidel Castro decreed harsh new restrictions on émigrés' ability to take money or other assets off the island, relatives, friends, priests, and local voluntary agencies scrambled to help impoverished refugees find shelter, food, and employment. As the increasingly desperate economic situation of the new Cuban arrivals was revealed, long-term Miami residents, already concerned about the changing racial and ethnic composition of their neighborhoods, also began to protest the negative effect of refugees on a depressed local economy. Cubans, they insisted, were taking jobs away from locals. Echoing charges often leveled at other racialized populations, including other Latina/os and African Americans, white Miamians accused Cuban refugees of moving into the overcrowded homes of their friends and relatives in Little Havana, turning the central city neighborhood into an ethnic ghetto, causing the deterioration of real estate values, and creating a potential public health risk.

Children played a central role in the construction of Cubans as poor and racially undesirable immigrants. Impoverished refugee parents found themselves unable to sustain the child-centered practices and performances that, on the island, had converted their sons and daughters into signifiers of their whiteness and socioeconomic privilege. Permitted only to take a bare minimum of clothing, shoes, toiletries, and medicine off the island and lacking money to replace them in the United States, parents and surrogate caregivers struggled to maintain the neat, well-clothed, and healthy appearance that would confirm their children's (and by extension their own) middle-class origins. However, as time passed, refugee boys and girls increasingly suffered the social stigma attached to their shabby clothing, footwear, inadequate school supplies, and meager bag lunches. These visible signs of material want transformed once privileged children into needy and neglected racialized bodies and reinforced the association of Cubans with other marginalized people of color.

Similarly, as Cuban parents struggled to find ways to continue their sons' and daughters' education, public debate about the growing numbers of refugee children attending public schools became a site in which white Miamians adapted preexisting notions of Cubanness to frame impoverished refugees and their children as a drain on municipal services. True to their middle-class origins, many Cuban parents believed that public schools were for children from lower socioeconomic backgrounds and preferred to enroll their sons and daughters in private and Catholic schools; however, few refugees could afford private education. Moreover, although some local Catholic schools offered free or subsidized tuition to refugee students, demand far exceeded available spaces. As a result, more refugees began to send their children to neighborhood schools. By the beginning of the 1960 academic year, as many as 2,000 Cuban students were attending elementary and secondary schools in Miami–Dade County. Over half had received fee waivers absolving their impoverished parents from paying the fifty-dollar fee the county school board charged nonresident students.

Disgruntled local residents complained about the growing cost of educating refugee children, calculating that the Dade County School Board had already spent more than $100,000 in order to allow Cuban children to attend public schools free of charge. Moreover, in a still racially segregated school system, phenotypically white Cuban children were enrolling in great numbers in schools reserved for Anglo-American students. White Miamians resented the presence of racially suspect and non-English-speaking refugee children in overcrowded classrooms, accusing them of taking instructional time and materials away from white students and negatively impacting their educational success. Public debates framing impoverished and linguistically deficient refugee students and their parents as an unfair burden on the Miami–Dade County school system would continue throughout the decade.[32]

Miami residents were equally worried about Cuban children who were not attending school. Local church and Miami–Dade County leaders were particularly worried about adolescent refugee boys and feared they might drive up juvenile delinquency rates.[33] Though delinquency was not in fact a significant problem among the early exile community, many refugee children—more often boys than girls—were in fact ill-supervised. Bored and restless refugee children waited for the return home of mothers, fathers, and other caregivers who worked long hours at menial jobs far from their central Miami neighborhoods. Those who had come to the United States as unaccompanied minors especially struggled to overcome loneliness during evenings and weekends spent alone or in the awkward company of foster families.[34] Many refugee children thus spent long unsupervised hours roaming the city or idling away time in parks, public libraries, and school playgrounds.[35]

Other children were driven into the streets by strained family relationships, the overcrowding of shared housing, and financial necessity. Young Cubans sought the company of other refugee and Spanish-speaking children or took part-time jobs cleaning, delivering groceries and newspapers, or selling comic books door-to-door. These experiences contrasted sharply with middle-class children's sheltered lives on the island, where the scrupulous vigilance of Afro-Cuban nannies and domestics had been a powerful signifier of both their whiteness and privilege. When they entered exile in Miami, however, a sudden and radical inversion of class and racial hierarchies converted refugee children and especially boys into a social problem, awakening mainstream American fears about the threat to order represented by working-class, immigrant, and minority youth in urban centers across the nation.

Public debate about neglected and unsupervised refugee children revealed the chasm between Cubans' own identities and the way they were initially perceived in Miami. Early exiles saw their sons and daughters as innocent victims of communism and understood themselves as heroic defenders of their children's spiritual, moral, and physical well-being; however, white Miamians persisted in framing anti-Castro Cubans as undesirably ethnic immigrants and imagined young refugees not as victims deserving of special care or compassion but rather as a social problem to be averted. Widespread anxiety about potentially delinquent refugee children further reinforced the racialized suspicion with which white Miamians regarded the growing Cuban population.[36]

Throughout 1960, as white Miamians continued to raise their voices against the growing influx of refugees and their children, Cubans came to a painful conclusion: locals did not recognize their middle-class origins and values or familiarity with North American ways but rather viewed them as socially inferior. Even more distressingly, despite the Cubans' phenotypical whiteness, Anglo-American Miamians did not acknowledge them as their racial equals. For refugees who had enjoyed a relatively privileged socioeconomic position in island society, this realization was more than a blow to their pride or racial identities. It jolted them into awareness of their collective vulnerability as impoverished foreigners in an increasingly unwelcoming city.

Cubans were well aware of the difficulties faced in the United States by other people of Latin American origin and were particularly troubled by the marginalization of New York's Puerto Ricans. Between 1959 and 1961, both revolutionary and exile newspapers decried discrimination against this other group of Caribbean Latina/os and structural barriers to socioeconomic mobility for African-origin and mixed-race peoples in the United States. The articles described North Americans who refused to rent to Puerto Ricans, charged them extravagant monthly rates, or took advantage of their lack of English and unfamiliarity with U.S. law— expressions of the anti-Latina/o prejudice that many Cubans were beginning to experience firsthand in Miami.[37]

Cuban refugees undoubtedly sympathized with Puerto Rican victims of U.S. ethnocentrism and racism; however, they also quickly realized that their well-being in exile depended on dissociating themselves from other Latina/os and African Americans. Growing intolerance thus awoke anti-Castro Cubans and their U.S. allies to the need to resist the marginalization of the refugee community by deemphasizing their ethnic and racial similarities to other Spanish-speaking peoples while simultaneously stressing their political, cultural, and class affinities with middle-class white Miamians. In order to accomplish this, exiles would turn once again to their children, adapting discourses and images at the heart of the counterrevolutionary politics of childhood to frame a morally and emotionally resonant appeal for the support of the American mainstream.

"LITTLE REFUGEES FROM INTERNATIONAL COMMUNISM": CHILDREN AND THE EXILE CREATION MYTH

By the summer of 1960, tensions between national foreign policy goals and local priorities came to a head in Miami, sparking citywide debate about the daily arrival of hundreds of new Cuban refugees at the same time that the Revolution's embrace of the Soviet Union drove ever greater numbers from the island. As U.S.-Cuba relations deteriorated, the federal government joined forces with state and municipal officials, refugee advocates, and exile leaders to ensure that Miami welcomed the tens of thousands fleeing "Castro-communism." Working hand in hand with anti-Castro Cubans, the U.S. government and media launched a carefully coordinated domestic public relations campaign that would create a class-based and political, rather than ethnic, identity for the exile community. They sought to change white Miamians' perceptions of Cubans as undesirable immigrants by asserting the affinities between refugees and their North American hosts, at the same time as they emphasized that exiles were guests who would return home once Castro was deposed.[38]

Aware that their survival in Miami depended on their ability to overcome Anglo-American fears of Cuban racial and cultural difference, refugees played an active role in the government-led campaign to define them in terms of their whiteness, Christian faith, middle-class family values, and commitment to a U.S. model of democratic-capitalism. Anti-Castro Cubans and their U.S. allies began to deploy child-centered discourses and images in order to construct a narrative of origin—a creation myth—that explained the emergence of a growing exile community in Miami. Government officials, refugee advocates, and U.S. journalists worked with exile leaders and media informants to disseminate the message that Cubans had left the island in order to save their children from communist oppression and indoctrination—thus emphasizing Cubans' political identity and downplaying aspects of their culture that might link them unfavorably to other U.S. Latina/os. Unlike other Latin American immigrants, they insisted, exiles had come to the United States not in search of economic opportunity but rather to protect their children from the red terror that had overtaken their island homeland, and to ensure their upbringing in accordance with the Christian democratic values that Cubans shared with their U.S. hosts.

To make certain that they would be perceived in terms of this politicized creation myth, refugees and their allies sought to ensure that public representations of the community focused on middle-class Cuban professionals and their families. Both exile and North American media featured frequent and prominent photographs of Cuban parents and their well-dressed, lovingly cared-for children, along with stories that narrated their harrowing escape from communism and newfound enjoyment of freedom in the United States. Though in many ways an accurate reflection of exiles' experiences, these narratives and the images that accompanied them were highly selective. To combat white Miamians' tendency to associate Cubans with other poor ethnic immigrants and minorities, neither exile *periodiquitos* nor the U.S. media published pictures of Cuban men sweeping factories or waiting tables. Nor did they acknowledge that some Cuban women had found employment alongside Puerto Rican migrants picking tomatoes on Dade County farms. And they most certainly did not feature photographs of exile children dressed in worn-out clothing or scuffed shoes, working after-school jobs to augment family incomes.

As late as the autumn of 1960, however, many Miami residents still lacked an in-depth understanding of the origins of the Cuban exodus and its importance to their nation's Cold War foreign policy goals. Miamians continued to focus on more immediate concerns: the perceived negative impact of refugees on a depressed local economy, the strain they placed on municipal health and educational facilities, and the social crises their growing numbers threatened to precipitate, especially in Miami's central city neighborhoods. Responding to a growing barrage of angry letters to the editor and to citywide disquiet, in October 1960 the *Miami Herald* joined forces with exile leaders and their U.S. allies to raise awareness about the plight of Cuban refugees in Dade County. The *Herald* invited local officials, public figures, and celebrities to form a panel to find rapid and effective solutions to the problems of the increasingly needy exile community. Exiles offered information and public testimony, and, reflecting Cold War America's growing acceptance of the energetically anticommunist Catholic Church, local clergy were also invited to speak about their efforts to provide aid and comfort to refugees and their children.

Politicians participating in the panel addressed their disgruntled constituents, seizing the opportunity to educate city residents about their patriotic obligation to embrace the anti-Castro refugees. Franklin Williams, member of the Miami City Council on Public Welfare, argued that the influx of Cubans offered Miami's citizens the opportunity to "show the world how we react here in the face of the communist problem created by the red regime that we have next door." Congressman Dante Fascell similarly asserted that "Miamians don't need to go to Latin America to do good work in the 'people to people' program. We have that work here in Miami; we can and must do it."[39]

The national media similarly deployed child-centered arguments to help mainstream Americans understand the broader geopolitical implications of the Cuban exodus and to garner sympathy for the growing exile community. They published photographs of hungry Cuban children on the island, dressed in threadbare clothing and lacking proper footwear, and wrote stories describing young boys and girls submitted to communist indoctrination in classrooms and nurseries, forced to carry pickets at revolutionary rallies or to participate in militia drills. These representations spoke powerfully to the fears and fantasies of many U.S. parents, who had come to idealize the post–World War II experience of a sheltered, consumption-oriented, middle-class childhood as an essential expression of the American way of life. Consumed within the broader context of the Cold War, newspaper articles, pamphlets, and speeches that drew on these child-centered discourses and images sparked moral outrage at the Revolution's efforts to mobilize innocent Cuban children for political, economic, and military efforts. This outrage fueled anticommunist sentiment and increased support for anti-Castro refugees across the nation.

Refugee advocates also drew on the exile community's child-centered creation myth to prepare Miami residents for the expansion of the exodus from the island in the months to come. Wendell Rollason, director of the Inter-American Affairs Commission, wrote to Joe Hall, superintendent of Dade County Public Schools, on November 7, 1960, describing the Revolution's interventions in the lives of children and the Counterrevolution's commitment to protecting innocent Cuban children from the sinister designs of Castro-communism. Echoing the morally and emotionally resonant discourses of the counterrevolutionary politics of childhood, he reminded Superintendent Hall of the enormous sacrifice that Cuban parents underwent in order to send their children to safety and freedom in the United States and urged him to extend all possible support to Cuban refugee students:

It is clear to even the most casual observer of the Cuban situation that Fidel Castro's government is following the party line of International Communism in most of its policies. This is particularly true concerning state control over children. The government has removed the discretionary control of the child's education from the hands of his parents. Our reliable sources in the Cuban underground state that additional "laws" are prepared that will remove virtually every vestige of parental authority from over every child in Cuba. Already, Cuban parents are sending their youngsters to Miami in increasing numbers. During the past two weeks, at least one-half of the children from that island have arrived in Miami unaccompanied by their parents, being consigned to the care of relatives in residence here. To avoid this despicable destruction of family life so dear to every free man, the Cuban parents can be expected to continue this exodus of their children at an ever-increasing tempo as long as the Castro government permits.

The letter advised Superintendent Hall that already overextended Miami–Dade County schools should expect an influx of upward of 10,000 Cuban children unaccompanied by parents in the year 1961. It also informed him that it was their shared patriotic duty to find ways of accommodating them in crowded local classrooms. "We, as avowed champions of personal freedom throughout the world, must meet the challenge by enthusiastically accepting these little refugees from International Communism."[40]

Patriotic duties notwithstanding, exile leaders and their allies recognized that the goodwill of local residents would depend on more than appeals to their anticommunist sentiments or sense of national pride. Miami's infrastructure was incapable of absorbing the ever greater number of arriving Cuban families and children; since federal asylum policy made it possible for refugees to settle in the city, they reasoned, the federal government should share the burden of caring for them. Continued pleas from the local Cuban Refugee Committee, municipal and state politicians, and Miami's Catholic Welfare Bureau received a federal response on December 2, 1960, when President Eisenhower allotted $1 million of discretionary funds to refugee aid and authorized the creation of the Cuban Refugee Emergency Center to coordinate the provision of relief and resettlement services to the growing exile population.

On February 3, 1961, a newly inaugurated President John F. Kennedy authorized $18 million in additional funds for the creation of the Cuban Refugee Assistance Program.[41] The program, housed at the Cuban Refugee Center (CRC) at 600 Biscayne Boulevard in central Miami, would provide financial assistance to Cuban families, supply them with health care, and help them find affordable housing and employment. It also worked to alleviate economic and social tensions in Miami by resettling refugees across the nation. Efforts to harmonize U.S. foreign policy goals and local needs also led President Kennedy to dedicate funds to support the Cuban Children's Program, founded under the auspices of the Catholic Welfare Bureau in November 1960 to provide shelter and aid to the unaccompanied minors whom the president called "the most troubled group among the refugee population."[42]

The directors of the Cuban Refugee Assistance Program quickly assumed leadership of the campaign, sponsored by the federal government, to create public support for anti-Castro refugees. In December 1960, an internal government memo dictated that the opening of the CRC should be announced "with as wide coverage as possible" and recommended that "the White House might [simultaneously] release the interim report on the Cuban refugee. . . . Copies of this report should be available at the Cuban Refugee Center press conference." It also instructed the center's leadership to meet privately with key executives of Miami newspapers, both English- and Spanish-language; chiefs of the various wire service bureaus and magazines; and radio and television station managers to outline future plans for alleviating the refugee problem.[43]

The CRC's Cuban staff members—most of them university educated, many in law, journalism, and social services—played an essential role in the CRC's public relations work. They dedicated themselves to translating the counterrevolutionary discourses of childhood disseminated in Spanish-language anti-Castro speeches, pamphlets, and *periodiquitos* for use in the U.S. media. They also worked tirelessly to produce images that portrayed Cubans as model immigrants—white, well-educated, hardworking, middle-class, and dedicated to freedom, capitalism, and family.[44] After January 1961, U.S. journalists coordinated closely with these exile public relations professionals to generate the child-centered messages that would inspire North Americans to open their hearts and homes to Cuban families and unaccompanied children.

Seeking to create support for its efforts, the CRC commissioned photographs of the youngest refugees to illustrate its widely distributed "Nine Points" mission statement. The photos drew special attention to Point 1, which called for the provision of daily necessities for refugees; Point 3, which called for funding and support for resettlement; Point 5, which called for the provision of essential health services, especially to children; Point 6, which called for federal assistance for public schools to offset the cost of educating refugee students; and Point 8, which called for the provision of financial aid for the care and protection of "defenseless . . . unaccompanied children."[45] These images of Cuban boys and girls sought to appeal to the emotions of U.S. citizens in Miami and across the nation and alleviate their concerns over the massive expenditures associated with this unprecedented federal assistance program.

Other photographs accompanied CRC appeals to U.S. citizens to become sponsors of refugees resettled across the nation. They leveraged North Americans' tenderness toward small children and babies and poignantly highlighted the intense bonds between parent and child. One publicity photo immortalized a Cuban exile father, relocated to Baltimore, embracing his toddler son. Another, which appeared in a CRC bulletin titled *Gracias, amigos!*, lovingly depicted a Cuban refugee mother holding a sleeping baby girl. These family portraits sought to drive home the importance of the universal bonds between parents and children, regardless of their origins, and emphasized the centrality of these bonds to Cubans' decisions to flee the Castro regime. Reflecting the middle-class family values of the Cold War era, photographs like these helped patriotic U.S. citizens identify emotionally with exiles as fellow parents and encouraged them to see their own children's futures reflected in the faces of innocent young refugees from communism.[46] In doing so, the images played a powerful role in a carefully coordinated campaign to urge white Miamians and Americans nationwide to welcome exiles into their communities.

The CRC staff similarly directed child-centered discourses and images at reluctant exiles in order to convince them that resettlement outside southern Florida was in their children's best interest. The center's monthly newsletters regularly included photographs of Cuban boys and girls, warmly bundled against the midwestern cold, smiling on the stoops of their new homes, perched on the hoods of secondhand cars local sponsors had helped their parents purchase, and gathered around Christmas trees laden with gifts donated by well-wishers in their new communities. These pictures additionally decorated the waiting room, corridors, and offices of the Cuban Refugee Center, through which all Cubans seeking assistance from the U.S. government necessarily passed.

At the request of the CRC, Cuban boys and girls relocated across the United States were also photographed by local voluntary agencies and their host families as they attended parties and classes at local schools, suited up for football games, and sledded happily in the snow. These photographs were distributed to civic associations, television and radio stations, and newspapers and magazines across the country, where they were published alongside articles explaining the mission of the Cuban Refugee Assistance Program; praising Cubans' faith, work ethic, and family values; and calling on Americans to offer their warmest welcome to exiles and their children.

During the spring of 1961, as relations between the United States and Cuba descended into open hostility, the few North American journalists remaining on the island worked to send home stories reinforcing the dangers faced by children in Castro's Cuba and detailing the threat that indoctrinated Cuban children represented to the future of democracy throughout the Western Hemisphere. Reporting from Havana on February 8, Jim Fontaine wrote: "At the same time as he lays siege to Catholic Education, Fidel Castro has said that he plans to send a thousand Cuban children to the Soviet Union. The goal, observe horrified parents and educators here, is to form a generation of 'mass-men,' communist automatons for the penetration of the Americas." Fontaine reminded U.S. and Cuban exile readers that this was not the first time innocent children had been kidnapped and trained to serve the nefarious purposes of international communism: "Today apparently Russians and Czechoslovaks that amble through Havana as 'technicians' and that speak Spanish so well, are the children that twenty-five years ago the Reds in Spain sent to Russia."[47]

During the April 1961 Bay of Pigs invasion and in its aftermath, the U.S. government and its media partners paid ever greater attention to the island's political transformation and the explosive growth of the Miami exile community. Journalists focused with rising urgency on the desperate plight of Cuban children under a regime that had now openly declared itself socialist. *New York Times* correspondent Tad Szulc reported on Castro's increasingly intimate bonds with the Soviet Union, while *Time* magazine described with distress the growing militancy of Cuban youth, who were being organized into juvenile patrols and militias charged with policing city and village streets at night.[48] Stories like these encouraged more North Americans to open their hearts to refugee families and to welcome unaccompanied minors as foster children in their homes.

Galvanized by events on the island and encouraged by this sudden outpouring of North American support, Cuban refugees launched new efforts to raise awareness of their needs, relying on the child-centered images and discourses that had helped to create them as an exile community in the American mainstream. They even drew on their own children to elicit sympathy and support. In June 1961, a recently arrived exile couple brought their six-month-old baby girl to the Cuban Refugee Center. Dressed in a crisp cotton sundress and bonnet, the baby wore a sign pinned to her dress: "I want to bring here my aunt," it read. "She doesn't want to be Red. Please help!" The baby girl was promptly photographed and the image was published in a leading exile *periodiquito*.[49]

A six-month-old exile, photographed at Miami's Cuban Refugee Center, pleads for help in bringing her aunt to the United States. From El Avance, June 2, 1961. Courtesy of the Cuban Heritage Collection, University of Miami Libraries, Coral Gables, Florida.

Though the photograph appeared first in the exile media, the fact that the sign was painstakingly printed in English suggests that the parents had deliberately targeted the English-speaking staff of the CRC and perhaps even the U.S. media, in search of the broadest possible audience for their anticommunist message.

It remains unknown whether this particular plea—as poignant as it was self-conscious—reached its desired English-speaking audience. However, by the spring of 1961, efforts by refugees and their advocates to disseminate the exile community's child-centered creation myth had clearly begun to bear fruit. Following the Bay of Pigs debacle, these efforts took on a greater urgency, even as they were received with a new alacrity by the American mainstream.

CHILDREN, "OUR CUBAN VISITORS," AND THE LIMITS OF ANGLO-AMERICAN HOSPITALITY

As public awareness of the exile plight grew, white Miamians began to demonstrate more support for anti-Castro refugees. By February 1961, many Anglo-Americans seemed increasingly willing to overlook the strain the Cuban influx placed on local infrastructure and services, choosing instead to respond "with cordiality to the problems of the exiles." Many even went to the airport to welcome the large number of Cuban families that arrived in the days after the United States severed diplomatic relations with Cuba. One vindicated exile leader exulted at the change of heart among the city's once less-than-welcoming residents. "For more than a year we've been trying to tell people that the government of Fidel Castro is a dictatorship worse than that of Batista," he said. "Now, finally, they are opening their eyes to the facts."[50]

After the disastrous failure of the Bay of Pigs invasion, residents of Miami and in cities and towns across the nation organized to demonstrate their solidarity with the tens of thousands of impoverished refugees fleeing the socialist Revolution. Local Lions and Rotary Clubs donated money to voluntary agencies for exile aid and provided badly needed medicines and household goods. As public sympathy for refugees grew, so did the scope of American efforts to welcome and assist new arrivals. In May 1961, eighty-eight Kiwanis Clubs from across the country organized a "Freedom Caravan for Cuban Refugees." More than twenty-five trucks bearing more than $100,000 worth of food and supplies, including a large quantity of children's clothing and toys, arrived in Miami, where local Kiwanis leaders distributed them among needy families. Organizer N. M. Harrison, a retired minister, told exile journalists that "there exists among the American people a deep feeling of compassion for the suffering of the people of Cuba," stressing that people in all the cities the caravan had visited were eager to help.[51]

Federal and state officials and journalists worked together to encourage Miamians' newfound sympathy for the refugees, reinforcing their increasingly positive perception of Cubans as well as their understanding of themselves and their nation as defenders of the victims of communism and their defenseless children. Praising the Miami community for its generous hospitality to "the victims of the Communist Tyranny," a *Miami Herald* editorial offered a succinct summary of the exile community's child-centered creation myth and reminded white Miamians of the class and cultural affinities linking refugees and middle-class Americans. It noted that "the Cuban visitors represent all phases of life and professions, having an excellent level of education. . . . More than half have their families with them, including children brought from Cuba to escape communist indoctrination in the schools."[52]

Addressing lingering concerns about Cubans' moral and political credentials, the editorial insisted that "they are honest persons that have refused to kneel before the Soviet boot ruling in Cuba, and they have come in search of Freedom among their American neighbors of the same ideas." Delighted that the English-language media had endorsed the exile community's strenuously proclaimed identity and recognized the sacrifices Cuban parents had made to protect their children, *El Avance* republished the editorial "in a place of honor" in its February 24 edition.[53]

An important subtext of the editorial, titled "Our Cuban Visitors," nonetheless went undiscussed. The repeated use of the word "visitor" subtly reassured white Miamians that the Cubans with whom they were temporarily coexisting would not become permanent residents of their city. Instead, even as it praised Cubans as "good" immigrants and reinforced locals' patriotic pride by describing the exiles' appreciation for the North American nation-making project, it simultaneously drove home the idea that refugees would soon return to their homeland. Thus, even in the emotional days following the failed Bay of Pigs invasion, when appreciation for democratically minded, hardworking, God-fearing Cuban families was at its highest, Miami residents continued to display a racialized distrust of "foreign" refugees that would only be assuaged by media references to their status as temporary guests in their city.[54]

CONTRARY TO POPULAR HISTORICAL MEMORY, the first wave of Cuban exiles were neither immediately recognized nor unconditionally accepted as white and middle-class by Anglo-Americans in Miami–Dade County. In fact, few Miamians initially perceived Cubans to be their racial or cultural equals. As a result, early interactions between refugees and their local hosts were characterized less by harmony or mutual respect and more by conflict, suspicion, and discrimination.[55]

Beginning in early 1960, Cuban refugees worked hand in hand with their U.S. allies to disseminate a child-centered creation myth that explained the origins of the emerging exile community to originally less-than-sympathetic Miami residents. They sought to adapt the discourses and images of a counterrevolutionary politics of childhood for use in a new context, in order to persuade Anglo Americans in the city that they had been compelled to undergo an involuntary exile in order to protect their vulnerable children from scarcity, physical danger, and Marxist indoctrination. This understanding of the Cuban exodus emphasized the harmony between refugees' political opposition to the Revolution, U.S. anticommunist foreign policy goals, and local priorities, ensuring that government officials and private citizens alike treated Cubans as political exiles from Communist persecution rather than undesirable "ethnic" immigrants.

Child-centered discourses and images also worked powerfully to counter white Miamians' concerns about the growing influx of racially and culturally suspect Cuban refugees. Representations of light-skinned, well-dressed, and carefully groomed refugee children enjoying their new-found freedom in the United States were crucial to securing a favorable reception for exiles—a welcome by no means inevitable—by coding their emerging community as white, middle-class, and sharing the Christian family values of Cold War America. However, not all Miami residents were enthusiastic about the seemingly never-ending flow of Cuban refugees into the city. Exiles' success in winning governmental support and assistance did not necessarily endear them to Miami's other Latina/o communities or to local African Americans, who in the midst of a prolonged local recession and ongoing civil rights troubles still struggled to overcome segregation and unequal access to employment, schools, and public facilities and resources.[56]

Moreover, the welcome that was eventually extended to Cuban "visitors" was not unconditional. Demonstrating the limits of the government-led public relations campaign to garner support for the exile community, white Miamians struggled to demonstrate their patriotic commitment to the nation's Cold War foreign policy goals while clinging to notions of Cuban difference that were more prevalent than has been acknowledged. Exiles were welcomed, not primarily because Anglo-Americans recognized their whiteness and middle-class Christian and democratic values but rather because of their perceived value in the global anticommunist struggle on which both U.S. foreign policy and the nation's collective identity were based. Miamians opened their arms to exiles because they believed official reassurances that the growing number of Cubans in their midst would not become permanent residents. Sharing this hope that their sojourn in the United States would be short, exiles would join hands with the U.S. government to launch a passionate struggle to depose the Castro regime, recover the *patria*, and reassert José Martí's vision of the moral republic. Their dream of a quick return home would prove elusive.

6
TO SAVE OUR CHILDREN
The Politics of Childhood in the Anti-Castro Struggle,
1959–1962

Between 1959 and 1962, a politically and socioeconomically diverse group of Cuban refugees launched the anti-Castro movement that they hoped would quickly topple the Revolution and allow them to return home as triumphant redeemers of the republic. However, weakened by political divisions and rivalries and lacking the resources necessary to execute a decisive campaign to free the *patria*, counterrevolutionary leaders entered into an asymmetrical relationship with the U.S. intelligence community that would increase exiles' dependence on the federal government, weaken the legitimacy of the anti-Castro movement on both sides of the Straits of Florida, and limit their ability to act autonomously and effectively to secure their nation's liberation. Though exile leaders insisted on their right to be treated with respect as Cold War allies of the United States, they were unable to prevent their exploitation and infantilization by U.S. politicians, military leaders, and intelligence agents whose commitment to Cuba's democratic future was less than clear.

Aware that a quick return to the homeland rested on mobilizing the material and political resources of the entire refugee population, a nascent exile media dedicated itself to the production of counterrevolutionary propaganda as a powerful complement to the exile paramilitary struggle, even as they resisted the federal government's subordination of the exile community's leadership by portraying them as the true protagonists of the anti-Castro movement. They targeted a hemispheric audience with morally and emotionally resonant child-centered messages, seeking to foment anti-Castro opinion and activity among Cubans on the island and to create consensus among the multiple counterrevolutionary factions in Miami. They also sought to discredit the Castro regime among Latin Americans whose progressive politics and latent anti-U.S. sentiment might otherwise predispose them toward sympathy for the Revolution. At the same time, the transplanted institutions of an emerging exile civil society rapidly reorganized in Miami and rallied around a shared objective: to promote the unity of the exile community, on behalf of its children and in service of the anti-Castro struggle.

Working together, the exile media and civil society would bring together a diverse population of Cuban refugees, forging a powerful moral consensus on the need to suppress political differences in order to defeat Castro and restore the Cuban nation to their sons and daughters. However, the community's growing sense of unity could not make up for the structural weaknesses of the anti-Castro movement, which would remain divided and ultimately dependent on the whims of the U.S. government. By 1962, when the resolution of the October Missile Crisis failed to produce the downfall of the Revolution, hopes of a triumphant homecoming were replaced by anger, disillusionment, and despair. Though bitterly regretting their misplaced trust in the U.S. government, anti-Castro Cubans nonetheless clung to their dreams of return to a redeemed republic and to their belief that exile must be endured in order to safeguard the future of their beloved children.

COLD WAR FOREIGN POLICY, THE POLITICS OF CHILDHOOD, AND THE ANTI-CASTRO MOVEMENT

On the eve of the 1959 Revolution, the southern Florida Cuban population was composed of individuals of widely varying racial identities, socioeconomic positions, levels of assimilation in American society, and diverse political affiliations. Cuban immigrants were nonetheless mostly united in their initial support for the Revolution. However, this political consensus was shattered during the first six months of 1959, when approximately 26,500 Batista-aligned exiles arrived in the United States.[1] Widely despised, these Batistianos initially sought to maintain a low profile, avoiding social contact with pro-Castro Cubans and Latin Americans while living off income from substantial U.S. investments and savings deposited in local banks. Alienated from their countrymen and -women, Batista supporters quietly nursed the bitterness of their lost power and status even as they hoped for a quick return home, organizing among themselves some of the earliest paramilitary efforts and sabotage campaigns against the Castro regime.[2]

Although the U.S. government sought to prevent Batistiano incursions against the island, President Eisenhower nonetheless approved CIA plans to promote opposition to the Castro regime as early as November 1959.[3] The agency began initial recruitment efforts among the increasing population of middle-class Cubans who, after the trial and imprisonment of Huber Matos, had become alienated from the Revolution and were swelling the ranks of Miami's expanding refugee population. These exiles had already begun to organize a rapidly proliferating number of groups that were passionately committed to the military overthrow of the Castro government and the reestablishment of democratic governance on the island.

The early anti-Castro movement encompassed a politically heterogeneous group that included many disenchanted members and supporters of the Movimiento 26 de Julio. It also included conservatives and liberals, socialists and Christian Democrats, unified only by their belief that the Revolution had exceeded its mandate and by their opposition to Fidel Castro, whom they believed had hijacked a broadly based moral crusade to renew the Cuban Republic. A majority had supported the anti-Batista insurgency, and as much as 23 percent of them had participated in resistance activities prior to the dictator's flight from the island.[4] Though sharing the passionately anti-Castro and anticommunist worldview of the Batistianos, they rejected any possibility of collaboration with those who had preceded them into exile.

Exiles were also initially divided by their differing attitudes toward the United States. A small number were *plattistas* who defended North American hegemony over their island and called both for the United States to support Castro's overthrow and for the restoration of Cuba's historical ties with its northern protector. However, many first-wave refugees were passionate Cuban nationalists who sympathized with the Puerto Rican independence movement and opposed U.S. interventions in Latin America. In order to secure greater autonomy for their own nation in the future, they believed, as José Martí had, that the struggle to establish democratic rule on the island must be undertaken by Cubans without outside help or interference.

Divisions among anti-Castro Cubans were also heightened by the emergence of competing exile factions led by representatives of a wide range of prerevolutionary political parties and urban resistance and guerrilla groups. Charismatic leaders drew on prestige and power derived from their prerevolutionary political activities to form a wide range of anti-Castro paramilitary and political organizations that reflected their individual priorities and distinct visions for the nation's future. These leaders and their devoted followers clashed over the direction of the struggle to depose Castro, seeking to promote their organizations in exile and to advance their claims to power in a postrevolutionary Cuba. By the summer of 1960, debate and animosity between these different organizations weakened an anti-Castro movement that was as fragmented as it was passionate and created a confused and highly politicized atmosphere in Cuban Miami.[5]

At the same time, the growing presence of communists in the revolutionary government and Castro's increasingly strident anti-U.S. rhetoric began to be perceived in Washington as a threat to inter-American solidarity on Cold War issues. In August 1960, President Eisenhower responded to CIA pressure to declare the Cuban Revolution a threat to hemispheric security. In order to prevent communist subversion in the region, he authorized funding for the covert anti-Castro Operation Pluto and authorized the Department of Defense to assist the agency in building a paramilitary exile force for a future invasion of the island.[6]

Divided among themselves and lacking the resources to launch a decisive campaign for the liberation of their homeland, exiles responded eagerly to U.S. government offers of support for the counterrevolutionary cause. Between 2,000 and 3,000 Cuban exile men had already signed up as CIA-supported anti-Castro combatants, and more would soon follow. In doing so, however, they acquiesced to an asymmetrical relationship with the U.S. intelligence community that would limit their ability to act as autonomous agents of their nation's liberation. It would also open exiles to manipulation, exploitation, and humiliation at the hands of U.S. power brokers who viewed Cubans through racialized and infantilizing lenses dating back to U.S. intervention in the 1898 war of independence, and whose commitment to the counterrevolutionary agenda was less than clear.

After 1959, Fidel Castro's increasingly forceful assertions of Cuban sovereignty threatened U.S. notions of Cubans as children who, incapable of determining their own national destiny, owed gratitude and obedience to their benevolent North American protector. U.S. leaders nonetheless refused to recognize the Revolution as an expression of Cubans' legitimate aspirations toward self-determination, aware that treating Cubans as adults and equals would threaten the objective and subjective foundations of U.S. hegemony on the island, in the Caribbean, and throughout Latin America.[7] As a result, U.S. politicians and public figures continued to describe Castro as an "overgrown boy" whose anti-U.S. posture revealed only his immaturity, irrationality, and emotional volatility; they also pointed to his growing dependence on Soviet trade and aid to vindicate their belief that he was incapable of leading without assistance from a powerful tutor and protector.[8]

Clinging to their right—indeed their duty—to intervene on the island to assure both their own economic and geopolitical interests and the well-being of Cuba's citizens, the federal government and the intelligence community sought to order interactions with the anti-Castro movement in accordance with the familiar parent-child dynamic of previous U.S.-Cuban relations. However, exiles resisted efforts to subordinate their leadership of the counterrevolutionary struggle. Imagining themselves at the front lines of a global Cold War struggle, they insisted on being treated as legitimate representatives of the Cuban nation in exile and demanded to be recognized as formal allies of the United States. However, they were unable to negotiate the terms of their partnership with the U.S. intelligence community from a position of strength.

Exile leaders needed the federal government to provide funds, logistical support, and training for a full-scale invasion of the island. Moreover, lacking access to the channels of international diplomacy, exiles needed the United States to take their campaign against the Castro regime to the Organization of American States and the United Nations. They were thus compelled to forge a strategic but unequal alliance with the U.S. government in order to pursue the liberation of their island.

The growing impoverishment of anti-Castro refugees and their precarious position in an unfriendly and economically depressed city further limited exile leaders' ability to forge an equal relationship with the intelligence community. Nowhere was this more evident than among recruits to the CIA-funded paramilitary force, whose reasons for volunteering included both political conviction and pragmatic considerations. One of the most powerful motivations for joining, however, was exile men's increasingly urgent need to provide for their families.

Ramón Puerto arrived in Miami in late 1959 with his wife and two small children. After several months of trying unsuccessfully to find employment, with no access to municipal or state relief programs, and with the establishment of the Cuban Refugee Program still a year in the future, the family's financial situation grew increasingly desperate. Finally, on the brink of destitution, the former army sergeant decided to go on the CIA payroll in July 1960. Though Puerto was ideologically anti-Castro, he ultimately resolved to translate his politics into action in order to ensure the day-to-day survival of his son and daughter. He recalled, "The man from the CIA said we would all get paid, even if we got caught, and the money would go to our families. Rosario and the children needed it. I joined."[9]

By 1961, capitalizing on the willingness of impoverished Cuban husbands and fathers to take up arms in order to defeat Castro *and* to feed their children, the CIA's newly established JM-Wave post in Miami began its expansion into the largest intelligence station in the world outside CIA headquarters in Langley, Virginia. Within years, the secret post would have an annual budget of between $50 million and $100 million and have as many as 15,000 Cuban employees on its payroll.[10] The well-being of the refugee community became increasingly tied to the expansion of JM-Wave, which provided well-paid, permanent, and contract positions for Cuban heads of household and created demand for goods and services from other exile businesses and service providers.

Many anti-Castro families relied on JM-Wave's indirect subsidies for their survival in Miami. CIA support for anti-Castro activities thus served, through the paychecks that fed, clothed, and sheltered refugee boys and girls, to harmonize U.S. Cold War foreign policy objectives with Cuban exiles' immediate concerns for the well-being of their children and their dreams of their future happiness in a liberated homeland. However, even before the establishment of the Cuban Refugee Program under President Kennedy, CIA dollars also contributed to institutionalizing exiles' growing dependence on the federal government.[11]

The asymmetrical relationship between the U.S. government and the anti-Castro movement was further manifested in the way officials engaged with exile leaders. Politicians, military leaders, and intelligence agents dismissed exiles' political differences, viewing them as evidence of Cuban immaturity, irrationality, and emotional volatility. They also subordinated exile leaders' principles and priorities to the nation's foreign policy objectives and their own instrumental goals.

In May 1960, the CIA supported the creation of the Frente Revolucionario Democrático (FRD) in order to coordinate the efforts of the major anti-Castro groups. However, the FRD soon foundered, weakened both by internal political differences and rivalries and by the lack of confidence expressed by its CIA overseers. Howard Hunt, assigned to assist in founding the anti-Castro umbrella organization, regarded the Frente's leadership with racialized contempt, dismissing them summarily as "shallow thinkers and opportunists" who "displayed most Latin faults and few Latin virtues."[12] Other agency handlers described the competing priorities of the distinct groups comprising the Frente's membership as "selfish interests" rather than legitimate expressions of political difference.[13] Interpreting divisions among exile leaders as evidence of Cubans' inability to understand their own best interests or act decisively in their own defense, intelligence agents reasoned that exiles' political immaturity precluded their participation as equals in the "adult world of Cold War politics."[14]

Military leaders and intelligence agents adopted similar positions, ranging from sympathetic condescension toward counterrevolutionary recruits to contempt for them. They thereby demonstrated that they viewed Cubans through racialized and infantilizing lenses inherited from their turn-of-the-century predecessors. At the first meeting of what would become the CIA's Bay of Pigs task force, Colonel J. C. King expressed his doubts about the exile force's competence, saying that he knew of "no Latin American country whose people were less secure operationally than Cubans." CIA agent Grayston Lynch agreed that Cubans were immature, highly emotional, and, like most children, unable to keep a secret. They were thus completely unequipped for the manly task of covert military action.[15] Captain Bradley Earl Ayers, a military instructor attached to JM-Wave, similarly characterized exile recruits as excitable and enamored of playacting the role of "commando freedom fighters"; he nonetheless insisted that a degree of paternal tolerance was in order, since exiles' "childish enthusiasm" was central to their morale and willingness to fight.[16]

By the summer of 1960, U.S.-backed guerrilla networks had begun conducting armed skirmishes in Cuba's interior. However, political divisions and hostilities among the major anti-Castro groups complicated the task of building a unified paramilitary force. To make matters worse, most exile men with military experience were former Batista-era soldiers and officers; their recruitment deepened the already serious divisions within the exile forces and heightened resentment of the CIA's dismissal of Cubans' desire to exercise control over the campaign to liberate their island. Tensions arose between Batistianos, former M-26-7 insurgents, and other non-Batista aligned men; training exercises led by officers of the Batista-era armed forces frequently led to disagreement, and many disintegrated into heated arguments and even physical violence.[17]

Disregarding the disunity among the exile community as well as intelligence reports that revealed the Revolution's military preparedness to be greater than expected, U.S. intelligence agencies persisted in preparations for the ill-fated invasion. Seriously underestimating Fidel Castro's popularity and capacity for leadership, CIA officials insisted that it would not be difficult to spark a national uprising against him. In January 1961, they assured the increasingly dubious Joint Chiefs of Staff that Castro enjoyed the support of less than 30 percent of the population. Moreover, they insisted—echoing racist arguments that had justified U.S. intervention in the 1898 war and the subsequent imposition of military rule over the new Cuban nation—the Revolution's main supporters were "the negroes, who have always followed the strong men in Cuba, but will not fight."[18]

Despite all evidence to the contrary, many exile recruits similarly believed that the invasion would result in a quick victory. They assessed the Revolution's chances of survival through a U.S.-centric lens that took for granted the reliance of their *patria* on its powerful northern patron and accepted uncritically the anti-Castro movement's dependence on U.S. support. Well aware of U.S. determination to maintain political and economic hegemony over the Americas, exiles were confident that the White House would never allow a communist regime to hold power within its self-proclaimed sphere of influence. CIA insistence on moving forward with the invasion thus reaffirmed anti-Castro Cubans' belief that the Revolution's days were numbered and their triumphant return home was imminent.

Confident that they enjoyed the full support of the United States, exile leaders nonetheless worried about their growing subordination within the CIA-sponsored anti-Castro movement. Taking over as military leader of the FRD in April 1961, Manuel Ray declared his opposition to the involvement of U.S. troops in the coming invasion because it would invite charges of collusion with the U.S. government.[19] Sensitive to Castro's frequent condemnations of the counterrevolutionary movement as a front for U.S. imperialist designs on the island, exiles struggled to assert the legitimacy and autonomy of their movement even as they became increasingly dependent on CIA aid and oversight.

In the weeks leading up to the Bay of Pigs invasion, exiles lost all control of the anti-Castro struggle. Widespread anti-Latina/o prejudice among the FRD's CIA handlers, combined with generally negative assessments of exiles' military and strategic competence, contributed to the decision to replace the Frente with a new exile umbrella group. Since the hastily organized Consejo Revolucionario Cubano (Cuban Revolutionary Council) was envisioned as a front for U.S.-led anti-Castro operations rather than as an organization coordinating the exiles' efforts to liberate their homeland, its leaders were prevented from playing a meaningful role in the invasion. During the brief battle at Playa Girón, they were sequestered—ostensibly in order to prevent them from leaking sensitive information—and prohibited from making public statements of any kind. Instead, the CRC's "war bulletins" were issued by Lem Jones Associates Inc., a New York public relations firm contracted by the CIA to script official announcements by the major anti-Castro groups.[20]

After the debacle at the Bay of Pigs, exile leaders were further denigrated by the invasion's U.S. organizers. Rather than acknowledging President Kennedy's failure to provide promised air support or admitting that the

CIA had endorsed a military mission that far exceeded its capacities, military leaders and agency personnel with little Latin American experience—many speaking no Spanish—heaped blame on exile leaders and recruits. They described the Cuban volunteers as untrustworthy, incompetent, and cowardly.[21] The CIA inspector general later recognized that North Americans bore much of the blame for the invasion's failure, largely because they had underestimated Cubans on both sides of the Straits of Florida and treated exiles as "incompetent children whom the Americans are going to rescue for reasons of their own."[22]

Antonio Rubio Padilla, an exile leader who had opposed both Batista and Castro, similarly denounced the intelligence community's contemptuous treatment of the FRD's leadership and critiqued the anti-Castro movement's dependence on the U.S. government. Insisting that the overthrow of communism in Cuba was as vital to U.S. interests as it was to Cubans', he rejected the notion that federal support for the anti-Castro movement was "a generous charitable act that Cubans have to accept along with unilateral conditions imposed by the United States." He concluded that exile leaders' "blind faith" in their North American protector had "proved to be a liability in the political and ideological struggle against Castroite nationalism."[23]

Rubio Padilla correctly identified the anti-Castro movement's greatest weakness—from its inception, it had been severely handicapped by an asymmetrical relationship with the U.S. government that mirrored the ties that had bound the island to its northern neighbor since the turn of the century. Dependent on U.S. funding, training, and logistical support for their efforts to liberate their homeland, anti-Castro volunteers were exploited by U.S. politicians, military leaders, and intelligence agents concerned with their own Cold War foreign policy priorities. At the same time, U.S. leaders continued to use historically grounded notions of childhood to assert Cubans' racialized inferiority and deny their aspirations toward leadership in the campaign to free their island from communism.

In the aftermath of the Bay of Pigs invasion, a devastated exile community was confronted with the weakness of the anti-Castro movement. Exiles would once again find strength and inspiration in their politics of childhood. In the same way that José Martí had called on Cubans to wage war in 1898 on behalf of the island's children, the anti-Castro movement's media and civil society allies would turn to self-affirming discourses of childhood to create unity from division, to preserve the exile community's dignity in the light of constant denigration and dismissal,

and to mobilize their countrymen and -women for the continuing battle
to recover the *patria*.

CHILDREN, THE EXILE MEDIA, AND
THE HEMISPHERIC ANTI-CASTRO STRUGGLE

In the early months of 1960, exile journalists established new Cuban
media outlets in Miami and reestablished newspapers that had been recently shut down on the island. These committed journalists viewed the
production of counterrevolutionary propaganda as a powerful complement to the exile paramilitary struggle. Understanding their fight against
Castro-communism as an essential battle in the global Cold War, they
targeted a hemispheric audience with morally and emotionally resonant
child-centered messages, seeking to foment anti-Castro opinion and activity among Cubans on the island and to create consensus among the
multiple counterrevolutionary factions in Miami. They also sought to discredit the new regime among progressive Latin Americans.

Taking advantage of the still relatively unimpeded flow of people, goods,
and information across the Straits of Florida, Miami's exile journalists and
their readers stayed obsessively up to date with events and debates in the
homeland and frequently sought to intervene in them, contesting articles
appearing in the revolutionary media through op-ed pieces and letters
to the editors of their own *periodiquitos*. Transported to Cuba by anti-
Castro agents and through international mail service, exile newspapers
quickly became one of the main vehicles for the dissemination of counterrevolutionary ideas on the island. Miami-based journalists and readers
collaborated to ensure that this flow of information continued unabated,
seeing the distribution of exile *periodiquitos* on the island as vital to their
struggle for control of their nation's destiny. Their shared belief in the
nation-making power of propaganda was succinctly expressed in the no-
tice that appeared in most editions of the exile newspaper *Patria* between
1960 and 1961. It read, "Make Revolution: When you finish reading this
edition of *Patria*, don't throw it away. Send it to someone in Cuba by mail.
Make the *patria* with *Patria*."[24]

The exile media organized itself around this understanding of propaganda as a necessary, effective, and morally justifiable tool in the Cold War
struggle for Cuba. On October 20, 1960, *El Avance*'s director Jorge Zayas
gave a speech to the sixteenth Congress of the Sociedad Interamericana
de Prensa (SIP) in Bogotá, in which he asserted the importance of the
press to the final outcome of the epic contest between the United States

and the Soviet Union. "The Cold War," he argued, "is basically ideological war, psychological war, a war of propaganda. Therefore journalists, more than those charged with pushing the buttons that fire rockets, are in the first lines of combat." Alluding more specifically to the threat of Castro-communist subversion in the Americas, he called on SIP to "form ranks in the defense of Western ideology against the new invasion of the barbarians. That this should not happen is the first responsibility of the press."[25]

In a January 1961 open letter to the U.S. State Department, noted exile journalist Ernesto Montaner made a forceful case for the deployment of child-centered messages in the battle to depose Castro and win the global Cold War. Montaner argued that the U.S. government and media's failure to counter Soviet discourses of childhood with similarly focused anticommunist propaganda had put all of the Americas at risk.

Montaner recognized that symbolic and actual children played a central role in communist propaganda:

> They specialize in presenting simple partial aspects of the great questions. . . . They present the millionaire who lives in opulence and luxury as the cause of the rural misery where children die, without medical assistance, annihilated by parasites. It moves one to indignation, doesn't it? The first just impulse is to hang the "guilty millionaire" from the tree nearest to the abandoned *bohío*. And one thinks: "Miserable bastard! Squandering a fortune in yachts and luxury cars, while that poor child was dying fully of parasites. . . ." And toward that point propaganda is directed. To awaken the idea of "a different way." So that—knowing the monstrosities of the capitalist regime—one will immediately think in communism as the only solution to the great evils of society. . . . Democracy . . . suffers the publicity barrage and carries the guilt of the millionaire while the communists harvest the cadaver of the child full of parasites.

In order to prevent communist appropriation of the symbolic figure of the child, Montaner continued, free-world journalists must be willing to follow the lead of the exile media in fighting fire with fire, putting discourses and images of childhood to work in the service of democracy. A vigorous child-centered propaganda campaign must be immediately launched to turn the tide of anti-Americanism in Latin America and to battle communism in Cuba, before "the diabolical affirmation of Nicolai [*sic*] Lenin blows up like an atomic bomb at the feet of the Statue of Liberty."[26]

Patria, one of the earliest and most stridently anti-Castro publications, quickly established itself at the forefront of efforts to deploy the figure of the child in support of the counterrevolutionary cause.[27] On May 13, 1960, the paper suggested that a shared concern for children had motivated the rapidly expanding body of anti-Batista insurgents, former revolutionary officials, religious and civic leaders, and everyday citizens, on the island and in exile, who had put aside their differences to join the fight against the Castro regime. "The rebellion grows larger by the minute," it claimed.

> Against the communist despot, traitor of the Revolution, thousands and thousands of men and women are mobilizing across the nation to launch the definitive battle, not just against Castro's regime but, something more grandiose, to exterminate communism in our homeland. No more are they the men of the past regime, more or less affected; no longer is this about "criminals of war, evil doers, great landowners," terms that Castro has been using against his adversaries. . . . Now, against the red Hyena . . . are mobilizing figures of recognized merit in the struggle against the past regime, who today are beginning to reinitiate the battle for a better Cuba. Here, against Castro, traitor and communist, we have Tony Varona; Aureliano Sánchez Arango; Arturo Hernández Tellaeche; Grau; Artime; Díaz Lanz; Huber Matos, Rasco; Márquez Sterling; the priests O'Farrill, Aguirre, and Pérez; organizations like SIP; Monsignor Pérez Serante; industrialists; homeowners; shopkeepers; workers with their salaries reduced; Catholics; thousands of prisoners; the very elements of the July 26 Movement . . . who fought for a Cuban, not a Russian, Revolution.

Revealing the masculinist bias of this socially conservative newspaper— a bias reflected to a greater or lesser degree in other exile publications— *Patria* went to great lengths to name the illustrious male leaders who had joined the counterrevolutionary ranks before concluding with a child-centered rhetorical flourish. Also represented in the counterrevolutionary ranks, *Patria* claimed, were thousands of nameless Cuban mothers, "tired of hearing talk of deaths, who think only about the children."[28]

In July, *El Avance Criollo*, an island newspaper recently reestablished in exile, offered its own child-centered critique of the Revolution. The newspaper attacked the hypocrisy of Castro's ostensibly antimilitary posture, most famously embodied in his broadly publicized campaign to convert Batista-era prisons and police stations into schools, since "at the same time, he was creating worker, peasant, and student militias" and carrying away "to the Sierra Maestra young students of both sexes, dressed in olive-green uniforms, on an exhausting march that, of course, also removed them from their classrooms." The attack continued: "Fidelista militarism didn't stop there. . . . It had to move on to the preparation of children, and the youth militias emerged, a tropical reproduction of the Spanish *flechillas* and the Nazi youth."

Fidel's emulation of communist and Nazi methods, the article claimed, did not end with the creation of youth militias. Castro had also launched a widespread brainwashing campaign that targeted children, basing the future of his despotic regime on the unconditional support and obedience of the island's youngest citizens: "It isn't just the military marches, the uniform of a markedly Nazi design. It's the indoctrination, the teaching of hard and implacable principles and dogmas of totalitarianism. That's the basis for the reading textbooks edited by the Ministry of Education, where the letter 'F' is taught with the word 'Fidel,' the letter 'Ch' with Che Guevara, and 'R' with Raúl, etc. Only textbooks from Soviet Russia and its most oppressed 'colonies' use this method. Fidel and his regime are setting up for a Nazi millennium."[29]

The newspaper used similarly child-centered language to make common cause with anticommunist student groups in Mexico in demanding that the Organization of American States (OAS) take a stand against the Castro regime. On the eve of the September 1960 meeting of American heads of state in San José, Costa Rica, *El Avance* joined the Feminine Democratic Union, the Mexican Federation of Democratic Youth, and the Feminine University Association in Favor of Peace and Liberty in a campaign to "save our children," declaring themselves "categorically opposed to the conspiracy that is being forged, against peace and the order of our Continent, by the present rulers of Cuba, conniving with the governments of Russia and China."

El Avance issued a blanket rejection of communism, which it said threatened "the destruction of the home and the separation of families," and demanded that the OAS oppose to its fullest "the imposition of the designs of the universal communist conspiracy in our Americas, that already has Cuba subjected to its hegemony and plans to impose its dominion over all the other nations of the Continent." It concluded, "We oppose the idea that any communist dictator who believes himself the only one worthy to think for the rest, and who imposes his ideas and resolutions with blood and fire, should govern the thoughts of our children."[30]

In the same month, new evidence of the revolutionary threat to children—not just Cuban children, but indeed all children of the Americas—shocked the exile community. During Castro's September 1960 visit to the UN headquarters in New York, a gang of revolutionary supporters opened fire on a group of exiles eating in a Cuban restaurant.

Nine-year-old Magadalena Urdaneta, a Venezuelan girl on vacation in the city with her family, was caught in the crossfire. Shot through the lungs, she died in her mother's arms.[31] Miami's exile journalists wasted no time in blaming the innocent child's murder on the leader of Cuba's communist Revolution, declaring, "The streets of New York are covered with children's blood, with 'red,' the footprint of a red that is not satisfied with destroying life in its homeland but rather has to destroy it . . . wherever it puts down its foot. . . . Fidel always causes death: in Moncada, aboard the *Granma*, in the civil war, in power, in Venezuela, in Bogotá."

While acknowledging that it "wasn't he who fired the gun," *Patria* insisted that it was Castro "who armed the criminal hand that, without conscience, has killed a girl who was the joy of her parents." This crime, moreover, was further proof of the Revolution's cruel disregard for life, its contempt for familial ties and indifference to the well-being of the young. At the same time, the journalist took the opportunity to shore up exiles' collective pride in their identity as parents and passionate defenders of children:

> What does Fidel know of these things of the heart? He doesn't love his own mother. He, in his demagoguery, insults his dead father. He reacts with the coldness of marble to the son agonizing in a hospital. . . . He can feel neither shame, nor pain, nor sadness, before the inanimate little body of a girl, murdered by his gangs. . . . He is incapable of being moved by the weeping of her parents, since in order to feel moved it is necessary to have a soul . . . and Fidel doesn't have a soul. . . . The poor little Magdalena, the unfortunate child vilely assassinated, could not possibly move Fidel Castro or his communists—feelings are bourgeois prejudices—but they definitely make us feel great sadness in the depths of our hearts. Because we have children and we love them more than our own lives, we know how to measure the deep and unending loss that the parents of Magdalena are feeling. While an innocent angel flies to the heavens to be taken in the loving and sweet arms of the Lord; on the earth, the diabolical figure of Fidel Castro will continue sowing suffering, hatred, rancor, and evil.[32]

Implicit in the article's concluding lines was the argument which underwrote the exile community's child-centered creation myth: loving Cuban parents had spirited their children off the island to save them from the Revolution. Stories like this kept ever present in refugees' minds the *fidelista* and communist threat to the young but also reinforced their sense of dignity, threatened by the racialized hostility directed toward them by

Anglo-American Miamians and by their awareness of the anti-Castro movement's growing dependence on the U.S. government. They also reminded exiles of the urgent need to unite across their differences, not only to restore the lost homeland to its smallest citizens but also to save all the children of the Americas from Castro's "satanic clutches."

Building on the fear and outrage that followed the story of Magdalena's death, *El Avance* informed refugees of an even more sinister threat to the island's children—and to their parents, relatives, and neighbors. In October the newspaper reported that the Revolution had begun training child-spies. The newspaper accused the director of the Cuban Ministry of Social Welfare, Raquel Pérez, of overseeing the establishment of "centers of indoctrination" in order to prepare "these children's brigades in the techniques of betrayal, ratting out, and espionage." After being submitted to courses of indoctrination that would help their childish minds to "mature" into revolutionary consciousness, children were divided into brigades and disguised as beggars and lottery ticket sellers before being set loose to gather intelligence on the streets of Havana. *El Avance* claimed that G-2 intelligence officers and the Ministry of Social Welfare had already put 250 child-spies to work in the capital's streets and were busily training another 250 children to join them. At least one citizen had already been shot on the basis of intelligence gathered by child-spies.[33] Accompanying the terrifying exposé, a photograph showed Fidel Castro hoisting a small girl into the air; the caption read, "First he praises them! Then he makes them into child-spies."[34]

As the 1960 holiday season approached, journalists continued to fan the flames of anti-Castro fervor with increasingly alarmist reports of the threat faced by Cuban children on the island. Then, in November, the counterrevolutionary cause received additional impetus when news of exile paramilitary training was leaked to the press. The campaign of covert action initially approved by President Eisenhower, always an open secret among Miami exiles, began to receive attention from national English-language media, bolstering refugees' confidence that a U.S.-backed invasion would take place within months. Exile political activities increased in preparation for the imminent landing on Cuba's coastline. This invasion, they believed, would give rise to a brief battle, sparking a general uprising and the collapse of the revolutionary regime, followed by exiles' triumphant return to the homeland.

In January 1961, Miami's Cuban journalists stepped up their activities to support the anti-Castro movement, proclaiming exiles and their media central players in the battle to prevent the penetration of international communism in the Western Hemisphere. As the date for the invasion of the island drew closer, Miami *periodiquitos* continued to strategically manipulate their readers' moral and emotional sensibilities through child-centered discourses and images, seeking to discredit the Revolution throughout the Americas.

In February, exile journalists challenged two of the Revolution's major claims to legitimacy, both centering on the new regime's paternal concern for the island's neediest children and young people. The first of these challenges responded to a January 23 speech by Fidel Castro, in which he condemned the death of youthful literacy volunteer Conrado Benítez at the hands of counterrevolutionaries in the Sierra Escambray. *El Avance* strenuously objected to Castro's claim that counterrevolutionaries "had executed him because he was poor, young, black, and a teacher." The exile newspaper especially rejected the idea that Benítez had lost his life because he was a teacher, framing this claim as yet another example of Castro's cynical campaign to frame the Revolution as the defender of children—and, conversely, to discredit its opponents as indifferent to the well-being of the island's youngest citizens.

Counterrevolutionaries, *El Avance* argued, would never have targeted an educator "because the national body of teachers is almost entirely against the gangsters of the Sierra Maestra and many dozens of them are in combat in the Sierra Escambray." Rather, the exile newspaper asserted, the Escambray insurgents responsible for Benítez's death had acted in order to protect rural boys and girls from brainwashing at the hands of a Soviet puppet. Anti-Castro guerrillas had killed Conrado Benítez for one reason alone: because he was a communist, "and one of the most dangerous communists, since he was dedicated to poisoning innocent Cuban childhood."[35]

El Avance also rejected Castro's child-centered declaration of 1961 as the "Year of Education," telling its readership in Miami, on the island, and throughout Latin America that it should more accurately be called El Ano del Paredón (The Year of the Firing Squad). Alternatively, Armando García Mendoza suggested, Cubans who were truly concerned with the well-being of young people could "call it the year of learning for slavery; year of communist indoctrination and of brainwashing; the year of the end of *patria potestad*, to prevent Cuban parents, so affectionate with their children, from inculcating in them the love of God and of family, consideration and sympathy for others, respect for friendship, and devotion to the homeland and to the truths that our heroes left us as a legacy."[36]

Articles like these resisted the revolutionary media's attempts to deploy the figure of the child in order to strengthen the legitimacy of the Castro regime; as such, they were an important component of the exile media's hemispheric campaign to discredit the Revolution, to shore up exiles' self-affirming identity as defenders of children, and to mobilize Cubans in Miami and Havana to become active participants in Castro's overthrow.

As preparations for an exile invasion of the island gained momentum, so too did the production of child-centered anti-Castro messages aimed directly at Cubans on the island. Exile leaders and journalists began to call directly on their countrymen and -women to rise up against the Castro regime. *Periodiquitos* stepped up their coverage of the problems and failures of the Revolution and praised Cuban parents' fight against the rumored imposition of the *patria potestad* law, the desertion of *milicianos*, and the escalation of civil protests and armed resistance against the regime, devoting special attention to forms of resistance that included children.

El Avance especially celebrated the efforts of Christian parents to ensure that their children continued to receive the religious and moral guidance of the clergy. In March 1961, the exile paper described the recent actions of the Junta Catequista Diocesana, an underground organization that had distributed anti-Castro and pro-Church leaflets throughout the city of Havana. Featuring a close-up of a wide-eyed boy's face, the leaflet asked, "This child, will he be a believer or an atheist? It depends on you. Cooperate with the catechism."[37]

Shortly after the leaflets' appearance, the article continued, Catholic schoolboys and -girls took to the streets and knocked on doors to sell small lithographs of the leaflet. *El Avance* claimed that the Cuban public responded overwhelmingly to the antirevolutionary efforts of these Catholic schoolchildren. "In businesses, in automobiles, on the walls, everywhere, the face of this interrogating child appeared like an invitation to the citizenry for their recapacitation in the face of what has been happening."

Demonstrating an up-to-the-moment knowledge of events on the island, the exile paper noted that a regime spokesperson had attempted to discredit this ostensibly grassroots expression of youthful faith by stating that the child on the flyer "wasn't black." *El Avance* roundly rejected this latest attempt to frame the anti-Castro movement as the sole province of the island's privileged white citizens. They ridiculed the Revolution's attention to the boy's race, "when it is well known that children, like souls, have no color," and denounced the Castro regime's subsequent attempt to suppress the clandestine Catholic movement. The regime reproduced the same announcement, with a "guerrilla" slogan: "This child, will he be a patriot or a traitor? It depends on you. Teach him the works of the Revolution. *Patria o Muerte. Venceremos.*" At the same time, *El Avance*

Este niño será CREYENTE O ATEO? De Ud. depende

coopere con el catecismo

JUNTA CATEQUISTICA DIOCESANA

This anti-Castro pamphlet calls on Cuban Catholics to resist the Revolution's efforts to eradicate religious education on the island. From El Avance, March 25, 1961. Courtesy of the Cuban Heritage Collection, University of Miami Libraries, Coral Gables, Florida.

reported, parents were ordered to tell their children to tear off the lithograph with the Catholic message wherever it was found and replace it with the revolutionary version. But this also failed, because Catholics immediately repasted the catechist announcement and made the "guerrilla" one disappear.

What did this latest struggle to control the ideological formation of the island's children mean? According to the exile paper, the episode demonstrated that "a totalitarian regime like the Fidelo-communist one won't allow the smallest expression of free thought." The exile media's coverage of the catechist movement sought to discredit the Revolution among Latin American readers, to present the virtuous young Catholics as a model for anti-Castro adults to follow in resisting Castro, and to convince Cubans on both sides of the Straits of Florida that his regime was losing its grip on the island's masses. It also revealed the centrality of child-centered images and discourses to both revolutionary and counterrevolutionary efforts to project their legitimacy and to mobilize support for their competing nation-making projects. The propaganda skirmish to interpret the activities of young Cuban catechists revealed the lengths to which both sides were willing to go to defend their exclusive right to control and manipulate representations of childhood. Moreover, the fact that Catholic insurgents and the Castro regime both put young boys and girls to work distributing competing versions of the leaflet further reveals their eagerness to deploy symbolic and actual children as proxies in an all-encompassing struggle for the nation's destiny.[38]

In tandem with calls to Cubans on the island to rise up against Castro, exiles also issued statements urging freedom-loving citizens of other Latin American nations to support the overthrow of his regime. They also drew on child-centered messages to emphasize that communism threatened all of the hemisphere's children and to chastise governments that had refused to stand against the Revolution. In an article appearing in *Patria* titled "America the Accomplice," Armando García Sifredo critiqued those who had failed to condemn Castro's crimes against children:

> Boys, almost children, are put in front of the firing squads. . . . In the year 1961, in an American Republic, they are murdering children and that is contemplated with indifference! Castro, the macabre specter who has placed his claws on the American Continent, is showing before the world, that in the Americas children can be murdered, they can be brought before firing squads, with the complicit silence of all the nations. . . . Faced with the martyring of children . . . all America responds with the complicity of silence. . . . To permit a country to officially murder innocent children, young people who could be great citizens of tomorrow, is to join in solidarity with such barbarity.

The journalist attacked Latin American governments for defending the "right of nonintervention" that guaranteed that these crimes against Cuba's young people would continue: "This America that permits in silence the ocean of blood that exists in Cuba cannot be the America of Lincoln, nor of Bolívar, nor of Martí, nor of Juárez. . . . This America, permitting in silence the murder of children, the jailing of thousands of men and women, the exodus of entire families . . . is a condemned Continent, irredeemably to be devoured by communism. . . . To speak of rights, of humanity, of justice and love in the Americas, is sarcasm, is irony! While in Cuba they continue murdering children and youth. . . . The blood that today is spilled in Cuba, splashes and stains all the governments of the Americas." Impatient with the subtleties of international diplomacy, García Sifredo used the symbolic figure of the Cuban child to frame the complex arena of Latin American relations in morally absolute terms—the hemisphere must stand against the Revolution or accept its guilt as an accomplice to the ongoing murder and torture of Cuban children. Making one final attempt to shame Latin American leaders into action, he concluded that even if the continent remained indifferent to exiles' pleas for help, "Cuba will know how to tear herself from the claws of communism. And when she is free again, SHE will offer aid to any country menaced by communism in the Americas."[39]

In early April, a period of frenzied political activity overtook Little Havana. Plans for the looming invasion were discussed openly by exiles on the streets and in restaurants, cafés, and churches as Cubans eagerly awaited word that the battle to reclaim their nation had been launched. And then, on the evening of April 17, the long-awaited action began. An expeditionary force of almost 3,000 men landed at Playa Girón. Exile journalists wasted no time in announcing that "the war against communism" was under way, rallying Cubans in Florida to unite in support of the fight to save the homeland and the future of its children. On April 18, *Patria* declared that "bullets have begun to fly" on the island and called on the entire exile community to dedicate itself to winning the war to defend freedom. This could only happen if the community came together in "the elaboration of a Cuban plan, without sectarianism," for the reconstruction of the homeland—something that persistent ideological divisions among exile groups had so far prevented.

"Let us leave aside jockeying for advantage, ambitions, rancor, hatred," *Patria* begged its readers. "There is a common enemy: communism." And there was a common motive for struggle that bound all exiles together and linked them to freedom-loving men and women on the island: their parental concern for the future of their sons and daughters. Cubans must unite in the fight "to guarantee to our children and the children of our children that, on achieving the total and definitive surrender of the communists, there will be in Cuba a provisional government . . . capable of deserving the support, the respect, and the consideration of all Cubans."[40]

Awaiting the imminent birth of Martí's moral republic, exiles instead were shocked by the invasion's disastrous failure, which resulted in the death, injury, or imprisonment of almost the entire exile paramilitary force. The media quickly rallied to respond to the grief and despair of the devastated community. Journalists struggled to articulate widespread anger at President Kennedy's failure to provide promised air support for the exile mission while asserting the need for continued collaboration between the anti-Castro movement and the U.S. government and intelligence community. On May 12, 1961, *El Avance* published a large photograph of a boy waving a Cuban flag, a U.S. flag positioned behind him, together with this commentary:

> The monster that enslaves Cuba and that has delivered it, without the slightest shame, to the insatiable bloody claws of the Kremlin dictator, has just announced his decision to take possession of the Cuban Private Schools—legitimate pride of our culture and our progress—to convert them into a center of Marxist indoctrination under the control of its "elite" communizing pseudo-intellectuals. In the face of this atrocity, the patriotism of Cubans in exile has been inflamed once again and they have expressed their energetic protests. And it is the Cuban children— the favorite prisoners of the insatiable Beast—who have comprehended this vile aggression, and have made public their sentiments.

Using two discursive motifs well-developed by the revolutionary media by the end of 1959, the exile journalist simultaneously depicted children as the innocent victims of a cruel and sinister state even as he framed the virtuous flag-waving boy as a model of courage and determination for the bereaved exile community. The newspaper praised the nationalistic conviction of "this little one who, with decisive gesture and strong arms, hoists the glorious colors of the solitary star and appears to be saying, defiantly, 'This is my only flag and nobody can tear it from my hands.'" It also called attention to the boy's strategic positioning in front of the Stars and Stripes in order to reinforce exiles' shaken faith in the U.S. commitment to their cause, noting that behind him, "as a symbolic support to his words, the victorious flag of the United States reveals its stars."[41]

The military failure of the anti-Castro movement positioned the exile media to take the lead in the battle to prevent communist penetration throughout the Americas. During the remaining months of 1961 and into 1962, child centered messages remained a constant feature of media efforts to restore the prestige and legitimacy of the counterrevolutionary leadership and to convert the exile community's humiliation, grief, and anger into an ever increasing anti-Castro fervor. They also sought to pressure U.S. and Latin American leaders into a deeper commitment to the struggle to restore democracy to their homeland. Miami *periodiquitos* dedicated themselves to describing the oppression and hardship that defined daily life on the island. Political cartoons showed

—Oiga, señor, ¿cuál de estas es la cola de la carne . . . ?

In this cartoon, a hungry child asks, "Which one is the line for meat?" During 1961, the exile media made repeated use of child-centered images in news articles, editorials, and political cartoons condemning new shortages of food and medical supplies on the island. From El Avance, June 30, 1961. *Courtesy of the Cuban Heritage Collection, University of Miami Libraries, Coral Gables, Florida.*

hungry children waiting in line for food rations. In one, a small toddler contemplated three interminable lines and asked the last person, a man dressed in ragged clothes, "Excuse me, sir, which one is the line for meat?"[42]

Journalists thus used cartoons and exposés to continually critique the Revolution's indoctrination of schoolchildren and the destruction of Cuban families. They also made frequent and forceful claims that the regime's failed economic policies had led to widespread shortages of food and medicine and were thus responsible for widespread childhood illness and death.[43] However, in its failure to acknowledge that child poverty and malnutrition had similarly threatened the legitimacy of the republic since independence, this coverage also revealed the privileged biases and the increasingly rigid conservative worldview of both the exile media and the majority of its readers. It nonetheless ensured that the suffering of Cuban children remained ever present in exiles' minds, providing powerful moral and emotional justification for the anti-Castro movement's continuing efforts to overthrow the Revolution.

CHILDREN, EXILE CIVIL SOCIETY, AND
THE ANTI-CASTRO MOVEMENT

During 1960, the mass movement of tens of thousands of Cubans to southern Florida went hand in hand with the transplanting of republican civil society to foreign soil. As the institutions of middle-class Cuban life, from the family to the Church to private schools and professional associations, were reestablished in Miami, they were simultaneously reorganized around a shared objective: to promote the unity of the exile community, on behalf of its children and in service of the anti-Castro struggle. In the months leading up to the Bay of Pigs invasion, exiled Cubans would further reassert the legitimacy of their prerevolutionary civic identities to ease the indignities of their downward socioeconomic mobility and marginalization by Anglo-American Miamians. Civil society would also become a crucial site in which exiles would counter Fidel Castro's charges that they were *gusanos* and *escoria*—worms and scum—and pawns of the imperialist United States, framing themselves instead as morally upright patriots, heroic defenders of children, and the spiritual heirs of José Martí's vision of the moral republic.[44] In the aftermath of the failed invasion, exile civil society would also rally around the community's children to come to terms with the U.S. government's betrayal of the anti-Castro movement and to gather strength to continue the fight to overthrow the Revolution.

In January 1961, determined to overcome persistent ideological divisions among factions of the anti-Castro movement, leaders of Cuban civic organizations in exile turned to the community's children for support in calling for counterrevolutionary unity. Including young boys and girls in positions of prominence in their public ceremonies and activities, exile civic leaders sought to drive home the unifying message of the exile creation myth: Cuban parents and grandparents had fled their beloved homeland to protect their innocent children from communist indoctrination, oppression, and deprivation. They stressed that anti-Castro Cubans must overcome their differences and work together for the same reason—for the children, in order to recover the island nation for all its victimized youth.

The approaching anniversary of José Martí's birthday provided an ideal opportunity to publicly link the fate of the island's children with exiles' desire to overthrow the Castro regime, and to link both to Cubans' long-deferred dreams of national autonomy, social justice, and representative government. Accordingly, the College of Cuban Educators in Exile, headed by director Isolina Diaz, organized a children's parade and ceremonies to honor the birth of the nation's apostle of independence. Advertising the event in advance and urging all Cuban refugees to attend, *Patria* stressed that the parade "should have the enthusiastic support of all those in exile, the same exile that José Martí suffered in his tireless struggle for the freedom of Cuba, who today struggle to reconquer our lost freedom. Children, women, and men should all answer 'Present!' to this homage to the great citizen of America that was Martí."

The community responded enthusiastically to this child-centered, nationalist, and counterrevolutionary message. At ten o'clock in the morning on January 28, 1961, a crowd of several hundred refugees gathered in central Miami to honor the apostle's birthday. Festivities began with a procession of painstakingly groomed refugee boys and girls dressed in their finest clothes; when the parade reached the small bust of Martí in Bayfront Park, children reverently deposited flowers at the feet of their national hero.[45] Local *periodiquitos* provided enthusiastic coverage of this and other events in which children played a visible role, ensuring that the community's child-centered creation myth remained salient in refugees' minds, where it would help maintain anti-Castro fervor and reinforce the need for unity in support of the counterrevolutionary cause. The increasingly hegemonic and conservative anticommunist messages that accompanied media reports of children's participation in public life thus worked to suppress differences among the diverse individuals and groups comprising the exile community and to blunt the forces of conflict and competition that threatened the fragile consensus on which the dream of a triumphant return to the *patria* rested.

Throughout the early spring of 1961, as the much anticipated exile invasion of the island approached, the leaders of a rapidly reconstituting exile civil society began to make plans for a return to the island. Civic organizations were eager to play an active role in the counterrevolutionary struggle and the establishment of Martí's moral republic. New pedagogical associations, many of them headed by displaced teachers, dedicated themselves to resisting Castro's interventions in the island's educational system and to preparing for the rehabilitation of its indoctrinated children. One of the first exile civic groups to explicitly link a child-centered agenda to the paramilitary anti-Castro campaign was the Federation of Cuban Private Schools. In late February 1961, the federation released its mission statement to the public, committing itself "to struggle to orient the private schools still functioning in Cuba" and to formulate plans for the "decommunization" and "detoxifying" of the minds of students exposed to the "destructive and immoral doctrines that have been forced on them by false teachers" and "bad Cubans."

The federation's statement stressed that its redemptive work with Cuban youth was part of its broader anticommunist mission; moreover, since the mission's realization was dependent on the success of the imminent invasion, federation leaders expressed "a sincere recognition for those Cubans involved in the clandestine struggle" and emphasized their resolve "to cooperate with all sectors of the struggle against communism." They also reinforced the community's growing belief that exiles must put aside their differences in order to restore the homeland to its youngest citizens, concluding the federation's mission statement by calling on all Cubans, "in a supreme effort, both in exile and in the island's clandestine struggle, [to] unite to achieve our principal objective: the extermination of communism."[46]

In conjunction with preparations for the exile invasion, exile civic leaders urged freedom-loving Cubans to work together to save the island's children from the terrors of communism. Their emotionally charged calls for unity, together with U.S. government pressure for exile organizations to form a cohesive anti-Castro front, began to bear fruit in mid-March, when the CIA-supported Consejo Revolucionario Cubano was formed. The council elected José Miró Cardona, prime minister of Castro's 1959 provisional government, as its president and charged him with coordinating the diverse activities of hundreds of small exile organizations in support of impending military action against the Revolution.[47]

Despite repeated calls for Cubans to come together, however, unity would remain elusive until after the Bay of Pigs. Devastated by President Kennedy's abandonment of the exile brigade and desperate for news of their killed or captured relatives, Cuban exiles finally came together in a collective response to the catastrophic failure of the invasion. Exile unity reached a high point in April and May 1961, led by Cuban refugee women who organized to provide aid and comfort to grieving widows, suffering families, and orphaned children, and to petition the U.S. government and the global community to secure the release of their prisoners from Castro's jails. Understanding their activities as an extension of their traditional roles as wives and mothers, refugee women articulated their concern for the well-being of Cuban families and children in tandem with an explicitly gendered commitment to the liberation of their homeland from Communist rule.

Women's groups like the feminine auxiliary of the Movimiento Rescate Revolucionario Democrático (Democratic Revolutionary Rescue Movement) already had more than a year's experience caring for Cuban refugee families and children; moreover, under the presidency of Emelina Ruisánchez de Varona, they had also dedicated themselves to supporting the exile forces' struggle to defeat communism on the island. Announcing that "they would have no problem taking arms to fight," they had nonetheless long insisted that they preferred to leave that work to the "honorable men" of the exile community. Instead, in the months leading up to the Bay of Pigs, they prepared for the women's work that would await them when they returned to the homeland: offering first aid to the wounded, reorienting "childish minds contaminated by the divisive theories of communism," and ensuring that Cuban militia women recovered their natural dispositions and roles in order to "become once again feminine, sweet, smiling, and friendly."[48]

In the aftermath of the failed invasion, the feminine section of Rescate and organizations like it turned their attention to meeting the more immediate needs of the women and children whose male relatives had been killed, wounded, or imprisoned on the island. At the same time, they mobilized for political action, relying heavily on representations of suffering mothers and children to press for the release of their prisoners and to compel U.S. and Latin American leaders to renew their commitment to the continuing struggle against Fidel Castro.

In the last week of April, Cuban women gathered in Miami's Bayfront Park. Setting up camp in front of the bust of José Martí, they vowed to remain in the park until the American continent changed its attitude toward the "case of Cuba," which they insisted was really the "case of the Americas." They organized their children to parade around the bust of the apostle of their independence, carrying placards that called on hemispheric heads of state to join their fight against Castro-communism. One of these signs explicitly linked the well-being of the continent's children with the destiny of the Cuban nation-state; it read, "Help us today and your children will be able to live tomorrow."

Patria reported approvingly on this political activism by the community's women, "symbol of maternity," and children, "symbols of the future of the nations." What's more, the newspaper echoed the Cuban mothers' claim that they were not simply struggling on behalf of their own children. They fought instead "for all the children of the American continent," as well as on behalf of all the mothers who would suffer "the same martyrdom that today those Cuban mothers suffer," unless communism was eradicated from Cuba and the Americas.[49]

Throughout May 1961, the relatives of men killed or captured at Playa Girón, most of them women and children, continued to gather in Bayfront

Park. They wept together and knelt in prayer before the monument to José Martí and the park's Torch of International Friendship, calling for the release of their fathers and brothers, husbands and sons, and for the liberation of the homeland. Refugee women also took their sons and daughters with them to rallies, marches, and demonstrations across the city in order to highlight their counterrevolutionary identities as martyred and suffering mothers and to remind people across the Americas of the communist threat to the hemisphere's young people.

That same month, Cuban women and children gathered at Dupont Plaza Center in Miami to demonstrate in front of the hotel where José A. Mora, secretary general of the Organization of American States, was staying. Demanding that the OAS support the exile struggle, mothers and their sons and daughters (a few fathers were also in attendance) carried signs proclaiming themselves "Con Cristo y contra Castro [With Christ and against Castro]"; they also called on the OAS (OEA in Spanish) to make a stand for freedom with signs reading, "OEA decídete por la democracia [OAS, decide in favor of democracy]" and "Cuba: Hungary of America."[50] The following month, children were among the hundreds of Cubans who awaited the arrival at Miami International Airport of Ricardo Chiriboga, former chancellor of Ecuador, on his way to take up a position at the Inter-American Development Bank in Washington, D.C. At this rally organized by the Consejo Revolucionario Cubano and the Frente Revolucionario Democrático, children carried signs, shouted slogans of solidarity with Ecuador, and praised Chiriboga for his efforts on behalf of democracy in the Americas.

Women and children also participated in May in a caravan of Cuban refugees that traveled by bus from Miami to Washington, D.C., to solicit President Kennedy's assistance in their continuing battle against Castro-communism. In the nation's capitol, exiles placed a wreath of flowers in front of the Lincoln Memorial, attended a special mass in Arlington Cemetery, and marched in front of the White House holding signs and waving Cuban and U.S. flags. Highlighting the importance of both symbolic and flesh-and blood children to the community's efforts to secure a deeper U.S. commitment to the anti-Castro struggle, children were featured prominently in exile media coverage of the caravan. *El Avance* published a large photograph of a "beautiful Cuban child," no more than two years old, who "waved the two sister flags in the fight for liberty: the American and the Cuban."[51]

Exile children also filled the pews of Miami's Catholic churches, brought by their mothers to pray and say the rosary for the safe return of their imprisoned loved ones and for the homeland's liberation. As many as 20,000 exiles gathered nightly in houses of worship and in public parks for masses dedicated to the anti-Castro struggle; photographs of children, babies and toddlers, and local parochial school students in attendance at religious services appeared regularly in *periodiquitos* that sought to remind Cubans of why they must continue the fight "for the total liberation of Cuba, for the defeat of Fidelo-communism, and the rescue of her freedoms and her sovereignty."[52] The public renewal of their religious faith, operating hand in hand with the continuous rearticulation of the community's child-centered creation myth, provided comfort and direction for Miami's Cubans.

Children also played an important role in strengthening exile solidarity and resolve after President Kennedy's decision to replace CIA plans for political change in Cuba with a limited covert campaign to destabilize the Castro regime. Though as many as 12,000 refugee men would remain on the agency's payrolls, exiles were outraged by the U.S. government's decision, in the light of global disapproval of their involvement in the Playa Girón invasion, to scale down future attacks on the Revolution. Well aware that another large-scale invasion would be impossible without U.S. support, anti-Castro Cubans bitterly regretted their misplaced faith in their U.S. patrons and despaired both for the freedom of their imprisoned relatives and for the future of their nation.[53]

Facing an uncertain future, exile civic leaders turned increasingly to discourses and images of childhood to strengthen the community's resolve to fight on, using the limited means still available to them, to restore the homeland to their sons and daughters. In honor of Mother's Day, 1961, the Directorio Magisterial Revolucionario (DMR), an organization of Cuban teachers in exile, reproduced a drawing an eleven-year-old Cuban girl had created during art class at Miami's Shenandoah Elementary School on an anti-Castro flyer distributed throughout the United States and Latin America. The sketch showed a church with its doors barred by a hammer and sickle; a shattered cross lay in the entryway. A Cuban girl in rags, a flag in her hands, sat weeping on the steps. The elementary school artist had written in bold letters "Ayúdanos" and "Please help us!" on the wall of the church. A second bilingual message—"Queremos abrir esta puerta. We want to open this door"—had also been stamped on the picture.[54]

The drawing vividly expressed the young exile's religious faith, her painful loss of home and homeland, and her desire to return to a democratic Cuba. Notwithstanding its apparent sincerity, however, what is most significant is not the artwork's message but rather its strategic deployment

QUEREMOS ABRIR ESTA PUERTA
WE WANT TO OPEN THIS DOOR

¡AYUDANOS!
PLEASE HELP US!

¡AYUDANOS!
AYUDANOS
AYUDANOS
AYUDANOS!

DIRECTORIO
MAGISTERIAL
REVOLUCIONARIO
2508 Biscayne Boulevard
FR 7-4002
Miami Fla. E. U. A.

Este original dibujo es un trabajo realizado por una niña cubana de 11 años en la clase de dibujo del colegio Shenandoah, en Miami.

The figure of a refugee child in this propaganda flyer further illustrates the relationship between exile Catholicism and the anti-Castro movement. From El Avance, *June 23, 1961. Courtesy of the Cuban Heritage Collection, University of Miami Libraries, Coral Gables, Florida.*

by an exile civic organization in service of the anti-Castro movement. Just as revolutionary publications featured letters written by children to articulate the values and aspirations of the Revolution, the DMR's dissemination of a young girl's art class project sought to press this refugee child into service as the ultimate *vocero* of the exile cause and to frame her as the symbolic embodiment of the victimized Cuban nation. In the same way that Fidel Castro's apologists deployed morally and emotionally resonant discourses of childhood in support of the Revolution's nation-making project, this DMR leaflet revealed the extent to which exile propaganda had similarly come to rely on children to promote its counterrevolutionary agenda.

Throughout the autumn of 1961 and into the New Year, children remained at the forefront of exile civic leaders' efforts to gather support for the anti-Castro cause. On February 23, 1962, refugee boys and girls were front-row attendees of a ceremony in Bayfront Park in honor of José Martí. During the patriotic event, community leaders made poignant reference to exile children and young people on the island, calling once again on the United States and Latin American nations to provide "the moral and material help that Cubans need" to restore democratic rule to their homeland. That April, children also participated in a hunger strike in Bayfront Park, accompanying their parents in demanding that the U.S. government supply them with weapons to liberate Cuba.[55] Ongoing civic activism, lovingly covered by the local Cuban media, thus continued to rely on symbolic and actual children to fan the flames of counterrevolutionary sentiment, bolstering exiles' commitment to securing the liberation of the *patria* and maintaining community cohesion in the face of political divisions that still threatened to pull it apart.[56]

Building on exile civil society's already entrenched practice of linking child-centered activism and advocacy efforts with the broader goals of the anti-Castro struggle, displaced Cuban educators led by María Gomez Carbonell, a former senator in the Cuban Congress, established the Cruzada Educativa Cubana (Cuban Educational Crusade, or CEC) in July 1962. The organization pledged itself to promoting the patriotic and religious education of refugee children by exposing them to the republic's intellectual and civic traditions, Cuban culture, and democratic and Christian values. Their mission, they asserted, was "a true crusade of patriotic impartiality, love for the family and an extraordinary vocation for the intellectual and moral formation of our children and adolescents—today torn away from the truth of God, respect for their parents, and love for their fellows."

From the beginning, however, the Cruzada revealed its militant commitment to the Revolution's overthrow and its belief that the education (and reeducation) of Cuban children was central to redeeming the island nation and establishing the moral republic. The Cruzada's first public manifesto, "Message to the People of Cuba," expressed the overlap between its moral and pedagogical vision and its far-reaching political agenda, predicting an imminent total war against Castro that would represent

the decisive battle against international communism, intrinsically perverse, and the legions of Democracy called on to inaugurate a new national era under the sacred historic rules of Faith, Law, and Culture. And when the noise of the weapons ceases and the forces of good have exterminated barbarity, we will confront, painfully, a homeland morally and physically undone; a family, dispossessed by those miserable ones who violated its sanctuary . . . a school prostituted by infamy, sickened by lies and oriented toward hatred, betrayal, and crime, the only patterns of human emulation known to Communism. The teacher will be—once this second War of Independence is won—the primary figure that will have to remake, with his virtues and his moral integrity, the future of the nation in ruins.

According to the Cruzada, the prerevolutionary institutions of the family and the school, "cornerstones of the homeland, destroyed by the galloping Communism that made her an easy prisoner in 1959," would play an essential role in the restoration of the republic. However, in order for this to occur, the exile community would first need to come together "without divisionary exclusions" and in solidarity with their freedom-loving countrymen and -women on the island. Only the total unity of all democratically minded Cubans, the manifesto concluded, would ensure the salvation of the homeland and of its children.[57] Throughout the summer and into the fall of 1962, this child-centered understanding of the counterrevolutionary mission would remain central to the self-definition of a rapidly reconstituting exile civil society and to its unceasing work to unify the persistently divided anti-Castro movement.

COLD WAR FOREIGN POLICY, THE POLITICS OF CHILDHOOD, AND THE CUBAN MISSILE CRISIS

In October, exiles' oft-repeated calls for a decisive battle against communism in Cuba and in the Americas took on a new urgency. On October 14, U.S. U-2 reconnaissance flights revealed the presence of interregional ballistic missile silos at several sites in Cuba, indicating U.S.S.R. plans to bring Cuba under its nuclear umbrella. A week later, President Kennedy condemned Soviet intervention in the Western Hemisphere and ordered an immediate naval blockade of the island. Fear of a possible nuclear showdown between the superpowers sent shock waves across the nation and around the world. Cuban exiles, however, saw the missile crisis in a different light. Vindicated in their predictions that the Castro regime intended to open the doors to Soviet infiltration of Latin America, they welcomed a confrontation between the United States and Cuba, which they were confident would produce the long-awaited demise of the Revolution.

However, after thirteen frightening days, the balance of Cold War power was restored—much to the chagrin of Cubans on both sides of the Straits of Florida, who had imagined the conflict as a final apocalyptic battle between good and evil for the destiny of their nation. The Kennedy-Khrushchev pact only added insult to injury. Just as in 1898, when Spain and the United States had signed the Treaty of Paris without consulting the leaders of the independence army, the superpower agreement to end the missile crisis revealed that Cubans still lacked the power to determine for themselves the fate of their homeland. It also exposed to the world the counterrevolutionary movement's humiliating dependence on the U.S. government. Nor did exiles take comfort in the fact that Fidel Castro had also been summarily excluded from the grown-up business of international diplomacy; Castro had once again defied the United States, and his socialist regime, now protected by a U.S. noninvasion guarantee and Khrushchev's promise to defend "little Cuba" from foreign aggression, appeared stronger than ever.

For Cuban exiles who already felt betrayed by Kennedy's vacillations during the Bay of Pigs, the end of the Missile Crisis was not simply another failure of resolve on the part of the U.S. president, whose soft stance on communism had cost them a decisive opportunity to liberate their nation. Anti-Castro Cubans believed that their U.S. patrons had abandoned their cause, this time irrevocably. Those fears were not totally unfounded. Shortly after the Missile Crisis, Indochina began to replace Cuba as the principal focus of U.S. Cold War foreign policy. By 1963, the United States discontinued much of the financial assistance it had been funneling to the anti-Castro movement since the summer of 1960 and proscribed involvement in future exile paramilitary operations. State Department and intelligence officials even debated the possibility of a negotiated settlement with Castro.

The reconsideration of its position on the Revolution revealed that the U.S. government's commitment to the anti-Castro movement rested almost entirely on concerns about a Soviet presence ninety miles from the United States and the threat of communist subversion throughout the Americas — and not, exiles realized, on any real commitment to the democratic future of the Cuban nation-state. Exile leaders struggled to come to terms with this betrayal of their faith in their U.S. government patrons, and with the humiliating realization that they would no longer be able to offer a credible threat to the Castro regime.

Once again, a despairing community returned to its religious faith and to its child-centered creation myth to articulate its anger and disillusionment, to assuage its wounded pride, and to rebuild its shattered dreams of return to a democratic homeland. On November 23, *Patria* columnist Armando García Sifredo began publishing weekly op-ed pieces on the anti-Castro struggle under the headline "For Our Children." García's first article about the Missile Crisis, titled "Nobody Is Crying Here!," was accompanied by a portrait of a small, fair-haired girl kneeling in supplication

¡AQUI NO LLORA NADIE!

Por Armando García Sifredo

Por Nuestros Hijos

In the aftermath of the Cuban Missile Crisis, this photograph of an exile girl praying for the liberation of her homeland challenged Patria's *readers to continue the anti-Castro struggle. From* Patria, *November 23, 1962. Courtesy of the Cuban Heritage Collection, University of Miami Libraries, Coral Gables, Florida.*

at the altar of a Miami Catholic church. The photograph lent moral and emotional resonance to the journalist's exhortation that the community put on a brave face and not succumb to despair: even if President Kennedy had chosen hemispheric security over Cubans' aspirations for freedom, he insisted, exiles must continue fighting to liberate their homeland, for however long it was necessary—"for our children."[58]

On December 7, García Sifredo offered his readers what he labeled "the best commentary that has been published in exile." "With true emotion," he ceded his weekly space to a handwritten letter by a young Cuban girl that he claimed had "moved my heart as a father and as a Cuban. She says everything; why say more?" The letter followed:

Dear Sir:

I am the little girl in the portrait that you put above your article "Nobody Is Crying Here!" and I want to thank you in the name of my little brothers and of all the children of the friends of my father who is in heaven. Our parents died for God, for Cuba, and for us, and for all the Cubans in "Playa Girón," and surely they applaud from heaven the call that you make to keep struggling. Neither do I cry. And when I feel very sad without my Daddy, I ask Father God and the Virgin that soon Cuba be free.

Myrna Maria Millan.[59]

The small girl had, in fact, said everything that could be said, communicating in a few short lines the poignancy and pathos of the exile community's creation myth and its defiance of the North American protectors who had abandoned them in their moment of need. Myrna's letter — whether written alone or with the help of her teacher or parents — worked powerfully to restore Cuban Americans' dignity by framing exiles as the legitimate protagonists of the anti-Castro movement and reasserting the exiles' self-affirming identity as the heroic protectors of their sons and daughters. Of equal importance to exiles still grieving the loss of family members and friends at the Bay of Pigs, the young girl's letter also honored the sacrifice of those who had died for Cuba and for the island's children.

The moral and emotional resonance of Myrna's letter nonetheless had its limits. The child's words, however galvanizing, could not dispel Cuban refugees' growing despair in the face of the Revolution's apparent invincibility, shielded from external aggression by the might of the Soviet empire. Nor would the girl's prayers alter a second, equally painful reality: refugees' decision to flee the island, which most imagined would be followed by a short stay in the United States and the swift overthrow of Fidel Castro, had led them down a path they had never contemplated. A cruel twist of fate had marked them for indefinite exile in a foreign land. In light of recent events, to believe otherwise was foolish — the dream of a child.

BETWEEN 1960 AND 1962, a politically and socioeconomically diverse group of Cuban refugees sought asylum in the United States. United only by their rejection of Fidel Castro's authoritarian regime and their desire to protect their children from communism, exiles quickly launched the anti-Castro movement that they hoped would quickly topple the Revolution and restore the republic. However, weakened by political divisions and rivalries and lacking the resources necessary to execute a decisive campaign to free the *patria*, counterrevolutionary leaders acquiesced to an asymmetrical relationship with the U.S. intelligence community that would increase exiles' dependence on the federal government, weaken the legitimacy of the anti-Castro movement on both sides of the Straits of Florida, and limit its ability to act as an autonomous and effective agent of their nation's liberation. It would also open exiles to manipulation, exploitation, and humiliation at the hands of North American power brokers who viewed Cubans through racialized and infantilizing lenses dating back to U.S. intervention in the 1898 independence war, and whose support had been based more on Cold War concerns for hemispheric security than on an unshakable commitment to Cuba's democratic future.

Aware that a quick return to the homeland would require mobilizing the entire refugee population in support of a unified anti-Castro movement, a nascent CIA-supported exile media dedicated themselves to the production of counterrevolutionary propaganda as a powerful complement to the exile paramilitary struggle. They targeted a hemispheric audience with morally and emotionally resonant child-centered messages, seeking to foment anti-Castro opinion and activity among Cubans on the island and to create consensus among the multiple counterrevolutionary factions in Miami. They also sought to discredit the Castro regime among progressive Latin Americans. At the same time, exile leaders and journalists sought to resist the anti-Castro movement's humiliating dependence on their federal government and CIA sponsors by portraying themselves as the legitimate protagonists of the anti-Castro movement.

At the same time, the transplanted institutions of an emerging exile civil society rapidly reorganized in Miami and rallied around a shared objective: to promote the unity of the exile community, on behalf of its children and in service of the anti-Castro struggle. In the months leading up to the Bay of Pigs invasion, exiled Cubans would further reassert their prerevolutionary civic identities to ease the indignities of their downward mobility and marginalization in an economically depressed and less-than-friendly U.S. city. Civil society would also become a crucial site in which exiles would counter Fidel Castro's charges that they were traitors and lackeys of the imperialist United States, framing themselves instead as morally upright patriots, heroic defenders of children, and the spiritual heirs of José Martí's vision of the moral republic.[60] In the aftermath of the failed Bay of Pigs invasion, women and children would take on an even more salient role in exile civil society, as a devastated community struggled to come to terms with the U.S. government's betrayal of the anti-Castro movement and to gather strength to continue the fight for the liberation of the *patria*.

The exile media and civic actors were strikingly successful in rallying the community around its child-centered creation myth. Their insistence on unity created a powerful moral consensus on the need to suppress political differences in order to defeat Castro and restore the Cuban nation to their sons and daughters. However, by 1962, they had also succeeded in imposing an increasingly hegemonic conservative worldview on a once progressive and pluralistic refugee population. This nascent ideology, as narrowly defined as its revolutionary counterpart, contributed powerfully to the forging of a collective identity and sense of purpose among diverse groups of exiles. However, the community's growing sense of unity could not make up for the structural weaknesses of the anti-Castro movement, which remained divided and ultimately dependent on the whims of the U.S. government.

In 1962, when the resolution of the October Missile Crisis failed to bring down the Revolution, the dream of Castro's defeat began to recede into the distance. Hopes of a quick return home were replaced by despair and resentment as exiles realized that the anti-Castro movement had been first betrayed and then abandoned by their U.S. protectors. Though bitterly regretting their misplaced trust in the U.S. government, Miami Cubans nonetheless clung to their faith in the democratic-capitalist nation-making project and to their belief that exile had been the right choice—a necessary evil to be endured in order to safeguard the well-being and future of their children. Struggling to reconcile themselves to the impossibility of future military action against the Revolution, exiles kept alive the dream that they would find a way, someday, to secure the next generation's return to a democratic homeland. In the meantime, they would continue to rely on their community's child-centered creation myth to make sense of their losses—of home, dignity, and homeland—even as they turned increasingly to their own sons and daughters for the strength to begin building new lives in the United States.

UNDERSTANDING ELIÁN

*The Politics of Childhood in Havana and Miami,
1959–2000*

After the October 1962 Missile Crisis, the survival of the island's socialist Revolution was assured. This newfound certainty freed the Castro regime to focus on preparing the new generation for citizenship in a future communist society. At the same time, Miami exiles dedicated themselves to ensuring that their vision of a moral Cuban republic remained alive in their children. During the decades to come, the bodies, hearts, and minds of exile girls and boys would serve as vessels in which their parents' and grandparents' political traditions, culture, and values could be preserved until the fall of the Castro regime. Between 1959 and the onset in 1999 of the Elián González custody battle, the politics of childhood in Havana and Miami would continue to articulate the processes of alienation, fragmentation, and reformation that led to the creation of Two Cubas on opposite shores of the Straits of Florida. The dialectic between revolutionary and exilic understandings, practices, and representations of childhood throughout this forty-year period reveals the persistent importance of the child as nation-maker both on and off the island.

"SEREMOS COMO EL CHE": CREATING THE REVOLUTIONARY CHILD IN CUBA

In December 1962, Fidel Castro declared himself a Marxist-Leninist and set his government the simultaneous tasks of building a socialist culture and constructing communism in Cuba. His ability to achieve both of these goals depended on establishing exclusive state control over the ideological formation of Cuban children. New policies and programs thus worked to redirect young people's loyalties away from the institutions of the family, the Catholic Church, and African-origin religious communities, while encouraging their commitment to the Revolution.[1] At the same time, education—and closely associated with it, the island's schoolchildren— became increasingly enshrined as one of the most important legitimizing symbols of the new regime.

As they had in the prerevolutionary era, child-centered policies claiming inspiration in José Martí's vision for an autonomous, egalitarian, and multiracial Cuban nation continued to play a central role in island citizens' aspirations for the future. Together with the dramatic expansion of educational services to impoverished *guajiro* children, repeated references to the Martían legacy of the Revolution's educational initiatives generated important reserves of support for the Castro regime, especially among rural, poor and working-class, and black Cubans.[2] However, the Revolution's educational objectives were ultimately guided less by Martí's principles than they were by the exigencies of constructing a socialist society, which had been used to justify (the apostle's antipathy toward the centralized state and its attendant bureaucracy notwithstanding) the regime's almost total control of an ever more ideologically rigid school system as early as mid-1961.

The Revolution's top-down, highly politicized approach to education was institutionalized by 1965, when Che Guevara's calls for the creation of a "New Man" became the explicit guiding force behind educational policy and children and youth programs. Primary and secondary instruction was redesigned to reinforce Marxist-Leninist interpretations in all subjects. The following year, the government also took over control of daycare centers from the Federation of Cuban Women, reorganizing their operations, curricula, and pedagogical methods to prioritize the fomentation of revolutionary *conciencia* in toddlers. They also made membership in the Pioneers league mandatory for all elementary school students in order to maximize the organization's ability to lead the ideological formation of Cuban children and mitigate the pernicious influence of nonrevolutionary parents on the next generation of the nation's citizens.[3]

In line with Martí's belief that rural education was central to the creation of a moral republic—but equally reflective of the priorities of Soviet pedagogy—the Ministry of Education also introduced the Escuela al Campo (School Goes to the Countryside) program in the first half of the decade, which required middle and high school students to combine study with agricultural labor in rural areas. The program certainly exposed children to the difficulties of life in the Cuban countryside, which the regime's leadership hoped would contribute to bridging the urban-rural divide that had plagued republican Cuban society; however, and perhaps more important, the Escuelas al Campo also removed privileged urban children from the bourgeois and potentially counterrevolutionary influence of their parents and extended families while providing an intense immersion, under the supervision of ideologically militant teachers, in revolutionary values.

Designed to prioritize rural education at the same time that improvements in urban elementary education and higher education were postponed—including the neglect of universities that had already lost their traditional autonomy—the Escuelas al Campo initiative was expanded when permanent Escuelas Secundarias Básicas en el Campo (Basic Secondary Schools in the Countryside), new rural boarding schools for urban high school children that were financed in part by students' labor, were established in the middle of the decade. By 1967, although approximately 85 percent of Cuban secondary students were participating in a School in the Countryside program, the initiative did not go unchallenged by parents.[4] Many, including committed revolutionaries, resisted sending their children—and especially their daughters—to boarding schools because they feared that unsupervised contact with the opposite sex, and especially with Afro-Cuban boys, would lead to sexual activity, loss of virginity, and possibly even pregnancy. At the same time, some young people viewed boarding school and other educational and extracurricular activities that took them away from home as an opportunity to exercise a greater degree of choice and control over their lives and to distance themselves from the conservative values and customs of the traditional patriarchal Cuban family—precisely the institution that many parents feared would be weakened by the regime's radical transformation of the educational system.

Other boarding school programs brought impoverished rural children to study in Cuba's cities. Known as *becados*, the recipients of state scholarships to these new boarding schools received both technical and political training under the careful supervision of fervently ideological teachers and staff. Living and studying in an environment of constant socialization and surveillance and inundated by messages stressing their ideological purity and importance to the emerging socialist society, the young *becados* learned to mimic the personal qualities, attitudes, and political values of the Revolution's leaders. Scholarship students also enjoyed access to a varied and ample diet and in-demand consumer goods like clothing, shoes, pencils, and books, living a privileged existence far removed from the struggles that defined their families' daily lives in a society plagued by economic stagnation, scarcity, and rationing. Not surprisingly, these *becados* were more easily identified with the Revolution and its presumed virtue than older Cubans, who, tainted by association with a corrupt and decadent past, had to earn this association through ideological conversion, participation in mass organizations, and volunteer labor.

The establishment of the Escuelas al Campo and the scholarship schemes that brought rural children to live and study in Havana helped forge revolutionary identities in impressionable young people even as they created new generational divisions in island-resident Cuban families.[5] The role of these boarding school–educated children in fanning the flames of revolutionary fervor throughout the 1960s cannot be overstated, since by 1965, Cubans between the ages of ten and twenty-five made up 40 percent of the population—and the overwhelming majority were enthusiastic *fidelistas*. However, by the end of the decade, the limits of the Revolution's efforts to deploy boarding school students in support of its broader socialist nation-making project were revealed, as thousands of peasant boys and girls, granted scholarships in the expectation that they would carry literacy, technical training, and revolutionary doctrine back to the *campo* after graduation, refused to return to live in the countryside.[6]

Rural children were not alone in demonstrating a degree of defiance to revolutionary dictates; by the mid-sixties, urban young people had also begun to express resistance to state-led attempts to remake them in the image of the Revolution. Emerging at a time of growing economic stagnation and declining political euphoria, persistently high rates of school absenteeism and sharp increases in juvenile delinquency, vandalism, and armed robbery, especially in poor urban and Afro-Cuban neighborhoods, threatened the Castro regime's legitimacy—precisely because it had worked so hard to associate the future of the socialist nation with the well-being of the island's youngest citizens. As a result, juvenile delinquents who had a few years earlier been portrayed as victims of social indifference were increasingly reframed as enemies of the revolutionary state and society.[7]

In line with this changing view of the island's youth, the government launched a broadly based ideological campaign directed at disciplining Cuban young people's persistently "unrevolutionary" cultural tastes and behaviors. Revolutionary leaders and the media joined hands with mass youth organizations to condemn a range of youth-oriented styles and activities, including young men's preference for long hair and the popularity of miniskirts and heavy jewelry among teenaged girls, all of which were considered evidence of "ideological confusion." They also criticized adolescents for frequenting nightclubs and dance halls and for listening to the Beatles and North American music and lamented the rising rates of adolescent sexual activity and births to single teenage mothers. In an attempt to eradicate these "antisocial" behaviors, members of the Union of Communist Youth were tasked with infiltrating groups of their peers suspected of antisocial behavior and reporting on them to Cuban intelligence agents. This practice led in 1968 to a series of police raids on public spaces frequented by young people and the arrests of hundreds of adolescents accused of truancy, drug abuse, and criminality. Many of these youth were sent to perform agricultural labor on the Isla de Pinos (Island of Pines), renamed that year the Isla de la Juventud (Island of Youth) after its state-directed repopulation by tens of thousands of school-age volunteers and "predelinquent" children in need of reeducation.[8]

Moreover, beginning in the middle of the decade and reflecting the regime leadership's belief in the linkages between masculinity, heterosexual virility, and military prowess—and conversely, between homosexuality, laziness, and decadence—the government decreed that "effeminate" boys be sent to reformatory schools, where they would be transformed into ideal revolutionary subjects through participation in sports, self-defense, and military drills. The military draft—suspended after Batista's overthrow in 1959—was also reinstated in 1964, with the age of mandatory three-year military service for Cuban males set at sixteen years. Promulgated during a time of relative peace, the new draft functioned primarily to secure cheap labor for the new state-run collective farms; however, it also offered a means of submitting nonconformist youth, and especially the sons of suspected counterrevolutionary peasants, to a militarized process of revolutionary reindoctrination.[9]

The revolutionary state also dramatically increased interventions in the home lives of the nation's young people. Beginning in 1963, the regime cracked down on evangelical Protestant parents, ostensibly for forbidding their children to salute the flag or swear the pledge of allegiance, and accused them of participating in a counterrevolutionary conspiracy with the CIA and the U.S. State Department. Initiation of children into Santería was also decreed a criminal offense, punishable by imprisonment. In 1967, television and radio programs, books and parenting manuals, and CDR study sessions began to target mothers and fathers directly with explicit instructions on how to raise their children as future citizens of a communist society. During that same year, the Federación de Mujeres Cubanas authorized its volunteers to enter the houses of truant and suspected "antisocial" children to "educate parents" in proper parenting. In 1968, the regime called on neighborhood vigilance committees to oversee the activities and attitudes of parents and their children, reinforcing the by now familiar exhortation that they should report any nonrevolutionary behaviors to the police.[10]

The state's growing power to shape domestic life was formalized in the 1975 Family Code, which stressed parents' obligation to assist in the state-directed socialization of children through the modeling of revolutionary values at home. By this time, in spite of the code's acknowledgment of the ongoing importance of the family unit within Cuban society, the revolutionary state had replaced the family as the preeminent institution in Cuba, taking on an unprecedented level of responsibility for the care, education, and socialization of the island's children. However, the regime's increasingly heavy-handed attempts to discipline the island's recalcitrant children and families suggest the limitations of revolutionary social control, at the same time as they contributed to the emergence of an underground youth counterculture of rebellion by the end of the decade.[11]

SAVING THE FUTURE: THE CARE AND EDUCATION OF EXILE CHILDREN

During the 1960s, South Florida's Cuban community continued to grieve the lost dream of a quick and triumphant return to the island. Exiles did not let their perhaps permanent separation from the *patria* undermine their commitment to its eventual liberation; however, in the light of decreasing U.S. support for the counterrevolutionary cause and a shift in foreign policy priorities to other Cold War battles in Indochina, the community found itself compelled to collectively reorder its priorities. Nursing their resentment of a U.S. government that they believed had gone soft on communism, the exile community turned increasingly inward, forging the strong community ties and an increasingly ironclad political consensus that would allow the exiles to continue the anti-Castro struggle. They also relied on the same social networks to begin building what would become a thriving economic enclave, establishing themselves as homeowners and proprietors of small businesses.

Anti-Castro Cubans worked hard to improve their socioeconomic position in Miami and to demonstrate their principled commitment to the U.S. democratic-capitalist nation-making project, both to counter Fidel Castro's accusations that they had chosen exile because they were cowardly, self-interested, and amoral traitors and to maintain their claims on the preferential immigration status that protected their community in southern Florida. At the same time, exiles sought to reestablish their middle-class status and identities in order to validate their assertions of raced, classed, and cultural affinity with the U.S. mainstream, maintaining the distance from other working-class Latina/o immigrants and minority communities that underwrote their conditional welcome by white Miamians. These efforts were motivated in large part by the overarching need to assure the well-being of their families, and especially of their children, in exile.

The first wave of Cuban refugees dedicated themselves to their parental duties as a means of continuing the struggle for their island's destiny. They committed themselves to instilling prerevolutionary political and cultural values in their children, transforming them into vessels of *cubanía* through which the nation in exile would be preserved until it could return home. Their preparation for positions of leadership in a democratic-capitalist nation with close ties to the United States was also central to the exilic nation-making project. With these goals in mind, exiles and their allies pressured the U.S. government to promote the educational success of the 21,000 Cuban refugee children enrolled in Miami–Dade County public schools for the academic year 1962. Their activism, framed strategically within a discourse that emphasized the value of the Cuban exile community to U.S. Cold War foreign policy, helped secure an additional $130 million in federal funds for bilingual education and multicultural awareness programs in Miami–Dade County, and it led to the government's commitment to subsidizing up to 60 percent of the cost of educating each exile pupil enrolled in county public schools.[12]

Exile activism also led to the establishment in 1962 of a bilingual immersion program at Coral Way Elementary. Inaugurated with local support and benefiting from plentiful funding and a well-trained staff, Coral Way Elementary and other Miami public schools offered the first federally funded bilingual programs of the post–World War II era, even as Puerto Rican and Mexican parents struggled with less success to secure equal educational opportunities for their own children in New York, Texas, and California.[13] Federal funds were also dedicated to hiring specially trained "orientation teachers" as well as more than 250 exile teacher aides to support refugee students in adapting to the routines and workload of Miami–Dade County elementary and secondary schools.[14] Hundreds more Cuban-born educators, taking advantage of new federally sponsored retraining programs for exiles, also quickly recertified as teachers and took positions in the Miami–Dade County school system. They dedicated themselves to supporting newly arrived Cuban students.

Though refugee children entered local schools frightened and disoriented by their rapid departure from the island and, in many cases, ill-prepared for their entrance into the English-language classroom, generous government funding, the provision of special services and support, and school district policy worked together to maximize their chances for success. District directives ensured that students were integrated into mainstream classrooms as quickly as feasible, but that they would not be graded in content areas until they demonstrated the ability to read and comprehend English-language texts at a functional level. Refugee students were also initially excluded from standardized testing requirements. Moreover, at the elementary school level, teachers were discouraged from preventing children with limited English from advancing with their class and urged to consider the age-grade relationship, arithmetic skills, and general progress in language development in their assessment of refugee students. In all cases, district superintendent Joe Hall insisted, teachers should err on the side of student promotion.[15]

Special funding and support thus helped exile students to quickly begin performing at relatively high academic levels. A 1963 Cuban Refugee Center report on refugee resettlement boasted of children's "remarkable adjustment" in the Miami-Dade school system, listing the academic distinctions and athletic letters awarded to CRC-enrolled high school students; they also congratulated a young refugee boy for winning a national math contest, and another for receiving his school's newly instituted Outstanding Cuban Student prize in honor of his straight-A average. The report also lauded an unnamed sixth grader—whose parents, it noted, were still in Cuba—for earning the national Daughters of the American Revolution Outstanding Student and Citizen Award. Finally, the CRC report recognized five Cuban students who had been elected to Junior American Citizens' Club offices—with no further comment on the seeming incongruity of the participation of noncitizen refugee children in such an organization.[16]

The celebration of these students' achievements, though it undoubtedly complemented the CRC's ongoing media campaign to maintain the positive image of the exile community, also reflected public support (albeit largely politically motivated) for Cuban children's integration in U.S. schools, in Miami and elsewhere. Mainstream America's sympathy for the academic challenges faced by exile children, however, stood in marked contrast with attitudes toward other Latina/o students, whose lack of access to bilingual education programs and supplementary services and continued segregation in underfunded and underperforming schools contributed to persistently high dropout rates. As late as 1968, 80 percent of Puerto Ricans on the U.S. mainland had failed to complete high school;

in the Southwest, few Mexican-origin children went beyond the seventh grade. These inequalities of opportunity in the public school system testify to the importance of Cold War foreign policy considerations in shaping markedly different educational outcomes among children from distinct Latina/o communities.[17]

In spite of the special consideration granted to refugee students in the Miami–Dade County district, however, Cuban parents were reluctant to leave the education of their children entirely to the U.S. public schools. Displaced exile teachers and administrators thus founded or reopened an extensive network of bilingual and Catholic Cuban schools in Miami, including the Edison School, Baldor, Lincoln, La Salle, Immaculata Academy, La Progresiva, Colegio La Luz, and, perhaps most famously, the Belén Jesuit Preparatory School.[18] Children attending these private schools participated in classroom activities, assemblies, school pageants, and events specifically designed to reinforce traditional Cuban values, customs, and faith and to deepen children's patriotism. By the mid-1970s, more than twenty-five private Cuban schools were operating in the greater Miami area, and a growing number had applied for and received the accreditation necessary to admit their pupils to U.S. universities.[19] By then, the rapidly expanding network of private schools had become an important site in which social networks among students and their families were established, evolving into one of the most enduring institutions of exiles' transplanted civil society, creating and re-creating the diasporic nation in the decades to come.

Committed Cuban teachers in both private and public schools made certain that exile children learned English and succeeded academically while otherwise resisting their assimilation, imagining every exile child educated into a continuing love for the *patria* as a small victory against communism and Fidel Castro. To that end, teachers monitored their exile students' Spanish-language skills and instructed them in an evolving exile version of Cuban history—one in which a newfound reverence for the achievements of the prerevolutionary era quickly replaced the story of Cubans' as-yet unfulfilled struggle to establish Martí's moral republic. By instilling their own version of Cuban history in their children, they sought to counter Castro's claims that his 1959 Revolution had been fought to free the island from persistent underdevelopment and an infantilizing dependence on the United States. Exiles also saw the academic success of refugee students as another means of resisting racially inflected notions about Latina/o, and by extension Cuban, inferiority that remained pervasive in Miami and across the country. Thus, while awaiting their return to the homeland, parents and teachers also dedicated themselves to preparing children for university and for lucrative careers as doctors, lawyers, and businesspeople. While clinging to the hope that the next generation would one day assume positions of prominence in a reconstituted Cuban republic, exile elders were nonetheless aware that the education and consequent social mobility of Cuban children in the United States would play an essential role in guaranteeing the survival and prestige of the emerging exilic nation.

Exile teachers' professional organizations like the Association of Cuban Teachers and the Federation of Cuban Educators also dedicated themselves to the care and education of exile children until a return to the homeland became possible. They raised funds to publish schoolbooks that reinforced their nationalist, Christian, and democratic-capitalist values—including three texts titled *Symbols, Dates, and Biographies*; *Elements of Cuban History*; and *Elements of Cuban Geography*—so that exile children, "far away from the homeland that we have temporarily lost," might "maintain some of their memories and know of its greatness."[20] Among the largest and most active of the growing exile community's educational associations, the Cruzada Educativa Cubana (CEC) continued to expand its membership base in Miami, across the United States, and into Latin America. By the time of its second general assembly on September 26, 1964, the organization boasted more than 200 members and would steadily increase that number throughout the decade.[21]

Since its founding in 1962, the CEC had lent consistent vocal support to armed efforts to restore democratic government on the island, collaborating during the first half of the 1960s with other exile educators and organizations to coordinate multiple curricular initiatives for the "decommunization of the Cuban schools" after the much anticipated overthrow of the Castro regime. However, as a swift return home became less likely, the Cruzada's membership became increasingly preoccupied with ensuring that "Cuba not die in our young people, neither its history nor its republican achievements, popular customs, and institutions." To that end, the CEC launched *La Escuelita Cubana* (The Little Cuban School), a weekly radio broadcast for exile children, which aired on Sundays as part of Miami station WMIE's Spanish-language program *El Periódico del Aire* (The Magazine of the Airwaves) in September 1963.[22]

The Little Cuban School appealed to its youthful audience with exciting and morally resonant stories about the island's history, republican political traditions, and customs. It also sponsored a weekly patriotic coloring contest. The first of these contests, organized around the theme "Cuba's

Flag and Coat of Arms," awarded a copy of José Martí's children's classic *La edad de oro* to Antolín García, a sixth-grader at St. Mary's Cathedral School. The Cruzada also sponsored Spanish-language clubs and a series of children's *tertulias* (cultural programs) under the banner "An Hour with Cuba." Staged in private homes and in the offices of anti-Castro organizations like Movimiento Rescate Revolucionario and Centinelas de la Libertad, the programs offered Miami's exile children the opportunity to savor Cuban history, music, poetry, and sweet treats, and featured performances by exile women who presented their own patriotic musical and literary compositions. In 1969, the CEC also launched a course directed at maturing exile youth in order to incorporate young people into the community's ongoing political and philosophical debates about the destiny of the nation. Over the next two years, it also collaborated with the Miami *municipios*, or exile hometown associations, to hold conferences and seminars at which exile high school, college, and university students presented papers on Cuban history, literature, and the future of the democratic republic.[23]

Throughout the 1960s and 1970s, the Cruzada also engaged in political activism to ensure that the future of the exile community's children remained a central concern of the federal government. It called for the creation of a federal commission to support Cuban exiles' artistic, cultural, scientific, and literary endeavors; advocated continuously to preserve and expand bilingual education in Miami-area public schools; and sought additional federal funding to support education preparing exile children for citizenship in a restored democratic republic. In May 1966, CEC president Vicente Cauce directed a letter on behalf of the organization's now 300-plus members to President Lyndon B. Johnson, urging him to instruct the Department of Education to sponsor supplemental courses in Miami–Dade County public schools in Cuban history, geography, civics, and literature. The letter argued that the establishment of these courses was essential to the fulfillment of exile educators' "sacred duty" to preserve the political and cultural values of the exile community's children and, through them, to secure the democratic future of their island homeland.

Perhaps aware of the audacity of requesting that the U.S. government fund educational programs within its borders for the formation of citizens of another nation, the letter further reminded President Johnson of the Cold War benefits to be accrued from such an unprecedented action. The care and education of exile boys and girls was not only "a task of transcendence for the future destiny of the Cuban nation," the letter argued; it would also pay important dividends in the ongoing U.S. fight against

communist subversion in the Americas. By demonstrating its "noble efforts to preserving for Cuba a brilliant reserve of future citizens, new
and clean blood necessary to the historic rehabilitation of our nation,"
it concluded, the United States would offer "a new and edifying example
of human love and understanding to the hemispheric [anticommunist]
cause." Moreover, future generations of Cuban leaders who were educated
in U.S. schools would be certain to "faithfully love and give thanks to
the United States for the favors and services received during the terrible
time in which they lost, along with their native soil, the cardinal goods of
freedom and dignity[,] . . . during which they were able to nonetheless
enjoy . . . under the shade of the Stars and Stripes, both security and
human decorum, even while feeling themselves intrinsically Cuban, proud
of their history and of their language and their homeland won after a century of sacrifice and struggle by the founders of the Republic."[24]

Other exile organizations and local allies provided exile children with
recreational opportunities that would help them become assimilated to
North American life without compromising their national identity and
culture. This was accomplished by integrating children into U.S. programs,
including the Boy and Girl Scouts, the Boys and Girls Clubs, the YMCA
and YWCA, and municipal athletic and recreational clubs, as well as by
establishing Cuban youth programs, many of them sponsored by local
Catholic churches.[25] Throughout the 1960s, as the exile community expanded, so too did the recreational options available to its youngest members. By the 1970s, parents could sign their daughters up for ballet classes
at one of numerous Cuban-operated studios, while little boys learned to
play baseball at one of Miami's seven Cuban-operated Little League acad-
emies before joining one of the many Cuban-sponsored teams. Teenagers
made new friends at youth social clubs and attended community-sponsored
mixers and dances. Young people enjoyed these new opportunities to participate in leisure activities in a familiar and friendly environment, under
the supervision of a community that remained deeply committed to preserving their children's cultural, political, and religious values; maintaining their Spanish-language skills; and fostering their identification with
their country of origin.[26]

"OUR YOUTH IS LOST": GENERATIONAL
CONFLICT IN THE TWO CUBAS

Within a few years of Cuban resettlement in the United States, what
Miguel de la Torre called the "imaginary nation of Exilic Cubans" began

to grow up in Miami alongside the first generation of refugee children.[27] As the first wave of island-born boys and girls began to come of age in the United States, however, new tensions also began to appear within Cuban American families as Cuban parents and grandparents found it increasingly difficult to sustain traditional family life and forms of childrearing in exile. By the late 1960s, though more than 54 percent of exile women had challenged traditional Cuban gender norms by taking full-time employment outside the home—resulting in a higher workforce participation rate than that of white American women and that of all other U.S. Latinas—multiple studies revealed that Cuban American mothers continued to attempt to enforce gender-specific rules of conduct for their sons and daughters. Some teenaged Cuban American girls resented a double standard that saddled them with heavier domestic responsibilities, placed differential restrictions on their behavior and dress, and allowed boys greater freedom to participate in activities outside the home and without adult supervision. In spite of this, Cuban elders often persisted in enforcing these gendered norms within their families, understanding the curtailing of their daughters' autonomy as necessary to shelter them from the dangers of an overly permissive U.S. culture, to preserve their reputation for feminine virtue, and, perhaps most important, to protect their virginity.[28]

Cuban American boys also sometimes expressed frustration with their parents' attempts to control their behavior and social lives. A study of Cuban high school students of both sexes in New Jersey found high levels of generational conflict, with an overwhelming majority of their parents reporting great difficulties in granting their children the same freedom and independence as other U.S. teenagers. It is safe to assume that these generational conflicts also existed in Miami. Moreover, they were likely to have been especially pronounced in relationships between parents reunited with children who had traveled unaccompanied to the United States in the early sixties and had experienced unprecedented autonomy while living with relatives or in foster homes. However, even among children who had never been separated from their families, parental insistence on the maintenance of Cuban cultural norms and traditions conflicted with young people's relatively faster integration into U.S. society and caused many exile teenagers to feel frustrated, isolated from their families, and marginalized among their politically and culturally progressive U.S. peers.[29]

During the turbulent second half of the 1960s, exile parents watched aghast as their host nation struggled to come to terms with a radical generational challenge to its sociopolitical structures and cultural values, reflected in a newly militant civil rights movement, renewed feminist and gay rights' activism, and anti–Vietnam War protests. Exiles who had fled the island in order to protect traditional middle-class and Catholic-inspired understandings of childhood and family life were horrified by the countercultural lifestyle their children were exposed to in the land that had been their refuge from the Revolution's godlessness and amorality. They increasingly took refuge in their conservative worldview, renewing their efforts to preserve the traditional patriarchal family and the virtue of their sons and daughters, working harder than ever to inculcate young people with a passionate sense of *cubanía* and with the values and ideals that had spurred their exodus from the island.

Since many Cuban parents and grandparents viewed the preservation of traditional Cuban family life and cultural values as part of a continuing struggle for the island's liberation from Castro-communism, they interpreted young people's rebellions and experimentations with alternative worldviews and lifestyles as a betrayal of not only their family values but also their beloved *patria*. Their persistent attachment to the exilic politics of childhood thus exerted enormous pressure on Cuban American children and teens, who struggled to negotiate the formidable challenges of adolescence in an unfamiliar society while simultaneously meeting the highly politicized expectations of a tightly bounded ethnic community. Exile elders and anti-Castro students involved in the Abdala movement widely condemned the involvement of Cuban American youth in the anti–Vietnam War movement, their radicalization alongside Chicana/o and Puerto Rican youth, and their foundation of the leftist journals *Areíto* and *Joven Cuba*, responding to their calls for dialogue with the Revolution with extraordinary displays of anger.

An even greater controversy erupted in the late 1970s, when radicalized Cuban American youth—many of them former Pedro Pan children—organized the Antonio Maceo Brigade. The young brigade members, who longed to reconnect with their native land and culture and to promote dialogue between the Two Cubas, provoked an unprecedented negative response in Miami. Anti-Castro Cubans interpreted the *brigadistas'* desire to return to the island as a repudiation of the personal and collective sacrifices exiles had made for their children. Moreover, the *brigadistas'* interest in the social gains of the Revolution cast doubt on the exile community's ability to preserve their competing vision of Martí's moral republic in the minds and hearts of their sons and daughters. The elders' failure to pass along their conservative Catholic values, pro-U.S.

worldview, and hatred for Fidel Castro to the youthful members of the Antonio Maceo Brigade constituted an imminent threat to the survival of the exilic nation-making project. Ironically, it was the elders' nostalgia for their lost homeland that inspired the young people's passionate desire to return to the island, a journey perceived by parents, relatives, and community members as treason against the nation that lived on only in exile.[30]

In contrast, political leaders on the island saw the visits of the Antonio Maceo Brigade as an opportunity to reinvigorate an increasingly institutionalized Revolution—and as a means of addressing the regime's growing difficulties with the island's young people, many of whom continued to resist state-sponsored efforts to ensure their revolutionary socialization. Following the failed 1970 sugar harvest—during which more than 100,000 children and adolescent volunteers performed unpaid labor— the Castro government struggled to combat a growing wave of disillusionment and apathy among youth. The government militarized the Pioneers children's organization and required middle and high school students to participate in expanded work-study and agricultural labor in the countryside. However, as discussions about youth malaise at the 1971 Congress on Education and Culture revealed, hopes that new educational methods and programs would create a socialist *conciencia* among the island's maturing revolutionary children had not been fulfilled. In fact, by the end of the decade, many students and youth resisted the regime's efforts to put them to work building and defending the Revolution, choosing instead to skip school, failing to show up for volunteer work and militia service, and engaging in theft, vandalism, and other crimes.[31]

Facing widespread social malaise, the Castro regime hoped that the brigade members' idealism and courage might reinspire in Cuba's much maligned "lost youth" a new commitment to the Revolution—or shame them into it.[32] Even as the U.S. and exile media continued to characterize every Cuban refugee arriving in Miami as a vote against communism, the revolutionary media portrayed each young exile who returned to the land of his or her birth as a vote against the U.S. democratic-capitalist nation-making project. Brigadistas returning to the island thus became exactly what their elders feared they would be—the latest in a series of youthful *voceros* deployed in defense of the socialist nation-making project. Some members of the brigade were aware of their instrumental value to the regime and were eager to contribute to efforts to renew the Revolution; others were disappointed to realize that the Castro regime sought to exploit their presence on the island and to manipulate their personal and family histories in the service of political goals not necessarily related to their motivations for returning.

Though the Antonio Maceo Brigade made several more highly publicized visits to Cuba, youth malaise on the island continued to deepen. Through the late 1970s and the early 1980s, a period of relative economic prosperity supported by generous Soviet aid, the creation of a socialist *conciencia* among young people remained an elusive goal. Twenty years after the triumph of the Revolution, the "children of Che" were still not always demonstrating the revolutionary commitment expected by their leaders. In the years that followed the visits of young exiles to the island, many disaffected young people, products of revolutionary schools and youth organizations, voted with their feet in the opposite direction, spurring yet another wave of emigration to the United States. They constituted the overwhelming majority of the 125,000 refugees who left the island during the 1980 Mariel Boatlift, some of whom may not have totally rejected the political values of the Revolution; however, their decision to emigrate indicated that they were no longer willing to make the sacrifices expected of the new socialist generations when freedom and economic opportunity beckoned in the United States.

FROM MARIEL AND BEYOND: THE CHANGING PARAMETERS OF THE POLITICS OF CHILDHOOD

The Mariel Boatlift sparked both legal controversy and moral panic in southern Florida and across the nation, revealing the decreasing influence of the politics of childhood on the U.S. government's shifting foreign policy goals and immigration policies. Anglo-American Miami's welcome of the Cuban refugees had always been conditional, however, dependent on government-sanctioned messages that deemphasized Cuban difference and reinforced the Cold War justification for federal, state, and municipal government generosity toward the exile community. By the 1980s, a changing political climate, increasing nonwhite immigration from Central America and the Caribbean, and a marked decline in media efforts to disseminate the Cuban American community's child-centered creation myth would reveal the limits of the exilic politics of childhood.

Throughout the first half of the 1960s, the U.S. media had continued to outrage readers with exposés of the communist indoctrination of children in Cuba and to charm them with exile families' success stories. Buoyed by public sympathy for these brave and resourceful refugees, between 1961 and 1971 the U.S. federal government spent more than $730 million on Cuban immigrant aid.[33] Nonetheless, although anti-Castro Cubans continued to enjoy the benefits of nationwide support, the limits of the exilic politics of childhood—and of Miami–Dade County's hospitality—were beginning to reveal themselves. Even as municipal and state politicians still expressed sympathy for the suffering of refugee children and solidarity with the exiles' anticommunist struggle, they began in 1963 to respond to their constituents' renewed concerns about the county's ability to absorb what appeared to be a never ending flow of Cuban refugees.

Then, in September 1965, as a second wave of refugees took advantage of government-funded "Freedom Flights" to reunite with their families in exile, thousands of newly arrived Cuban children entered Miami's public schools. An overwhelmed district struggled at first to accommodate them, but it was unable to meet the demand for seats in classrooms already filled to capacity. Reversing his previous patriotically inspired declarations of support for the refugee community, Miami-Dade school superintendent Joe Hall threatened to suspend enrollment of Cuban students unless the federal government provided immediate and expanded funding to offset the district's expenditures.[34] In a similar reversal, Dante Fascell, a Miami Democratic delegate to the Florida House of Representatives and a previous advocate of the exile community, made a speech on the House floor demanding U.S. congressional hearings to set a limit on the number of Cuban refugees admitted to the country.[35]

As Dade County sank deeper into economic recession, struggling local residents also began to complain about the federal government's apparent preoccupation with the well-being of Cuban refugees. Black Miamians, hardest hit by the lack of employment opportunities and increasingly angry about persistent racial segregation in the city's schools, the inaccessibility of safe and affordable housing, the destruction of African American neighborhoods by urban renewal and expressway developments, and unfair treatment by Miami police, were particularly bitter about the generous assistance provided to the exile community. These frustrations boiled over in 1968 during the Liberty City Riots, which a local task force later determined were sparked at least in part by black frustration at the government's seemingly preferential concern for recently arrived Cubans. Juanita Greene, urban affairs editor of the *Miami Herald*, articulated the anger of local African American residents, stating, "There is no doubt that the federal government has done more for Cuban refugees than for black Americans in this community."

Similarly, in a September 1969 statement to the *Miami Herald*, T. Willard Fair, executive director of the Greater Miami Urban League, condemned the federal and state government and racist white Miamians who treated Cuban immigrants better than they treated black citizens. Alluding to the hundreds of millions of dollars that had been invested in bilingual education programs in Miami–Dade County schools while black students attended classes in underfunded and poorly maintained facilities, Fair concluded, "When we can teach English as a foreign language here and not understand the need to teach black history, it tells me our society is morally bankrupt." While avoiding discussions of the racial politics of government assistance to Miami–Dade County's needy residents, even exile advocates at the Cuban Refugee Center acknowledged the seeming inequity of the way resources were being distributed. Conceding that "the unemployed local citizen's sense of frustration, and possible hostility, is heightened by comparison of the social welfare programs available to him with the social welfare program available to the Cuban refugee through the federal government," they committed themselves to an increased effort to resettle new arrivals outside southern Florida.[36]

In the decades to come, recurrent public debates over each new influx of Cuban refugees to the city repeatedly laid bare the tension between the federal government's Cold War foreign policy objectives and local exigencies. White and black Miamians alike, albeit for different reasons, found common cause in expressing their resentment at having to absorb a disproportionate share of the costs associated with the resettlement of a steady stream of Cuban arrivals. Moreover, in the 1970s, during a period of relative détente between the United States and the Soviet Union, they also increasingly voiced their displeasure with the cultural and linguistic transformation of their city as a result of the exile community's growing demographic, political, and economic power. These tensions culminated in 1980—just as the first wave of Mariel refugees began to arrive in Miami—with the passage of a county ordinance eliminating local funding for multicultural programs or services and requiring government business to be conducted exclusively in English.

Although Ronald Reagan's election as president renewed U.S. enthusiasm for the Cold War, new political priorities at the municipal, state, and federal level would conspire to deprive the Marielitos of the warm government-sponsored welcome and sympathetic media coverage that the first two waves of anticommunist Cuban refugees had enjoyed. Instead, newly arrived refugees were detained in makeshift camps and military bases throughout the United States. Their immigration status remained uncertain, and they did not receive the generous assistance extended to first- and second-wave exiles through the Cuban Refugee Emergency Program, which had been suspended in 1973. Meanwhile, their sons and daughters languished in boredom during prolonged stays in the poorly equipped camps, few of which offered services or recreational activities for children. Of those placed in schools, many had only a few years of formal education. They struggled to adapt to a more challenging academic environment and had difficulty making English-speaking friends. Concerns about the racial, linguistic, and scholastic differences between Marielito children and their U.S. classmates became a justification for school leaders to segregate them in separate classrooms, only compounding their sense of isolation from their peer group.[37]

Between 1980 and 1981, even as Mariel refugees were being dispersed to makeshift facilities in Wisconsin, Pennsylvania, and Arkansas, more immediate hemispheric considerations compelled the U.S. government to rethink a well-established practice of allowing unlimited Cuban immigration. At the height of the Cold War in the 1960s, the argument that Cubans had been allowed unrestricted entry into the United States to protect their innocent children from communist indoctrination, oppression, and deprivation had resonated powerfully with the self-affirming belief that U.S. immigration laws and foreign policy were motivated by moral and humanitarian rather than strategic geopolitical concerns. However, during the 1980 Mariel exodus, the simultaneous influx of a wave of Haitian and Central American refugees brought into stark relief the diminishing foreign policy returns and the rising domestic cost of the continued deployment of the exilic politics of childhood. Given U.S. reluctance to provide asylum or assistance to a growing influx of impoverished and racially and culturally undesirable refugees, it quickly became apparent that, universal moral claims notwithstanding, the emotionally resonant discourses of childhood which had justified the government's embrace of anti-Castro Cubans would not bring a refugee policy that privileged the well-being of all children, regardless of their race, class, or national origin.

The federal government thus began to disinvest in the exile community's politics of childhood at exactly the moment that it struggled to explain the humanitarian calculus behind the deportation of hundreds of thousands of Central American refugees fleeing political violence at the hands of U.S.-allied regimes in El Salvador and Guatemala—especially when return often meant death or destitution.[38] Unable to assert historic claims about the defense of Cuban children without opening themselves to charges of situational morality and a racist immigration policy, U.S.

politicians and journalists downplayed exiles' insistence that Mariel refugees were political refugees who fled the island to protect their children, even as they insisted on categorizing Haitian, Salvadoran, Guatemalan, and even anticommunist Nicaraguan asylum seekers as economic migrants—in spite of the fact that many Nicaraguans requesting asylum in the United States did so because they feared that their children would be drafted into military service by the socialist Sandinista regime.[39]

Denied the preferential immigration status that first- and second-wave exiles had received, the Marielitos also provoked widespread public hostility because they did not meet the racial, political, or cultural expectations for Cuban refugees, expectations produced in the early 1960s by the coordinated campaign of the federal government and the exile community to stress the affinities between anti-Castro Cubans and Anglo-Americans. The working-class, mixed-race, and Afro-Cuban Mariel refugees did not reflect the early exile community's hard-earned white, middle-class image but rather revived earlier tendencies to associate Cubans with poor Latina/o immigrants and African Americans. Moreover, as products of revolutionary schools and youth organizations, the Marielitos lacked the first- and second-wave exiles' anticommunist political credentials. Arriving during a moment of heated public debate over language policy and bilingual education programs in local schools, this latest wave of refugees exacerbated a growing anti-Cuban backlash in Miami.[40]

Attempting to ease the hostility toward their newly arrived countrymen and -women—and by extension toward the entire Cuban American community—while justifying the continued need for Cubans' preferential immigration status, exile leaders and journalists sought to portray Marielitos through the interpretive lens provided by preexisting discourses of childhood. However, since a significant number of Marielitos were unmarried men who had no children or had left them on the island, it was difficult for exiles to assert the continuing relevance of the child-centered creation myth on which the community still relied to assuage Miami residents' concerns about their city's growing Cuban population. Mainstream America, distressed by the racial and class composition of the Marielitos, met claims that they were in fact political refugees with deep skepticism and responded to them in the same way as it did to other "undesirable" Caribbean and Central American immigrants.

Public outcry over the Mariel exodus awoke exiles to the limitations of the exilic politics of childhood, revealing their vulnerability to the vagaries of shifting U.S. foreign policy. It also reminded them that their acceptance by white Miamians had been hard-earned and remained conditional at best. Cuban Americans, who had long shunned involvement in U.S. domestic politics in order to dedicate their political energies entirely to the anti-Castro cause, began organizing to defend their community's interests in Miami. Throughout the 1980s, they naturalized in large numbers, launched a number of successful campaigns for municipal offices, and joined the Republican Party, which they viewed as taking a harder stance against communism. They also established the Cuban American National Foundation in 1981, organizing a powerful lobby in order to press for a greater federal government commitment to the anti-Castro cause.

A decade after the Mariel Boatlift, the politics of childhood in Havana and Miami were reshaped once again by the collapse of the U.S.S.R. In 1991, the Revolution suddenly lost the Soviet subsidies on which it had come to depend, resulting in a sudden and massive contraction of the Cuban economy that produced hunger and deprivation across the island. During the subsequent "Special Period," characterized by severe austerity measures, political restructuring, and social unrest, Cuban young people began to demonstrate unprecedented levels of disaffection from the Revolution, giving birth to a new and youth-centered culture of noncompliance, individualism, and materialism, as well as an upsurge in political dissent, human rights activism, and a return to the Christian and Afro-Cuban religious practices that had been effectively prohibited by the Revolution.[41] These phenomena, combined with the deterioration of the public health and school systems and diminishing access to postsecondary education, cast serious doubt on the Revolution's historic claims to a special relationship with young people, one of the foundations of the Castro regime's legitimacy.

On the other side of the Straits of Florida, the end of the Cold War dealt a death blow to exile efforts to use child-centered discourses and images to justify the preferential immigration policies that preserved their claims to being distinct from and superior to other ostensibly economic migrants. During the summer of 1994, when tens of thousands of Cubans took to the sea on homemade rafts or *balsas*, the U.S. government confronted a fourth wave of Cuban refugees. But these *balseros* had no strategic value to a U.S. government no longer engaged in a battle against international communism. Abandoning previous administrations' pretenses of humanitarian concern for Cuban children, President Bill Clinton reversed the thirty-five-year-old practice of allowing unrestricted entry to the United States to all Cubans fleeing Fidel Castro and instituted a policy that would intercept rafters at sea and transport them to U.S. Navy detention camps at Guantánamo Bay.

Stunned by this reversal, exiles sought to defend their unconditional right to asylum in the United States by resurrecting their child-centered creation myth. Miami Cubans turned once again to the media to expose the Revolution's ongoing victimization of innocent Cuban children and to remind the United States of its moral obligation, as leader of the free world, to provide shelter and protection to the island's young people. On October 15, 1994, the following letter appeared in the *Miami Herald*:

Dear Mr. President, Mrs. Clinton, and fellow Americans:

A scene I watched on television last week has been haunting me since. A young Cuban girl in the Guantanamo naval base had just learned to play "The Star Spangled Banner" on her only worldly possession—a violin. I was both spellbound and wretched by the irony of it all. There she was, surrounded by almost three thousand other children, behind barbed wire fences, yet still pursuing the ideal of liberty and justice for all. As a father, I know you understand, Mr. President, these children beseech you to open the doors of the land of the free.

PLEASE, MR. PRESIDENT, DON'T LET THESE CHILDREN DOWN.

Respectfully yours,

Dr. Manuel Rico Pérez and my six children

Pérez's pleas employed child-centered discourses that had moved previous generations of U.S. politicians and parents and remained central to the exile community's identity. However, in the more pragmatic post–Cold War era, they failed to influence the federal government's handling of the *balsero* crisis. Undeterred by the prospect of indefinite detention at Guantánamo, the rafters kept coming, until May 1995, when President Clinton announced that he would release the detainees and process them for entry to the United States. However, he announced, the United States would no longer accept unlimited numbers of refugees from the island. A newly established immigration quota, while generous in comparison with other Latin American quotas, would nonetheless require Cubans to apply for visas like other would-be entrants. Shocked exiles saw Clinton's actions as yet another betrayal by a Democratic administration that had gone soft on communism, repudiating U.S. values as well as the cause of Cuban liberation at the moment when the Castro regime was at its weakest.[42]

UNDERSTANDING ELIÁN: THE ENDURING POWER OF THE POLITICS OF CHILDHOOD

Since 1959, children consistently played a starring role in the newly established metanarratives of both revolutionary and exilic nationalism. Moreover, as Cubans on opposite sides of the Straits of Florida repeatedly took to the streets to assert or defend their competing nation-making projects, the prevalence of children in public demonstrations ensured that the politics of childhood remained fundamental to both the territorial and the diasporic nations' structures of feeling and *razónes de ser*. Less constant, however, was the response of the U.S. government and mainstream America to the evolving politics of childhood in Havana and Miami. By the middle of the 1990s, the limits of the politics of childhood in Havana and Miami were obvious to island and U.S.-resident Cubans alike. And then, on the eve of the new millennium, a small shipwrecked boy was rescued off the coast of Florida. Since his mother had died during the dangerous crossing from Cuba, he was taken to the home of his Miami relatives. The boy's name was Elián González.

Cuban leaders in Miami and Havana immediately mobilized, seeing in this traumatized orphan child the salvation of their frustrated nation-making projects. In Miami, Elián quickly became what Miguel de la Torre called "the poster child" of the exile community.[43] Cuban Americans of all ages came together to demand that Elián remain with his Miami relatives, where he would enjoy the maternal attention of his devoted cousin Marisleysis and the freedom his mother had died to give him. In Cuba, young Pioneers marched through the streets of cities and towns, carrying placards demanding that the boy be returned to his classroom, to his Camagüey home, and to his distraught father.

Elián provided an aging Fidel Castro with an undreamed-of opportunity to inflame public sentiment against the United States and the exile community and to rally support for his struggling socialist regime. Remaking the child into a symbol of the revolutionary nation's historic victimization at the hands of CIA-sponsored saboteurs and terrorists and almost forty years of economic embargo, Cuban officials and the media used Elián to rekindle support for a Revolution mortally wounded by the collapse of the Soviet Union.[44] However, not everyone was convinced. Declining to join the public demonstrations demanding the boy's return were an untold number of disaffected youth who saw the young *balsero*'s story in a different light and created a rallying cry of their own: "Elián, amigo! Queremos estar contigo! [Elián, friend! We want to be with you!]."[45]

In Miami, the child became a symbol of first- and second-wave exiles' continued sense of victimization by Castro, who had deprived them of their *patria*, their culture, their ancestral homes and extended families, and their dreams of being laid to rest in a free Cuba. The struggle for the child's destiny allowed older and politically intransigent exiles to reconcile with their politically diverse "Yuca" (Young Urban Cuban American) and

"ABC" (American-Born Cuban) children and grandchildren; it also offered younger Cuban Americans and their second- and third-generation sons and daughters a way to connect on a powerful emotional level with the community's child-centered creation myth, creating a climate of political unity and ethnic solidarity in Cuban Miami that had not been seen since the early 1960s.

Revolutionary and exile leaders' manipulation of the Elián custody battle was consistent with their historical use and abuse of children in pursuit of mutually antagonistic nation-making projects. The politics of childhood in Havana and Miami had nonetheless been irrevocably altered by the end of the Cold War and changing U.S. foreign policy priorities. In a strange reversal, Castro—who had once railed against the family as a bourgeois institution that impeded the socialist formation of children—had taken on the role of protector of traditional family values, arguing that international law and universal humanitarian norms demanded Elián's return to the loving care of his island-resident father and grandparents. And U.S. public opinion—which forty years earlier had shown overwhelming support for exiles' commitment to saving their children from communist indoctrination and oppression, even when it meant separating them from their families, as in the case of Operation Pedro Pan—now favored the child's repatriation.

An enraged exile community fought back, categorically rejecting Castro's oft-repeated claims that all he cared about were Elián's best interests. A group known as "Misión Elián" organized to testify to the Cuban government's deliberate policy of separating children from their families and to "unmask Fidel Castro's manipulation [of the custody battle] before the world." Understanding the Elián saga as the latest episode in their forty-year struggle to protect innocent Cuban children from Castro-communism, exiles staged demonstrations at Freedom Tower—the former home of the Cuban Refugee Center—in downtown Miami. Waving placards that read, "Castro Separates Families with Distance and with Death" and "These Children Are Hostages," group members called attention to the plight of hundreds of nameless Cuban boys and girls who had been denied permission to leave the island to be reunited with their parents in the United States.[46]

Miami's Spanish-language media also featured interviews with Cuban immigrants who had been forced to endure years of separation from their children. *El Nuevo Herald* told the story of Luís Grave de Peralta, a scientist who had arrived in the United States in 1996 and whose sons, four years later, were still in Cuba. Though twelve-year-old Gabriel and seven-year-old César both had U.S. immigrant visas, the Cuban government had yet to grant permission for their departure. Grave de Peralta called Castro's demands for Elián's return "totally hypocritical" and condemned his regime for presenting itself as the guardian of the integrity of the family, insisting that "there are hundreds of parents and children separated by the express will of that same government. . . . It's an act of calculated cruelty, to create conflicts and familial divisions."[47] Other Cuban American parents testified publicly to the Castro government's policy of family separation. Milagros Cruz, an exile woman whose nine-year-old daughter had also been denied permission to leave the island, staged a hunger strike to denounce the hypocrisy of demands for Elián's return while countless émigrés waited to be reunited with their own children.[48]

The exile community's politics of childhood now held little credibility outside Little Havana, however. Pleas that Elián be allowed to stay with his local family fell on deaf ears. In March 2000, Attorney General Janet Reno announced the Justice Department's ruling in favor of repatriation. The exile community organized to resist the court order, forming a human barricade around the home of Elián's great uncle Lázaro González. Cuban American celebrities, including Gloria Estefan and Andy García, joined the crowds that gathered outside Elián's home to express solidarity with the boy's suffering Miami relatives and an unceasing commitment, forty years later, to the child-centered creation myth that remained so central to Cuban Americans' collective identity. On Good Friday, demonstrators marched through Little Havana, chanting Catholic prayers and shouting anti-Castro slogans. They also staged a mock crucifixion symbolizing the shared martyrdom of Elián and the exile community.[49]

Increasingly confused and alienated by exiles' emotional protests, non-Cubans in Miami also organized counterdemonstrations that expressed white and black Miamians' shared resentment of exiles' growing economic and political power and their perceived proprietary attitude toward the city.[50] Those who retained a degree of sympathy for exiles nonetheless saw their passions as anachronistic, failing to understand the extent to which the Cuban American identity revolved around a politics of childhood that demanded the continuation of struggle, by any and all means possible, against the Castro regime. Characteristic U.S. historical amnesia perhaps explains this lack of empathy for a community whose children the U.S. government had long exploited in the pursuit of its Cold War goals; it nonetheless reveals a widespread willingness to disregard the priorities of a community of politically and economically privileged but still racially and culturally suspect immigrants who no longer fulfilled any instrumental purpose to the nation's foreign policy objectives.

Official impatience with the exile community was vividly expressed the morning that Elián was removed from the custody of his Miami relatives. Before dawn on April 22, Immigration and Naturalization Service agents stormed the home of Lázaro González and retrieved the boy at gunpoint. His removal under force of arms demonstrated both a profound disrespect for the exile community's sensibilities and a shocking disregard for the physical safety and emotional well-being of a five-year-old child. It also arguably reflected the Clinton administration's desire to discipline the exile community for defying a federal court order, thereby transgressing the bounds of a historically asymmetrical relationship that required Cuban Americans to earn their privilege and favor through public demonstrations of support for the U.S. government and its democratic-capitalist nation-making project.

Word of the raid on the González home spread like wildfire. Humiliated Cuban Americans took to the streets to express their fury, accusing the Clinton administration of betraying the very community that, for more than forty years, had been the federal government's most loyal supporter. Crowds carried placards declaring Bill Clinton a communist; Cuban flags flew all over the city, as did many U.S. flags—upside down. Businesses on Calle Ocho were shuttered. Bomb threats were issued, and one-third of students in Miami-Dade public schools stayed home from classes. Masses were said in Elián's name, and Miami's Cuban American faithful wept for the loss of the child.

On the island, tens of thousands of Cubans also took to the streets, joyfully hailing the return of the small boy who had been snatched from the jaws of the imperialist monster. Parades and ceremonies were organized, and Elián's first day back at school and his reunion with his jubilant classmates was televised across the nation. Photographs of Fidel Castro embracing the boy appeared in every newspaper. The Castro regime's troubled relationship with the island's young people was reinvigorated as the shipwrecked boy who had unwittingly come to symbolize all Cuban children—and indeed the nation itself—was reunited with the Revolution in the loving arms of the socialist *patria*.

In the aftermath of the battle for Elián, the González home in Miami was turned into a museum; the young *balsero's* bedroom—filled with toys, clothes, and gifts given to him by well-wishers—remains untouched, his shiny racing car bed neatly made and awaiting the boy's return. For many visitors, however, the humble Little Havana home is much more than a museum. It is instead a memorial to the lost innocence of all who have been victimized by Castro's Revolution, and a monument to the courage and self-sacrificing love of exile parents who have been willing to go to any lengths for their children. On the island, in Elián's hometown of Cárdenas, the revolutionary government established the "Museum of the Battle of Ideas" in July 2001 to commemorate its own version of the transnational custody struggle. The museum features a life-sized bronze statue of the small boy, clenched fist raised in defiance of his Miami captors.[51] The statue pays silent homage to an idealized vision of the island's children, militant in their rejection of the United States and fervent in dedication to the Revolution; it reminds all who see it of an aging regime's claims to legitimacy, embodied in its oft-repeated slogan, "La Revolución es para los niños."

DURING THE LAST DECADE, Elián has remained the subject of public scrutiny and debate on both sides of the Straits of Florida, most recently in 2008, when the fourteen-year-old boy joined Cuba's Union of Communist Youth.[52] Continued interest in Elián's life—not to mention his enduring ability to evoke grief, rage, patriotic pride, and even religious rapture—reveal the extent to which revolutionary and exilic Cubans understood the battle for the small *balsero* as the continuation of a fifty-year struggle, not only for the minds, bodies, and hearts of their children but also for the destiny of their nation.[53] However, this book demonstrates that the highly publicized custody battle was but the most recent manifestation of a politics of childhood that dates back at least to 1898, when José Martí inspired Cubans to wage a third and final war of independence against Spain on behalf of their sons and daughters, ensuring that children would remain at the heart of a century-long competition between competing Cuban nation-making projects.

Throughout the first half of the twentieth century, Cuban children played a starring role in the frustrated nationalist aspirations that propelled their island inexorably toward a second Revolution. During the pivotal year of 1959, the politics of childhood achieved a new prominence as Fidel Castro's provisional government worked to immediately alleviate the suffering of the island's neediest boys and girls, bolstering Castro's popularity and reinforcing the legitimacy of his leadership through the slogan "La Revolución es para los niños." In 1960, however, as dissenting voices began to be raised with more frequency in Cuba, Castro and his allies also began to use children to attack a still vibrant civil society. The revolutionary media took the lead in disseminating an increasingly hegemonic discourse of childhood that linked children's well-being to the survival of the Revolution and demonized its detractors for their supposed indifference to the island's youngest citizens, even as the Revolution accelerated its movement toward socialism and the pursuit of a strategic alliance with the Soviet Union. By 1961, new revolutionary initiatives sought to radicalize children and to use child-centered programs and policies—as well as the bodies of actual children—to advance broader political goals associated with the Revolution's rapid turn toward socialism.

This prompted the emergence of a U.S. and Catholic Church–supported Counterrevolution that similarly relied on symbolic and actual children in implementing its anti-Castro agenda. Children were also central to the exodus from the island to Miami between 1959 and 1962. Received with open arms by U.S. politicians and journalists who recognized the propaganda value of families fleeing "communist terror" on the island, the emergent exile community forged the child-centered anticommunist creation myth through which its members articulated their decision to emigrate, interacted with the federal and state agencies that oversaw their settlement, and secured their less-than-inevitable welcome by white Miamians. Children were also central to the anti-Castro movement's efforts to negotiate what became an asymmetrical relationship with the U.S. intelligence community and to unify a politically fragmented exile population around their struggle to liberate the island.

After the 1962 Missile Crisis, the politics of childhood that had propelled the Revolution and the formation of the southern Florida exile community between 1959 and 1962 continued to influence events in the Two Cubas. Now under Raúl Castro's leadership, the island regime continues to make deliberate use of symbolic and actual children to enforce a Manichaean view of the Revolution as a totalizing struggle between the forces of good and evil. Cuban exiles similarly continue to rely on their own understandings and practices of childhood to reinforce the epic myths of political terror and martyrdom, heroic exodus, and dreams of future return and redemption that sustain their displaced community.[54]

Interpreted in the light of this history, Elián's story is less exceptional than it first appears. In spite of the radical transformation of children's lives on both sides of the Straits of Florida since 1959, many of the understandings, practices, and representations of childhood in the Two Cubas remain largely consistent. This consistency stems from their common origins in metanarratives implicit in and essential to the founding of the territorial and diasporic nations—metanarratives that also underwrite the national histories of the United States and what remains of the socialist world and, more broadly, the nation-building projects that encompass so much of what we think of as modernity.

The transnational politics of Cuban childhood, in all its historical specificity and contingency, nonetheless reaffirms the enduring power of the child-as-nation-maker across time, ideological constructs, and territorial borders. But at what cost to actual children?

Much remains unknown about the ways that hundreds of thousands of flesh-and-blood Cuban and Cuban American children have been affected by their experiences as supporters or opponents of the Revolution, as refugees, and as members of the exile community in the United States. I hope future research will address the myriad questions raised but not answered by this study about the gap between representations of children and their lived experience. This gap, facilitated by children's limited political agency, voicelessness, and vulnerability, remains the most troubling aspect of the politics of childhood in both Havana and Miami. However, in light of conditions on the island, continuing revolutionary and exilic resistance to nonhegemonic versions of their history, and the U.S. government's slow progress in declassifying information about exiles and their children, answers to these questions may have to wait until processes of political opening and reconciliation take place on both sides of the Straits.[55]

In the meantime, Elián's story reminds us of the extent to which the minds, bodies, and hearts of Cuban and Cuban American children have been inscribed with the historical asymmetries of U.S.-Cuban relations, by the euphoria and terror of revolution, and by the pain and possibilities of exile. His story thus speaks poignantly to the ways successive generations of the island's children have been victimized in the name of nationalist politics. But it also offers silent testimony to the suffering of millions of nameless and voiceless boys and girls around the world, trapped in the political machinations of adults who have claimed, in a consistently cruel irony, to be acting in their best interests.

This book evokes their presence in the hopes that they will motivate us to historicize claims made about and on behalf of the future generations, and to adopt a more critical view of initiatives undertaken—with no disrespect to the memory of José Martí—"for the children." It looks to the ghostly figure of a five-year-old Elián González, doomed to forever drift between the physical and spiritual borders of the Two Cubas, to open the way toward a deeper understanding of the consequences of the politics of childhood, and to a critical reconsideration of the roles of nationalism and the nation-state in the world our children will inherit.

NOTES

INTRODUCTION

1. Quoted in Levander, *Cradle of Liberty*, 167.

2. Louis Pérez, *Cuba in the American Imagination*.

3. Bardach, *Cuba Confidential*, xvii; Torres, *In the Land of Mirrors*.

4. Portes, "Dilemmas of a Golden Exile." This imagining is changing as a result of recent middle-class South American migration to the United States.

5. Fagen, Brody, and O'Leary, *Cubans in Exile*; Lisandro Pérez, "Growing Up in Cuban Miami."

6. Llanes, *Cuban Americans*, ix; de la Torre, *La Lucha for Cuba*; Loescher and Scanlan, *Calculated Kindness*.

7. May, *Homeward Bound*; Weldes et al., *Cultures of Insecurity*.

8. Ariès, *Centuries of Childhood*.

9. Mitterauer and Sieder, *The European Family*; Shorter, *The Making of the Modern Family*; Stone, *The Family, Sex, and Marriage in England*; DeMause, *The History of Childhood*; Ozment, *Ancestors*.

10. Dillon, *The Gender of Freedom*, 145.

11. Cunningham, "Histories of Childhood"; Mintz, *Huck's Raft*; Fass and Mason, *Childhood in America*; Richardson, *The Century of the Child*.

12. Zahra, *Kidnapped Souls*; Zahra, "Lost Children"; Stargardt, *Witnesses of War*; Mickenberg, "The New Generation and the New Russia"; Gorsuch, "Soviet Youth and the Politics of Popular Culture during NEP."

13. Hecht, *Minor Omissions*; Premo, "How Latin America's History of Childhood Came of Age."

14. Kelley, *Learning to Stand and Speak*; Thorne, "Re-visioning Women and Social Change."

15. Stephens, *Children and the Politics of Culture*.

16. Louis Pérez, "The Imperial Design"; Louis Pérez, *On Becoming Cuban*.

17. Wald, *Children of Che*; Sutherland, *The Youngest Revolution*.

18. Bunck, *Fidel Castro and the Quest for a Revolutionary Culture in Cuba*; Medin, *Cuba*; Guerra, *Visions of Power in Cuba*, 317, 320.

19. Vicki Ruiz, *From out of the Shadows*; Briggs, *Reproducing Empire*.

20. Sánchez, *Becoming Mexican-American*; Alvarez, *The Power of the Zoot*.

21. San Miguel, *Brown, Not White*; Nieto, *Puerto Rican Students in U.S. Schools*.

22. Chávez, *The Latino Threat*.

23. María Cristina García, *Havana USA*; Masúd-Piloto, *From Welcomed Exiles to Illegal Immigrants*; Louis Pérez, "Cubans in Tampa"; Poyo, "*With All, and for the Good of All.*"

24. Pedraza-Bailey, *Political and Economic Migrants in America*; Pedraza, *Political Disaffection in Cuba's Revolution and Exodus*; Conde, *Operation Pedro Pan*; Triay, *Fleeing Castro*.

25. Torres, *The Lost Apple*.

26. Hunt, *Ideology and U.S. Foreign Policy*, 17; Eley, "Nationalism and Social History," 92, 104.

27. Polletta, *It Was Like a Fever*; Connerton, *How Societies Remember*; Samuel, *Past and Present in Contemporary Culture*; Zeruvabel, *Time Maps*; DeRojas, "*La Cubanía* in Exile."

28. Anderson, *Imagined Communities*; Wallerstein, *World Systems Analysis*; Ariès, *Centuries of Childhood*; Stephens, *Children and the Politics of Culture*, 6.

29. Anderson, *Imagined Communities*; Brubaker and Cooper, "Beyond 'Identity'"; Brubaker, *Nationalism Reframed*; Alonso, "The Politics of Space, Time and Substance."

30. Waldinger and Fitzgerald, "Transnationalism in Question."

31. Basch, Glick-Schiller, and Szanton Blanc, *Nations Unbound*; Lao-Montes and Dávila, *Mambo Montage*, 13; Duany, *The Puerto Rican Nation on the Move*, 4; Flores, *The Diaspora Strikes Back*.

32. Wimmer and Glick-Schiller, "Methodological Nationalism, the Social Sciences, and the Study of Migration."

33. Frederick, *Cuban-American Radio Wars*.

34. Scott, *Gender and the Politics of History*; Foucault, *History of Sexuality*.

35. Stuart Hall, "What Is This 'Black' in Black Popular Culture?," 111; Roediger, "The Pursuit of Whiteness," 590.

36. Guerra, *Visions of Power in Cuba*, 41–42.

37. *Revolución*, February 8, 1961, 1.

38. Torres, *The Lost Apple*, 2.

39. Zelizer, *Pricing the Priceless Child*; Marx, *The Early Economic and Philosophical Manuscripts*; Lenin, *On Youth*.

40. Magnússon, "The Singularization of History," 704.

41. Horowitz, *The Long Night of Dark Intent*; McGillivray, *Blazing Cane*.

42. Max Castro, "The Trouble with Collusion."

43. Rosen, *Empire and Dissent*; Peter Smith, *Talons of the Eagle*; Schoultz, *Beneath the United States*.

44. Gutiérrez, *The Columbia History of Latinos in the United States since 1960*.

CHAPTER 1

1. Martí, "Our America," 293.

2. José Martí, "Our Ideas," *Patria* (New York), March 14, 1892.

3. Dana, *To Cuba and Back*, 205, 268.

4. Manners, "Cuba," 15, 44.

5. Jacobson, *Barbarian Virtues*.

6. Ibid., 237–39; Louis Pérez, *Cuba in the American Imagination*, 95–174.

7. *New York Times*, August 1, 1898, 6.

8. Cabrera, *Cuba and the Cubans*, 272–73.

9. Levander, *Cradle of Liberty*, 166, 168.

10. Martí, "Our America," 293.

11. Levander, *Cradle of Liberty*, 167. The phrase "moral republicanism" is taken from the Manifesto of Montecristi, the statement of principles that would guide the third Cuban War of Independence. José Martí and General Máximo Gómez signed the manifesto on March 25, 1895.

12. Hagedorn, *Leonard Wood*, 371.

13. Epstein, "The Peril of Paternalism," 8, 9.

14. Ibid., 6–7.

15. Sutherland, *The Youngest Revolution*, 150; Epstein, "The Peril of Paternalism," 4, 7, 9.

16. Epstein, "The Peril of Paternalism," 4, 15.

17. Ibid., 10.

18. Gutiérrez-Boronat, "Cuban Exile Nationalism," 50–51.

19. Ibid., 51.

20. Platt, "The Solution of the Cuban Problem," 730.

21. Damián Fernández, "Cuba and *lo Cubano*," 80–82; Ferrer, "Rethinking Race and Nation in Cuba," 63.

22. Gutiérrez-Boronat, "Cuban Exile Nationalism," 44–46.

23. Ibarra Guitart, *El Tratado Anglo-Cubano de 1905*.

24. Pérez-Stable, *The Cuban Revolution*, 37; de la Fuente, *A Nation for All*, 10.

25. De la Fuente, *A Nation for All*, 10–13, 15, 46.

26. "Crimen por brujería?," *La Lucha*, July 26, 1906; "La brujería en La Habana," *La Lucha*, June 14, 1907; "Los crímenes de la brujería," *La Lucha*, March 20, 1910, quoted in Palmié, *Wizards and Scientists*, 214–25; Helg, *Our Rightful Share*, 107–16, 238–39.

27. Betancourt, *Doctrina negra*, 13, 78.

28. Dye and Sicotte, "U.S.-Cuban Trade Cooperation and Its Unraveling."

29. Epstein, "The Peril of Paternalism"; Louis Pérez, "Incurring a Debt of Gratitude."

30. Louis Pérez, *On Becoming Cuban*, 230.

31. Ibid., 251–52.

32. *Commercial Appeal*, September 27, 1915, 6; *Havana Post*, September 28, 1915, 2; quoted in Louis Pérez, "Incurring a Debt of Gratitude," 383–84.

33. De Leuchsenring, *Cuba no debe su independencia a los Estados Unidos*.

34. Ortíz, *La decadencia cubana*, 6.

35. Bailey, *Report: Education in Cuba*.

36. Agustín Tamargo, "Quien injuria a Martí y a Maceo no puede ser amigo de Cuba," *Bohemia*, August 26, 1956, 49–50. See also Louis Pérez, "Incurring a Debt of Gratitude."

37. Phillips, *White Elephants in the Caribbean*, 129; quoted in Louis Pérez, *Cuba in the American Imagination*, 206.

38. Torres, *The Lost Apple*, 38; *Constitución de la República de Cuba, 1940*, in de la Cuesta, *Constituciones cubanas desde 1812 hasta nuestros días*.

39. Marinello, *La cuestión racial en la Constitución*, 18.

40. Marinello, "La Constitución cubana y la enseñanza privada."

41. Louis Pérez, *On Becoming Cuban*, 400.

42. Torres, *The Lost Apple*, 38.

43. Truslow, *Report on Cuba*, 404.

44. Lugris y Beceiro, *Los problemas de la niñez actual*, 17.

45. Louis Pérez, *On Becoming Cuban*, 177, 287.

46. O'Brien, *The Revolutionary Mission*.

47. Louis Pérez, *On Becoming Cuban*, 177, 287.

48. Ibid., 76, 257, 275, 285.

49. Lugris y Beceiro, *Los problemas de la niñez actual*, 32.

50. Louis Pérez, *On Becoming Cuban*, 474–76.

51. Matthews, *Revolution in Cuba*, 181.

52. Quoted in Chadwick, *Cuba Today*, 55.

53. Torres, *The Lost Apple*, 38.

CHAPTER 2

1. Masúd-Piloto, *From Welcomed Exiles to Illegal Immigrants*, 32.

2. De la Campa, *Cuba on My Mind*, 26.

3. Pedraza, *Political Disaffection in Cuba's Revolution and Exodus*, 71.

4. Amaro, "Mass and Class in the Origins of the Cuban Revolution"; Pedraza, *Political Disaffection in Cuba's Revolution and Exodus*, 36.

5. Bonachea and Valdés, *Cuba in Revolution*.

6. After Castro's failed attack on the Moncada barracks in 1953, the archbishop of Santiago, Monseñor Enrique Pérez Serantes, interceded on his behalf with the Batista dictatorship, saving him from a death sentence. On the relationship between Fidel Castro and *Bohemia* magazine, see also Guerra, *Visions of Power in Cuba*, 42.

7. *Revolución*, February 16, 1959.

8. Jorge I. Domínguez, "Crisis in Central America 2: Castro's Challenge," *FrontLine News*, PBS, April 10, 1985; Pedraza, *Political Disaffection in Cuba's Revolution and Exodus*, 49, 59.

9. *Revolución*, February 25, 1959, 4.

10. Fidel Castro, *Pensamiento de Fidel Castro*, 5.

11. *Revolución*, September 17, 1959, 1; October 14, 1959, 1; October 15, 1959.

12. Federación de Mujeres Cubanas, *Nada hay más importante que un niño*, 62, 70.

13. Pedraza, *Political Disaffection in Cuba's Revolution and Exodus*, 56, 57, 64.

14. Ibid., 58.

15. "Un influyente batistiano, preso por realizar actos criminales de hechicería," *Hoy*, January 29, 1959, 2.

16. Guerra, *Visions of Power in Cuba*, 81; *Bohemia*, November 8, 1959, 19.

17. Pedraza, *Political Disaffection in Cuba's Revolution and Exodus*, 59, 60.

18. A *caballería* was about 33 acres; properties of less than 5,000 acres were not initially nationalized.

19. Pedraza, *Political Disaffection in Cuba's Revolution and Exodus*, 64.

20. *Revolución*, September 19, 1959, 12; September 30, 1959, 8.

21. Torreira Crespo and Buajasán Marrawi, *Operación Pedro Pan*, 42.

22. *BBC World News*, July 20, 1959.

23. Matos, *Cómo llegó la noche*, 325–52; Pedraza, *Political Disaffection in Cuba's Revolution and Exodus*, 62–63. It should be noted that Fidel Castro was not a member or ally of the prerevolutionary Partido Socialista Popular.

24. *Bohemia*, November 8, 1959, 64.

25. *Bohemia*, November 29, 1959, 51, 132.

26. *Bohemia*, November 8, 1959, 74.

27. Ibid., 45.

28. *Bohemia*, November 1, 1959, 90.

29. *Bohemia*, November 29, 1959.

30. *Bohemia*, December 20, 1959, 69.

31. Brinton, *The Anatomy of Revolution*.

CHAPTER 3

1. Quiroz, "The Evolution of Laws Regulating Associations and Civil Society in Cuba," 18; Damián Fernández, "Cuba and *lo Cubano*," 82–83; Keane, *Civil Society*; Fraser, "Rethinking the Public Sphere"; Skocpol and Fiorina, "Making Sense of the Civic Engagement Debate."

2. Suárez, *Cuba*, viii.

3. Guerra, "'To Condemn the Revolution Is to Condemn Christ,'" 74; Draper, *Castro's Revolution*; Llerena, *The Unsuspected Revolution*; Montaner, *Fidel Castro and the Cuban Revolution*; Paterson, *Contesting Castro*; Pérez-Stable, *The Cuban Revolution*, 61–75; Farber, *The Origins of the Cuban Revolution Reconsidered*.

4. Guerra, "'To Condemn the Revolution Is to Condemn Christ,'" 76; "Ministerio de Hacienda: Honradez con honradez se paga"; "Informe al pueblo: Colecta de la libertad: $2.111.628,94," *Bohemia*, July 5, 1959, 74–77; Antonio Nuñez Jiménez, "Dos años de reforma agraria," *Bohemia*, May 8, 1961, 37.

5. "There's a Warm Sun and an Ocean of Foam," *Havana Post*, July 4, 1959; "$7 Million Earmarked for Rural Cuban Schools," *Havana Post*, July 7, 1959.

6. "3,000 camas para niños son necesarias en los hospitales," *Diario de la Marina*, September 30, 1959, 12.

7. Quiroz, "Martí in Cuban Schools."

8. "Julio Lobo Announces Country School Plan," *Havana Post*, September 20, 1959, 3.

9. *Diario de la Marina*, September 25, 1959, 13.

10. "Moa Bay Mining Company Builds Public School in Oriente Town," *Havana Post*, September 24, 1959, 10.

11. "Una gran obra de acción social católica: El Colegio Salesiano 'Don Bosco' de Guanabacoa," *Diario de la Marina*, September 17, 1959.

12. "La actualidad: La reforma de la enseñanza," *Diario de la Marina*, September 18, 1959, 4.

13. *Bohemia,* November 8, 1959, 133.

14. Pedraza, *Political Disaffection in Cuba's Revolution and Exodus,* 56, 57, 64.

15. "El día de la Juventud Católica Cubana en La Habana," *Diario de la Marina,* September 29, 1959, 17.

16. Gervasio G. Ruiz, "Una cruz gigantesca arderá sobre La Habana," *Carteles,* November 22, 1959, 30.

17. Guerra, "'To Condemn the Revolution Is to Condemn Christ'"; Crahan, "Salvation through Christ or Marx," 161; U.S. House of Representatives, "International Relations" (testimony of Margaret E. Crahan).

18. *Bohemia,* November 8, 1959, 103.

19. "Los niños y la Navidad," *Bohemia,* November 11, 1959, 75, 86.

20. *Hoy,* January 10, 1960, 10.

21. "Navidades en Cuba Libre!," *Bohemia,* December 20, 1959.

22. *Bohemia,* December 20, 1959, 51.

23. *Hoy,* January 3, 1960, 1.

24. *Hoy,* January 5, 1960, 5.

25. *Hoy,* January 7, 1960, 7.

26. *Revolución,* January 5, 1961, 4.

27. *Hoy,* January 5, 1960, 1.

28. *Hoy,* January 9, 1960, 7.

29. Ramonet and Castro, *Fidel Castro.*

30. *Hoy,* January 3, 1960, 4.

31. "Con tres mil nuevas escuelas se aumenta a siete mil el número de las creadas," *Hoy,* February 17, 1960.

32. "Convertido en centro escolar el Cuartel Goicuria," *Revolución,* May 2, 1960, 18; García Gallo, "Educar."

33. *Bohemia,* January 8, 1960.

34. See "Campesinos de Guantánamo hacen sus propias escuelas," *Hoy,* February 4, 1959; and "Escuela concedida," *Bohemia,* November 8, 1959, 133.

35. "A los profesores, estudiantes y empleados de la Universidad de La Habana," *Revolución,* July 2, 1959, 8.

36. The newspaper was subsequently reestablished in exile in Miami but ceased publication there after little more than a year.

37. *Hoy,* January 29, 1960, 4.

38. "En Jesús de Miramar," "El suceso de la Catedral," and "Los detenidos," *Información,* July 19, 1960; "Al pueblo cubano," *Juventud Obrera,* September 1960, 2.

39. "Declaraciones del Episcopado cubano," *Juventud Obrera,* September 1960, 9.

40. See *Juventud Obrera,* June 1960, 15; and "Actividades jocistas," *Juventud Obrera,* April 1960, 5.

41. "Es cristiana la revolución social que se está verificando en Cuba?," *La Quincena,* October 30, 1960, 3, 33.

42. The accusation of Francoist sympathies was one of Castro's most damning condemnations of the Church. However, for every Francoist priest who ministered to a Cuban congregation, another had fled Spain during or after the Civil War, fearing that

his loyalty to the Socialist Republic marked him for execution. Guerra, "'To Condemn the Revolution Is to Condemn Christ,'" 104–5.

43. "En Cuba," *Bohemia*, December 11, 1960.

CHAPTER 4

1. This book takes the position that the Revolution's socialist turn was less a response to U.S. hostility and more the necessary precursor to Fidel Castro's efforts to forge ties with the U.S.S.R. According to this perspective, Castro moved to the left to secure Soviet support as a means of consolidating his personal power and in order to propel a radical remaking of Cuban society far exceeding anything envisioned by the insurgent anti-Batista coalition. Soviet support also facilitated his goal of exporting revolution throughout Latin America—and later to the developing nations of Asia and Africa. See Suárez, *Cuba*, vii–x.

2. "Del Cté. de las Organizaciones Juveniles de la U.R.S.S. a la juventud socialista," *Hoy*, January 1, 1960.

3. *Hoy*, February 11, 1960.

4. Nicolás Guillén, "Visita extraordinaria," *Hoy*, February 14, 1960, 2.

5. Guerra, *Visions of Power in Cuba*, 109–17.

6. Monahan and Gilmore, "How the Kremlin Took Cuba," 5.

7. Conde, *Operation Pedro Pan*, 16.

8. Ministerio de Relaciones Exteriores, "Trabajo, estudio y fusil," *Boletín Cultural*, January/February 1961, 6.

9. Quoted in Louis Pérez, "Incurring a Debt of Gratitude," 395.

10. *Revolución*, January 4, 1961, 6.

11. *Revolución*, January 6, 1961, 17.

12. *Revolución*, January 18, 1961.

13. "Niños de Leningrado se dirigen a Fidel," *Revolución*, February 3, 1961, 16.

14. "Discurso pronunciado en el acto de clausura de la Plenaría Nacional de Secretarios Generales de Sindicatos sobre los Círculos Sociales Obreros y Círculos Infantiles," *Revolución*, December 17, 1960.

15. "En manos de los profesores, como en las manos del pueblo, está el porvenir de la Revolución," *Revolución*, February 6, 1961, 6.

16. *Revolución*, February 6, 1961, 6.

17. Ibid., 6.

18. *Bohemia*, January 8, 1961.

19. Sutherland, *The Youngest Revolution*, 114.

20. Ibid., 119.

21. "Ha conquistado el derecho a la educación la juventud," *Revolución*, February 27, 1961, 7.

22. *Revolución*, February 27, 1961, 7.

23. Federación de Mujeres Cubanas, *Nada hay más importante que un niño*, 84; Guerra, *Visions of Power in Cuba*, 161–62.

24. *Alfabeticemos*; Guerra, *Visions of Power in Cuba*, 83.

25. *Revolución*, February 27, 1961, 7.

26. *Revolución*, February 1, 1961.

27. Sutherland, *The Youngest Revolution*, 36.

28. Julián Iglesias, "Jóvenes patriotas salvan una escuela," *Verde Olivo*, February 26, 1961, 15.

29. Pérez Serantes, *La voz de la iglesia en Cuba*, 135–41.

30. *La Quincena*, November 30, 1960, 9, 43–44, 48.

31. Torreira Crespo and Buajasán Marrawi, *Operación Pedro Pan*, 35.

32. Ibid., 26.

33. Ibid., 26, 91–92, 94.

34. Guerra, *Visions of Power in Cuba*, 212–13; Dewart, *Cuba, Church and Crisis*, 160.

35. Torreira Crespo and Buajasán Marrawi, *Operación Pedro Pan*, 93.

36. *Revolución*, December 26, 1960, 1.

37. Conde, *Operation Pedro Pan*, 26.

38. "Cómo fue el crimen," *Verde Olivo*, March 12, 1961; *Bohemia*, March 5, 1961, 73; *Verde Olivo*, March 19, 1961, 72–73; *Hoy*, March 1, 1961.

39. Speech by Fidel Castro, March 4, 1961, reprinted in *Verde Olivo*, March 19, 1961, 42–43.

40. *Revolución*, February 27, 1961, 7.

41. Quoted in Torreira Crespo and Buajasán Marrawi, *Operación Pedro Pan*, 51–52.

42. *Revolución*, April 12, 1961, 8.

43. *Bohemia*, April 2, 1961, 32–34; *Verde Olivo*, April 2, 1961, 48–49.

44. "Asesinado un niño por un grupo contrarevolucionario," *Revolución*, December 12, 1960, 1, 8; "Grave el niño balaceado por esbirros en el avión," *Revolución*, October 31, 1960, 1, 8; "Ante el brutal acto de Flogar," *Revolución*, December 28, 1960, 1, 12.

45. Walsh, "Cuban Refugee Children," 384; Torres, *The Lost Apple*, 58.

46. Harold H. Martin, "Angry Exiles in Florida, *Saturday Evening Post*, April 8, 1961, Theodore Draper Papers, Box 1, Envelope 5, Hoover Institution Archives.

47. "We Who Tried," *Life*, May 10, 1963, 69.

48. Bunck, *Fidel Castro and the Quest for a Revolutionary Culture in Cuba*.

49. Sanche de Gramont, "Red Mess in Cuba—III . . . And the Young Beginning," *New York Herald Tribune*, September 11, 1963, Theodore Draper Papers, Box 17, Envelope 15, Hoover Institution Archives.

50. Tad Szulc, "Castro's Regime Moves to Solidify Links to Soviets," *New York Times*, April 30, 1961.

51. "Foreign Relations: Grand Illusion," *Time*, April 28, 1961, 21, Theodore Draper Papers, Box 9, Folder D14, Hoover Institution Archives.

52. Tad Szulc, "Castro's Regime Moves to Solidify Links to Soviets"; "Castro Rules Out Elections in Cuba," *New York Times*, May 2, 1961.

53. Torreira Crespo and Buajasán Marrawi, *Operación Pedro Pan*, 60–61.

54. Ibid., 63.

55. Grau Alsina and Ridderhof, *Mongo Grau*, 137.

CHAPTER 5

1. Louis Pérez, "Cubans in Tampa"; Poyo, *"With All, and for the Good of All."*

2. Boswell and Curtis, *The Cuban-American Experience*, 39–41.

3. José Yglesias, "The Radical Latino Island in the Deep South," *Nuestro* 1 (1977): 1–10.

4. Ingalls, *Urban Vigilantes in the New South*; Gene Burnett, "Death and Terror Scar Tampa's Past," *Florida Trend* 18 (1975): 76–80.

5. Olson and Olson, *Cuban Americans*, 43.

6. Ibid., 44.

7. Ibid., 43.

8. Ibid., 39.

9. Ibid., 39. Others estimate that as few as 10,000 to 12,000 Cubans lived in the greater Miami area just prior to the 1959 Revolution. Boswell and Curtis, *The Cuban-American Experience*, 71–74.

10. Boswell and Curtis, *The Cuban-American Experience*, 71–74; Dunn, *Black Miami in the Twentieth Century*, 320.

11. *Diario las Américas*, January 1, 1959, 4; January 7, 1959, 4; March 29, 1959, 5.

12. Olson and Olson, *Cuban Americans*, 40–41.

13. Ibid., 47.

14. Winsberg, "Housing Segregation of a Predominantly Middle-Class Population."

15. Ramos García, *Operation Wetback*; Gutiérrez, *Walls and Mirrors*; Ngai, *Impossible Subjects*.

16. Loescher and Scanlan, *Calculated Kindness*.

17. Duany, *Blurred Borders*.

18. Elliston, *Psywar on Cuba*, 15–22.

19. Ibid., 81–82, 105.

20. *U.S. News and World Report*, March 21, 1960; *New York Times*, June 8, 1960.

21. Walsh, "Cuban Refugee Children"; U.S. Senate Committee of the Judiciary, "Cuban Refugee Problems."

22. Walsh, "Cuban Refugee Children"; "Cuban Refugees," *New York Times*, February 4, 1961, 1; U.S. Senate Committee of the Judiciary, "Cuban Refugee Problems."

23. The "first wave" of Cuban refugees, arriving between January 1959 and October 1962, totaled approximately 280,000; Batista-aligned exiles represented slightly less than 10 percent of this total. Llanes, *Cuban Americans*, 8.

24. Pedraza, *Political Disaffection in Cuba's Revolution and Exodus*, 62–63.

25. Boswell and Curtis, *The Cuban-American Experience*, 71–78.

26. U.S. Department of Health, Education, and Welfare, "Cuban Refugee Program."

27. Boswell and Curtis, *The Cuban-American Experience*, 45–47, 71–78; María Cristina García, *Havana USA*, 15.

28. Eire, *Learning to Die in Miami*, 17, 99–100.

29. "Effects of the Cuban Situation on the Economic and Social Life of Dade County, Florida," 6; Miguel González-Pando, "Interview with Cuban-American Banker and Community Leader Luís Botifoll," in González-Pando, *The Cuban Americans*, 35.

30. De la Torre, *La Lucha for Cuba*, 34.

31. Scholars disagree about how Anglo-Americans perceived first-wave Cuban exiles. José Llanes asserts not only that first-wave Cubans were white but that they were unequivocally recognized as such by Anglo-Americans. In contrast, Cheris Brewer

Current argues that Cuban exiles' anticommunism, whiteness, and middle-class attributes were strategically broadcast by the U.S. government and media in order to secure support for refugees throughout the 1960s and 1970s. However, Current's assertion that Cuban exiles occupied a variety of socioeconomic, racial, and political positions overstates the diversity of first- and second-wave exiles. Miguel de la Torre acknowledges the problems of ethnic discrimination in housing and employment but insists that the social class of exiles spared them from the minority status of other Latina/os. Llanes, *Cuban Americans*, 29–30; Brewer Current, "Normalizing Cuban Refugees"; de la Torre, *La Lucha for Cuba*, 34–36.

32. "Cuban Refugees in Florida."

33. Ibid.

34. Eire, *Learning to Die in Miami*, 133–53.

35. Pérez-Firmat, *Next Year in Cuba*, 54–55.

36. Alvarez, *The Power of the Zoot*.

37. *Bohemia*, November 29, 1959, 51, 132; José Montes Q., "Discriminan a portorriqueños en N.Y.," *El Avance*, February 24, 1961, 12; "Effects of the Cuban Situation on the Economic and Social Life of Dade County, Florida."

38. "Practical Patriotism," *Waltham (MA) News-Tribune*, January 15, 1962; *Public Information Activities Report, Cuban Refugee Center, Miami*.

39. *El Avance*, November 11, 1960, 9.

40. Joe Hall, *The Cuban Refugee in the Public Schools of Dade County, Florida: A Report Covering the Period from Early 1960 to December 1961*.

41. Levine and Asís, *Cuban Miami*, 24; José del Cueto, "La unidad hay que practicarla," *El Avance*, August 25, 1961, 24.

42. "Cuban Refugees," *New York Times*, February 4, 1961, 1.

43. Foster, "Immediate Recommendations for Establishing the Work of the Cuban Refugee Center in the Minds of the General Public."

44. Brewer Current, "Normalizing Cuban Refugees," 63.

45. Cuban Refugee Center Collection 0218 (Series 6, Box 43, Folders 28, 30, 34, and 35; Box 44, Folder 91, CHC, University of Miami Otto G. Richter Library); Cuban Refugee Center, "Nine Points Mission Statements."

46. Cuban Refugee Center Collection 0218 (Series 6, Box 44, Folder 86, CHC, University of Miami Otto G. Richter Library).

47. Jim Fontaine, "Why Castro Asphyxiates Catholic Education," original source of publication unknown, reprinted as "Por qué Castro asfixia a la educación de tipo católico," *El Avance*, March 3, 1961, 45.

48. Tad Szulc, "Castro's Regime Moves to Solidify Links to Soviet," *New York Times*, April 30, 1961; "Foreign Relations: Grand Illusion," *Time*, April 28, 1961, 21, Theodore Draper Papers, Box 9, Folder D14, Hoover Institution Archives.

49. *El Avance*, June 2, 1961, 17.

50. *El Avance*, February 10, 1961, 48.

51. *El Avance*, May 19, 1961, 18–19.

52. "Our Cuban Visitors," *Miami Herald*, February 9, 1961.

53. *El Avance*, February 24, 1961.

54. Honig, "Immigrant America?," 3.

55. Max Castro, "The Trouble with Collusion."

56. Dunn, *Black Miami in the Twentieth Century*, 319–20.

CHAPTER 6

1. Llanes, *Cuban Americans*, 8.

2. De la Torre, *La Lucha for Cuba*, 34; Díaz Briquets and Pérez, *Cuba*, 26.

3. De la Torre, *La Lucha for Cuba*, 105–6.

4. Fagen, Brody, and O'Leary, *Cubans in Exile*, 51; O'Leary, "Cubans in Exile," 33.

5. María Cristina García, *Havana USA*, 3.

6. Olson and Olson, *Cuban Americans*, 56.

7. Louis Pérez, *Cuba in the American Imagination*, 239.

8. Ibid., 241.

9. Llanes, *Cuban Americans*, 66–67.

10. Arguelles, "Cuban Miami," 31.

11. Ibid.

12. Schoultz, *That Infernal Little Cuban Republic*, 151.

13. Elliston, *Psywar on Cuba*, 60.

14. Louis Pérez, *Cuba in the American Imagination*, 241.

15. Schoultz, *That Infernal Little Cuban Republic*, 147.

16. Arguelles, "Cuban Miami," 32.

17. "Castro Building Drab Red State as Internal Opposition Falters," *New York Times*, July 21, 1963, 1, 7.

18. Schoultz, *That Infernal Little Cuban Republic*, 148.

19. Solomon, *Breaking Up with Cuba*, 203.

20. Elliston, *Psywar on Cuba*, 47.

21. Schoultz, *That Infernal Little Cuban Republic*, 157–58.

22. Ibid., 159.

23. Quoted in Gutierrez-Boronat, "Cuban Exile Nationalism," 119.

24. *Patria*, January 17, 1961, 2.

25. *El Avance*, May 12, 1961, 3.

26. Ernesto Montaner, "Memorandum al State Department: Rusia a 90 millas de Estados Unidos," *Patria* (Miami), January 24, 1961, 1.

27. *Patria* was a socially and politically conservative newspaper believed to be supported by Batistianos. However, aware that most exiles wanted nothing to do with Batista-aligned Cubans, *Patria* denied any relationship with the former dictator. "La toga verde olivo," *Patria* (Miami), May 13, 1960, 1; Arguelles, "Cuban Miami," 38.

28. "Inevitable la guerra en Cuba," *Patria* (Miami), May 24, 1960, 1.

29. "Las patrullas juveniles," *El Avance*, July 8, 1960, 2.

30. *El Avance*, September 2, 1960, 6.

31. Solomon, *Breaking Up with Cuba*, 189.

32. Armando Garcia Sifredo, "Magdalena," *Patria* (Miami), September 27, 1960, 2.

33. "Entrenando niños como espías," *El Avance*, October 21, 1960, 9.

34. *El Avance*, October 21, 1960, 8.

35. "Por qué mataron al 'maestro rural,'" *El Avance*, February 10, 1961, 2.

36. *El Avance*, February 10, 1961, 2; Armando García Mendoza, "La tiranía de Castro y la enseñanza cívica en Cuba," *El Avance*, February 17, 1961, 27.

37. *El Avance*, March 25, 1961, 9.

38. "Otra derrota que sufre Castro," *El Avance*, March 17, 1961.

39. Armando García Sifredo, "América cómplice," *Patria* (Miami), March 14, 1961, 2.

40. Armando García Sifredo, "Ahora, las balas," *Patria* (Miami), April 18, 1961, 2.

41. *El Avance*, May 12, 1961, 1.

42. *El Avance*, June 30, 1961, 12.

43. "Mueren niños en Matanzas por falta de antibióticos," *El Avance*, August 4, 1961.

44. Gutierrez-Boronat, "Cuban Exile Nationalism," 128–30.

45. "Invitan los educadores," *Patria* (Miami), January 17, 1961, 2.

46. "Por la patria: Por la escuela," *Patria* (Miami), February 21, 1961, 3.

47. *Cuban Revolutionary Council.*

48. "Intensa labor patriótica realiza la sección femenina de 'Rescate,'" *El Avance*, April 21, 1961.

49. "Damas cubanas reclaman ayuda," *Patria* (Miami), May 2, 1961, 5.

50. *El Avance*, May 5, 1961, 6, 7.

51. *El Avance*, May 19, 1961, 14–15.

52. "Misa solemne en Bayfront Park el Día Panamericano," *El Avance*, April 28, 1961, 10; "Oraciones y lágrimas por los que cayeron," *El Avance*, May 5, 1961, 1; *El Avance*, May 5, 1961, 4, 9.

53. Olson and Olson, *Cuban Americans*, 57; González-Pando, *The Cuban Americans*, 28.

54. *El Avance*, May 26, 1961, 9.

55. *El Avance*, April 6, 1962, 39.

56. *El Avance*, March 30, 1962, 38.

57. Provisional Executive of Cruzada Educativa Cubana, "Mensaje al pueblo cubano."

58. *Patria* (Miami), November 23, 1962, 2.

59. "El mejor comentario del exilio," *Patria* (Miami), December 7, 1962, 2.

60. Gutierrez-Boronat, "Cuban Exile Nationalism," 128–30.

EPILOGUE

1. Bunck, *Fidel Castro and the Quest for a Revolutionary Culture in Cuba*, xi, 2–7.

2. Quiroz, "Martí in Cuban Schools," 79.

3. Leiner, *Children Are the Revolution*, 15; see also Wald, *Children of Che*.

4. Paulston, "Education," 387; Quiroz, "Martí in Cuban Schools," 79; Guerra, *Visions of Power in Cuba*, 239.

5. Hamilton, *Sexual Revolutions in Cuba*, 31, 81.

6. Guerra, *Visions of Power in Cuba*, 175, 205, 216–18.

7. Ibid., 258, 260, 264.

8. Ibid., 239.

9. Leiner, *Sexual Politics in Cuba*, 33–34; Guerra, *Visions of Power in Cuba*, 190.

10. Salas, "Juvenile Delinquency in Post-revolutionary Cuba"; Guerra, *Visions of Power in Cuba*, 195, 262–63.

11. Leiner, *Sexual Politics in Cuba*, 33; Hamilton, *Sexual Revolutions in Cuba*, 32–37; Guerra, *Visions of Power in Cuba*, 252.

12. Olson and Olson, *Cuban Americans*, 64–65; James T. Peterson, "The Cuban Refugees in Dade County," February 18, 1963; Joe Hall, *The Cuban Refugee in the Public Schools of Dade County, Florida: Supplementary Report Covering the Period January–October 1962*.

13. Mackey and Beebe, *Bilingual Schools for a Bicultural Community*, 6, 59.

14. Joe Hall, *The Cuban Refugee in the Public Schools of Dade County, Florida: Supplementary Report Covering the Period January–October 1962*.

15. Ibid.

16. "'Remarkable Adjustments' by Cuban Students Are Reported."

17. San Miguel, *Contested Policy*; MacDonald, *Latino Education in the United States*.

18. Louis Pérez, *On Becoming Cuban*, 502.

19. Arboleya, "The Cuban Colony."

20. Espinosa, *Símbolos, fechas y biografías*; Gutierrez-Boronat, "Cuban Exile Nationalism," 128.

21. Gómez Carbonell, "Informe rendido por la secretaría de organización de 'Cruzada Educativa Cubana.'"

22. "Address by Tuduri to the 10th Anniversary of the Cruzada"; "Asamblea General 29 de septiembre 1966."

23. Gómez Carbonell, "Informe rendido por la secretaría de organización de 'Cruzada Educativa Cubana'"; Gómez Carbonell, "Establecimiento de delegaciones de 'C.E.C.' en capitales de E.U.A. y países latino-americanos."

24. Cauce and Gómez Carbonell, "Letter"; "Address by Tuduri to the 10th Anniversary of the Cruzada."

25. Casados, "Cuban Culture."

26. Arboleya, "The Cuban Colony."

27. Lipset, *The First New Nation*, 18; quoted in Bunck, *Fidel Castro and the Quest for a Revolutionary Culture in Cuba*, 1; de La Torre, *La Lucha for Cuba*, 31–33.

28. Harrison, "Changes in Feminine Role"; U.S. Department of Labor, *Manpower Report of the President*; Rogg, *The Assimilation of Cuban Exiles*, 82, 178.

29. Gil, "The Assimilation and Problems of Adjustment to the American Culture of One Hundred Cuban Refugee Adolescents Attending Catholic and Public High Schools in Union City and West New York, New Jersey."

30. Torres, *The Lost Apple*, 15–16.

31. Bunck, *Fidel Castro and the Quest for a Revolutionary Culture in Cuba*, 11; Guerra, *Visions of Power in Cuba*, 305.

32. The expression "Our youth is lost" circulated widely among disaffected young people during the 1970s. *Granma Weekly Review*, May 6, 1990, 12, and September 23, 1990, 12.

33. Olson and Olson, *Cuban Americans*, 64–65.

34. Pete Mann, "U.S. Foots Cuban School Bill: Hall Orders 300 Children Admitted," *Miami Herald*, November 23, 1965; "And Other Cuban School Costs?," *Miami Herald*, November 25, 1965; Pete Mann, "Battle Brewing on Paying for Exile Students," *Miami Herald*, December 19, 1965; "School Aid Talks Due in Dade," *Miami Herald*, December 23, 1965; Louise Blanchard, "U.S. School Funds for Exiles Argued," *Miami News*, January 6, 1966.

35. "Exiles in Miami Still Need Aid," *Miami Herald*, February 9, 1965.

36. Egerton, *Cubans in Miami*, 4–5, 10–11.

37. Eckstein, *The Immigrant Divide*, 45; Macdonald, *Latino Education in the United States*, 204–7.

38. María Cristina García, *Seeking Refuge*, 114, 118, 162.

39. Masúd-Piloto, *From Welcomed Exiles to Illegal Immigrants*, 121.

40. Dunn, *Black Miami in the Twentieth Century*, 321.

41. John Newhouse, "A Reporter at Large: Socialism or Death," *New Yorker*, April 27, 1992, 52–83.

42. Masúd-Piloto, *From Welcomed Exiles to Illegal Immigrants*, 143.

43. De la Torre, *La Lucha for Cuba*, 3.

44. Revolutionary journalists and scholars drew explicit connections between Elián's victimization and U.S. victimization of previous generations of Cuban children through Operation Pedro Pan. The most explicit attempt to do so was published at the height of the custody battle and sold with an accompanying bookmark that proclaimed it the "story of 14,000 Eliáns." Torreira Crespo and Buajasán Marrawi, *Operación Pedro Pan*.

45. I heard this chant in Havana in December 1999.

46. Ivette M. Yee, "Llaman la atención sobre 'niños rehenes' de Castro," *El Nuevo Herald*, January 8, 2000.

47. "Científico cubano sufre separación familiar," *El Nuevo Herald*, December 12, 2000.

48. Cubas, "Performing Cubanidad," 100.

49. Ibid. 98–101.

50. Ibid., 62.

51. "Elián's Miami Home Turned into Shrine," *BBC World News*, October 22, 2001, http://news.bbc.co.uk/2/hi/americas/1612785.stm.

52. "Elián González Joins Communist Youth," *New York Times*, June 16, 2008, http://www.nytimes.com.

53. D'Arcus, *Boundaries of Dissent*, 116; Damián Fernández, "Elián as Metaphor."

54. Medin, *Cuba*, 39–52.

55. Torres, *The Lost Apple*, 19; Masúd-Piloto, *From Welcomed Exiles to Illegal Immigrants*, xvii–xviii.

BIBLIOGRAPHY

PRIMARY SOURCES

Cuban Heritage Collection, University of Miami Libraries, Coral Gables, FL

"Address by Tuduri to the 10th Anniversary of the Cruzada, Miami, 1972." Cruzada Educativa Cubana Collection 302, Series 1, Box 1, Folder 1.

Arboleya, Carlos J. "The Cuban Colony: Past, Present and Future." Cuban Refugee Center Collection 0218, Series IV, Box 38, Folder 64, 1975.

"Asamblea General 29 de septiembre 1966." Cruzada Educativa Cubana Collection 302, Box 3, Folder 39.

Casados, Ernest M. "Cuban Culture." Report prepared on behalf of the Boy Scouts of America, Miami, Florida, Cuban Refugee Center Collection 0218, Series IV, Box 38, Folder 67, November 29, 1967.

Cauce, Vicente, and María Gómez Carbonell. "Letter." Cruzada Educativa Cubana Collection 302, Series 1, Box 1, Folder 7.

Cuban Refugee Center. "Nine Points Mission Statements." Cuban Refugee Center Collection 0218, Series 6, Box 42, Folder 19.

"Cuban Refugees in Florida." Cuban Refugee Center Collection 0218, Series 4, Box 38, Folder 71, November 8, 1960.

"Effects of the Cuban Situation on the Economic and Social Life of Dade County, Florida." Memorandum to Honorable Chuck Hall, mayor, Metropolitan Dade County, from Hoke Welch, acting county manager, Vertical File, "Dade County Public Schools," February 5, 1965.

Egerton, John. *Cubans in Miami: A Third Dimension in Racial and Cultural Relations.* Report to the Race Relations Information Center, Nashville, TN, Cuban Refugee Center Collection 0218, Series IV, Box 38, Folder 70, November 1969.

53 Resettlements: African Descent. Cuban Refugee Center Collection 0218, Series 6, Box 44, Folder 63.

Foster, Mark. "Immediate Recommendations for Establishing the Work of the Cuban Refugee Center in the Minds of the General Public." Circular Letter, December 9, 1960. Cuban Refugee Center Collection 0210, Series 1, Box 5, Folder 74.

Gómez Carbonell, María. "Establecimiento de delegaciones de 'C.E.C.' en capitales de E.U.A. y países latino-americanos—su reglamentación—'Clubes de español.' Carta-circular a la familia Cuba desterrada." Cruzada Educativa Cubana Collection 302, Series II, Box 3, Folder 50.

———. "Informe rendido por la secretaría de Organización de 'Cruzada Educativa Cubana.'" Cruzada Educativa Cubana Collection 302, Series II, Box 3, Folder 50.

Hall, Joe. *The Cuban Refugee in the Public Schools of Dade County, Florida: A Report Covering the Period from Early 1960 to December 1961.* Cuban Refugee Center Collection 0218, Series 4, Box 39, Folder 99, January 1962.

———. *The Cuban Refugee in the Public Schools of Dade County, Florida: Supplementary Report Covering the Period January–October 1962.* Cuban Refugee Center Collection 0218, Series 4, Box 39, Folder 99, October 1962.

Peterson, James T. "The Cuban Refugees in Dade County." Cuban Refugee Center Collection 0218, Series IV, Box 39, Folder 99, February 18, 1963.

Photographs from U.S. and exile media that adorned the walls of the Cuban Refugee Center. Cuban Refugee Center Collection 0218, Series 6, Box 43, Folders 28, 30, 34, and 35; and Box 44, Folder 91.

Photographs in the Cuban Refugee Center Collection 0218, Series 6, Box 44, Folder 86.

Photographs of Miami's non-Catholic faith-based agencies at work. Cuban Refugee Center Collection 0218, Series 6, Box 44, Folders 62 and 79.

Provisional Executive of Cruzada Educativa Cubana. "Mensaje al pueblo cubano." Miami, July 1962, Cuban Exile Collection 302, Series 1, Box 3, Folder 39, July 1962.

Public Information Activities Report, Cuban Refugee Center, Miami: For Period January 1–August 20, 1963. Cuban Refugee Center Collection 0218, Series 1, Box 1, Folders 12 and 16.

"'Remarkable Adjustments' by Cuban Students Are Reported." Supplement to "Resettlement Re-cap." Cuban Refugee Center Collection 0218, Box 1, Series I, Folder 16, August 1963.

Government Hearings, Documents, and Studies

Alfabeticemos. Havana: Imprenta Nacional de Cuba, 1961.

Bailey, Carlton. *Report: Education in Cuba.* Havana, December 10, 1926. U.S. National Archives, Washington, DC, RG 59, 837.42/21.

Cuban Revolutionary Council: A Concise History. Appendix to Hearings by House Select Committee on Assassinations, vol. 10, 4–57. Washington, DC: U.S. Government Printing Office, March 1979.

Elliston, Jon. *Psywar on Cuba: The Declassified History of U.S. Anti-Castro Propaganda.* New York: Ocean, 1999.

Federación de Mujeres Cubanas. *Nada hay más importante que un niño: Cuba, año 20 de la Revolución.* Havana: ORBE, 1979.

U.S. Department of Health, Education, and Welfare. "The Cuban Immigration, 1959–1966, and Its Impact on Miami–Dade County, Florida." Research Institute for Cuba and the Caribbean, Center for Advanced International Studies, University of Miami, Coral Gables (1967).

———. "Cuban Refugee Program." Fact sheet. Social and Rehabilitation Service. Miami, December 1, 1969.

———. *Cuba's Children in Exile: The Story of the Unaccompanied Cuban Refugee Children's Program.* Social and Rehabilitation Service, Children's Bureau. Washington, DC: U.S. Government Printing Office.

U.S. Department of Labor. *Manpower Report of the President*. Washington, DC: U.S. Government Printing Office, 1973.

U.S. Department of State. *The Continuing Need to Aid Refugees and Escapees: Judiciary Hearings on Cuban Refugee Problems*. Bulletin 45, 87th Congress, 1961.

U.S. House of Representatives, Subcommittee on International Organizations of the Committee on International Relations. "International Relations: Hearings on H.R. 6382" (testimony of Margaret E. Crahan). 94th Congress, 1976.

U.S. Senate Committee of the Judiciary, Subcommittee to Investigate Problems Connected to Refugees and Escapees. "Cuban Refugee Problems." 87th Congress, 1961, 1962.

Voorhees, Tracy S. *Report to the President of the United States on the Cuban Refugee Problem*. Washington, DC: U.S. Government Printing Office, January 18, 1961.

Publications of Church and Civic Organizations

Espinosa, Rolando. *Símbolos, fechas y biografías*. Miami, 1969.

Institute of International Education. *Report on International Exchange*. 1958.

Lugris y Beceiro, Plácido. *Los problemas de la niñez actual*. Havana: Manuel Martín, 1949.

Pope Pius XI. *Atheistic Communism: Divini Redemptoris*. Encyclical letter. New York: Paulist, 1937.

Memoirs and Oral Histories

Barrios, Flor Fernández. *Blessed by Thunder: Memoir of a Cuban Girlhood*. Seattle: Seal, 1999.

Castro, Fidel. "Democracia: Gobierno de las mayorías." In *El pensamiento de Fidel Castro*. Vol. 1, part 2, 393. Havana: Política, 1983.

———. *Pensamiento de Fidel Castro: Selección temática*. Vol. 1. Havana: Editora Política, 1983.

de la Campa, Román. *Cuba on My Mind: Journeys to a Severed Nation*. New York: Verso, 2000.

de León, Rodolfo. "Leaving Cuba." In *First Generation: In the Words of Twentieth Century Americans*, rev. ed., edited by June Namias, 154–63. Chicago: University of Illinois Press, 1992.

Didion, Joan. *Miami*. New York: Simon & Schuster, 1987.

Draper, Theodore. Papers. Hoover Institution Archives, Stanford University, Stanford, CA.

Eire, Carlos. *Learning to Die in Miami: Confessions of a Refugee Boy*. New York: Free Press, 2010.

———. *Waiting for Snow in Havana: Confessions of a Cuban Boy*. New York: Free Press, 2003.

Fernández, Alina. *Castro's Daughter: An Exile's Memoir of Cuba*. New York: St. Martin's, 1997.

García, Luís M. *Child of the Revolution: Growing Up in Castro's Cuba*. Crows Nest, New South Wales: Allen & Unwin, 2006.

Lewis, Oscar, Ruth M. Lewis, and Susan M. Rigdon. *Four Men: Living the Revolution—An Oral History of Contemporary Cuba*. Chicago: University of Illinois Press, 1977.

———. *Four Women: Living the Revolution—An Oral History of Contemporary Cuba*. Chicago: University of Illinois Press, 1977.

———. *Neighbors: Living the Revolution—An Oral History of Contemporary Cuba*. Chicago: University of Illinois Press, 1978.

Ojito, Mirta. *Finding Mañana: A Memoir of a Cuban Exodus*. New York: Penguin, 2005.

Ramonet, Ignacio, and Fidel Castro. *Fidel Castro: My Life: A Spoken Autobiography*. New York: Scribner, 2006.

Randall, Margaret. *To Change the World: My Years in Cuba*. New Brunswick, NJ: Rutgers University Press, 2009.

Fiction, Essays, and Poetry

Cabrera, Raimondo. *Cuba and the Cubans*. Translated by Laura Guiteras. Philadelphia: Levy-Type, 1896.

Dana, Richard Henry. *To Cuba and Back: A Vacation Voyage*. Boston: Ticknor and Fields, 1859.

Du Bois, W. E. B. *Darkwater: Voices from within the Veil*. New York: Scribner's, 1919.

Hawkes, Francis L. "Narrative of the Expedition of an American Squadron." In *Major Problems in Asian American History: Documents and Essays*, edited by Lon Kurashige and Alice Yang Murray, 445–53. New York: Houghton Mifflin, 2003.

Manners, Robert. "Cuba: An Incident of the Insurrection." In *Cuba: And Other Verse*, 7–44. Toronto: William Briggs, 1898.

Martí, José. "Our America." In *Jose Marti: Selected Writings*, edited by Esther Allen, 288–95. New York: Penguin Classics, 2002.

Obejas, Achy. *We Came All the Way from Cuba So You Could Dress Like This?* San Francisco: Cleis, 1994.

Otero, Lisandro. *Arbol de la vida*. Mexico City: Siglo XXI, 1990.

Miscellaneous Published Works

Hibbard, M. Eugénie. "Cuba: A Sketch." Parts 1 and 2. *American Journal of Nursing* 4, no. 9 (June 1904): 696–702; no. 12 (September 1904): 939–43.

Marinello, Juan. "La Constitución cubana y la enseñanza privada." *Confederación de Trabajadores de Cuba* 6 (July 1945): 26–29.

———. *La cuestión racial en la Constitución*. Havana, 1940.

"Ministerio de Hacienda: Honradez con honradez se paga." *Revolución Anuario* (1960): 11–12.

Ortíz, Fernando. *La decadencia cubana*. Havana: La Universal, 1924.

Platt, Orville H. "Our Relation to the People of Cuba and Porto Rico." *Annals of the American Academy of Political and Social Science*, vol. 18, *America's Race Problems*, April 12–13, July 1901, 145–59.

———. "The Solution of the Cuban Problem." *World's Work* 2 (May 1901): 730.

Stapleton, Judith. "A Visit to Cuba." *Hispania* 34, no. 2 (May 1951): 187–88.

Sutherland, Elizabeth. *The Youngest Revolution: A Personal Report on Cuba*. New York: Dial, 1969.

Tuthill, R. L. "An Independent Farm in Cuba." *Economic Geography* 25, no. 3 (July 1949): 201–10.

Periodicals

Atlantic Monthly	*Marriage and Family Living*
El Avance (Exilio)	*Miami Herald*
BBC World News	*Miami News*
Bohemia	*El Mundo*
Boletín Cultural	*New Yorker*
Boston Gazette	*New York Herald Tribune*
Carteles	*New York Times*
Commercial Appeal	*Nuestro*
Diario de la Marina	*El Nuevo Herald*
Diario las Américas	*Patria (Miami)*
Florida Trend	*Patria (New York)*
Granma Weekly Review	*La Quincena*
Havana Post	*Revolución*
Havana Times	*Saturday Evening Post*
Hoy	*Scientific Monthly*
Información	*Time*
Juventud Obrera	*U.S. News and World Report*
Life	*Verde Olivo*
La Lucha	*Waltham (MA) News-Tribune*

SECONDARY SOURCES

Aguirre, Benigno E. "Differential Migration of Cuban Social Races: A Review and Interpretation of the Problem." *Latin American Research Review* 11, no. 1 (1976): 103–24.

Aguirre, Benigno E., and Roberto J. Vichot. "The Reliability of Cuba's Educational Statistics." *Comparative Education Review* 42, no. 2 (1998): 118–38.

Alonso, Ana María. "The Politics of Space, Time and Substance: State Formation, Nationalism and Ethnicity." *Annual Review of Anthropology* 23 (1994): 379–405.

Alvarez, Luis. *The Power of the Zoot: Youth Culture and Resistance during World War II*. Berkeley: University of California Press, 2009.

Amaro, Nelson R. "Mass and Class in the Origins of the Cuban Revolution." In *Cuban Communism*, 8th ed., edited by Irving Louis Horowitz, 31–54. New Brunswick, NJ: Transaction, 1989.

Anderson, Benedict. *Imagined Communities: Reflections on the Origins and Spread of Nationalism*. London: Verso, 1983.

Arguelles, Lourdes. "Cuban Miami: The Roots, Development, and Everyday Life of an Emigré Enclave in the U.S. National Security State." *Contemporary Marxism*, no. 5 (Summer 1982): 27–43.

Ariès, Philippe. *Centuries of Childhood: A Social History of Family Life*. New York: Alfred A. Knopf, 1962.

Babún, Teo A., and Victor Andrés Triay. *The Cuban Revolution: Years of Promise*. Gainesville: University Press of Florida, 2005.

Badillo, David A. "Catholicism and the Search for Nationhood in Miami's Cuban Community." *U.S. Catholic Historian* 20 (Fall 2002): 75–90.

Banet-Weiser, Sarah. "Elián González and 'The Purpose of America': Nation, Family, and the Child-Citizen." *American Quarterly* 55, no. 2 (2003): 149–78.

Bardach, Anne Louise. *Cuba Confidential: Love and Vengeance in Miami and Havana*. New York: Random House, 2002.

Basch, Linda, Nina Glick-Schiller, and Cristina Szanton Blanc. *Nations Unbound: Transnational Projects, Postcolonial Predicaments, and Deterritorialized Nation-States*. Langhorne, PA: Gordon and Breach Science, 1994.

Batista, Fulgencio. *The Growth and Decline of the Cuban Republic*. New York: Devin-Adair, 1964.

Becker, Marvin B. *The Emergence of Civil Society in the Eighteenth Century*. Bloomington: Indiana University Press, 1994.

Behar, Ruth, and Lucía M. Suárez, eds. *The Portable Island: Cubans at Home in the World*. New York: Palgrave Macmillan, 2008.

Belleli, Gugliemo, and Mirella Amatulli. "Nostalgia, Immigration and Collective Memory." In *Collective Memory of Political Events: Social Psychological Perspectives*, edited by James W. Pennebaker, Dario Paez, and Bernard Rimé, 209–20. Mahwah, NJ: Lawrence Erlbaum, 1997.

Betancourt, Juan René. *Doctrina negra: La única teoría certera contra la discriminación racial en Cuba*. Havana: P. Fernández, 1954.

Beveridge, Alfred J. "Cuba and Congress." *North American Review* (April 1901): 540–55.

Blanton, Carlos Kevin. "The Strange Career of Bilingual Education: A History of the Political and Pedagogical Debate over Language Instruction in American Public Education, 1890–1990." PhD diss., Rice University, 1999.

Bodnar, John. *The Transplanted: A History of Immigrants in Urban America*. Bloomington: Indiana University Press, 1985.

Boli-Bennett, John, and John W. Meyer. "The Ideology of Childhood and the State: Rules Distinguishing Children in National Constitutions, 1870–1970." *American Sociological Review* 43, no. 6 (1978): 797–812.

Bonachea, Rolando E., and Nelson P. Valdés, eds. *Cuba in Revolution*. Garden City, NY: Doubleday, 1972.

Boorstein, Edward. *The Economic Transformation of Cuba: A First-Hand Account.* New York: Monthly Review Press, 1968.

Boswell, Thomas D., and James R. Curtis. *The Cuban-American Experience: Culture, Images, and Perspectives.* Totowa, NJ: Rowman & Allanheld, 1984.

Boutcher, Warren. "The Analysis of Culture Revisited: Pure Texts, Applied Texts, Literary Historicisms, Cultural Histories." *Journal of the History of Ideas* 64, no. 3 (2003): 489–510.

Boyden, Jo. "Children and the Policy Makers: A Comparative Perspective on the Globalization of Childhood." In *Constructing and Reconstructing Childhood,* edited by Allison James and Alan Prout, 184–216. London: Falmer, 1990.

Brewer Current, Cheris. "Normalizing Cuban Refugees: Representations of Whiteness and Anti-communism in the USA during the Cold War." *Ethnicities* 8 (2008): 42–67.

Briggs, Laura. *Reproducing Empire: Race, Sex, Science and U.S. Imperialism in Puerto Rico.* Berkeley: University of California Press, 2003.

Brinton, Crane. *The Anatomy of Revolution.* New York: Vintage, 1965.

Bronfenbrenner, Urie. *Two Worlds of Childhood: U.S. and U.S.S.R.* New York: Russell Sage Foundation, 1970.

Brubaker, Rogers. *Nationalism Reframed: Nationhood and the National Question in the New Europe.* Cambridge: Cambridge University Press, 1996.

Brubaker, Rogers, and Frederick Cooper. "Beyond 'Identity.'" *Theory and Society* 29 (February 2000): 1–47.

Bunck, Julie Marie. *Fidel Castro and the Quest for a Revolutionary Culture in Cuba.* University Park: Pennsylvania State University Press, 1994.

Castañeda, Claudia. *Figuration: Child, Bodies, Worlds.* Durham, NC: Duke University Press, 2002.

Castro, Max J. "The Trouble with Collusion: Paradoxes of the Cuban-American Way." In *Cuba, the Elusive Nation: Interpretations of National Identity,* edited by Damián J. Fernández and Madeline Cámara Betancourt, 292–309. Gainesville: University Press of Florida, 2000.

Chadwick, Lee. *Cuba Today.* New York: Lawrence Hill, 1976.

Chávez, Leo R. *The Latino Threat: Constructing Immigrants, Citizens, and the Nation.* Stanford, CA: Stanford University Press, 2008.

Cole, Johnetta B., and Gail A. Reed. "Women in Cuba: Old Problems and New Ideas." *Urban Anthropology and Studies of Cultural Systems and World Economic Development* 15 (Fall/Winter 1986): 321–53.

Coles, Robert. *The Political Life of Children.* Boston: Atlantic Monthly, 1986.

Conde, Yvonne M. *Operation Pedro Pan: The Untold Exodus of 14,048 Cuban Children.* London: Routledge, 1999.

Connerton, Paul. *How Societies Remember.* Cambridge: Cambridge University Press, 1989.

Cortés, Carlos E., ed. *Cuban Exiles in the United States.* New York: Arno, 1980.

———. *The Cuban Experience in the United States.* New York: Arno, 1980.

Crahan, Margaret E. "Cuba: Religion and Revolutionary Institutionalization." *Journal of Latin American Studies* 17, no. 2 (November 1985): 319–40.

———. "Salvation through Christ or Marx: Religion in Revolutionary Cuba." *Journal of Interamerican Studies and World Affairs* 21, no. 1 (February 1979): 156–84.

Cubas, Mario Anthony. "Performing Cubanidad: Identity and Expressive Culture in Cuban Miami." PhD diss., University of Wisconsin–Madison, 2007.

Cunningham, Hugh. "Histories of Childhood." *American Historical Review* 103, no. 4 (October 1998): 1195–1208.

D'Arcus, Bruce. *Boundaries of Dissent: Protest and State Power in the Media Age.* New York: Routledge, 2006.

de Genova, Nicholas, and Ana Y. Ramos-Zayas. *Latino Crossings: Mexicans, Puerto Ricans, and the Politics of Race and Citizenship.* New York: Routledge, 2003.

de la Cuesta, Leonel-Antonio, ed. *Constituciones cubanas desde 1812 hasta nuestros días.* New York: Exilio, 1974.

de la Fuente, Alejandro. *A Nation for All: Race, Inequality, and Politics in Twentieth-Century Cuba.* Chapel Hill: University of North Carolina Press, 2001.

———. "Race, National Discourse, and Politics in Cuba: An Overview." *Latin American Perspectives* 25, no. 3 (May 1998): 43–69.

———. "Race and Inequality in Cuba, 1899–1981." *Journal of Contemporary History* 30, no. 1 (January 1995): 131–68.

del Aguila, Juan M. *Cuba: Dilemmas of a Revolution.* Boulder, CO: Westview, 1984.

de la Torre, Miguel A. *La Lucha for Cuba: Religion and Politics on the Streets of Miami.* Berkeley: University of California Press, 2003.

de Leuchsenring, Emilio Roig. *Cuba no debe su independencia a los Estados Unidos.* Havana: Sociedad Cubana de Estudios Históricos e Internacionales, 1950.

DeMause, Lloyd, ed. *The History of Childhood.* London: Souvenir, 1976.

DeRojas, Alma. "*La Cubanía* in Exile." In *Cuba Transnational*, edited by Damián J. Fernández, 179–204. Gainesville: University Press of Florida, 2005.

de Tocqueville, Alexis. *Democracy in America.* New York: Penguin Putnam, 2001.

Dewart, Leslie. *Cuba, Church and Crisis: Christianity and Politics in the Cuban Revolution.* London: Sheed and Ward, 1964.

Dewey, John. *Democracy and Education: An Introduction to the Philosophy of Education.* New York: Macmillan, 1916.

Díaz, Guarione M. *The Cuban American Experience: Issues, Perceptions, and Realities.* St. Louis: Reedy, 2007.

Díaz Briquets, Sergio, and Lisandro Pérez. *Cuba: The Demography of Revolution.* Population Bulletin, 36, no. 1. Washington, DC: Population Reference Bureau, April 1981.

Dillon, Elizabeth. *The Gender of Freedom: Fictions of Liberalism and the Literary Public Sphere.* Stanford, CA: Stanford University Press, 2004.

Draper, Theodore. *Castroism: Theory and Practice.* New York: Frederick A. Praeger, 1965.

———. *Castro's Revolution: Myths and Realities.* New York: Frederick A. Praeger, 1962.

Drouillard, Lisa. "Cuban Miami: Exile Nation in a Global City." MA thesis, Carleton University, 1997.

Duany, Jorge. *Blurred Borders: Transnational Migration between the Hispanic Caribbean and the United States*. Chapel Hill: University of North Carolina Press, 2011.

———. *The Puerto Rican Nation on the Move: Identities on the Island and in the United States*. Chapel Hill: University of North Carolina Press, 2002.

———. "Revisiting the Cuban Exception: A Comparative Perspective on Transnational Migration from the Hispanic Caribbean to the United States." In *Cuba Transnational*, edited by Damián J. Fernández, 179–204. Gainesville: University Press of Florida, 2005.

Dubois, Laurent. *Avengers of the New World: The Story of the Haitian Revolution*. Cambridge, MA: Harvard University Press, 2004.

Duignan, Peter J., and L. H. Gann. *The Spanish Speakers in the United States: A History*. Lanham, MD: University Press of America, 1998.

Dunn, Marvin. *Black Miami in the Twentieth Century*. Gainesville: University Press of Florida, 1997.

Dye, Alan, and Richard Sicotte. "U.S.-Cuban Trade Cooperation and Its Unraveling." *Business and Economic History* 28 (Winter 1999): 19–31.

Eckstein, Susan Eva. *The Immigrant Divide: How Cuban Americans Changed the U.S. and Their Homeland*. New York: Routledge, 2009.

Eley, Geoff. "Nationalism and Social History: Review Essay." *Social History* 6, no. 1 (January 1981): 83–107.

Eley, Geoff, and Keith Nield. "Farewell to the Working Class?" *International Labor and Working-Class History* 57 (Spring 2000): 1–30.

Elkins, Stanley M. *Slavery: A Problem in American Institutional and Intellectual Life*. Chicago: University of Chicago Press, 1976.

Epstein, Erwin H. "The Peril of Paternalism: The Imposition of Education on Cuba by the United States." *American Journal of Education* 96, no. 1 (November 1987): 1–23.

Erikson, Erik. *Childhood and Society*. New York: W. W. Norton, 1950.

Espiritu, Yen Le. *Home Bound: Filipino American Lives across Cultures, Communities and Countries*. Berkeley: University of California Press, 2003.

Ette, Ottmar. *José Martí, apóstol, poeta, revolucionario: Una historia de su recepción*. Translated by Luís Carlos Henao de Brigard. Mexico City: UNAM, 1995.

Fagen, Richard R., Richard A. Brody, and Thomas J. O'Leary. *Cubans in Exile: Disaffection and the Revolution*. Palo Alto, CA: Stanford University Press, 1968.

Farber, Samuel. *The Origins of the Cuban Revolution Reconsidered*. Chapel Hill: University of North Carolina Press, 2006.

Fass, Paula S. "Is There a Story in the History of Childhood?" In *The Routledge History of Childhood in the Western World*, edited by Paula S. Fass, 1–14. New York: Routledge, 2013.

Fass, Paula, and Mary Mason, eds. *Childhood in America*. New York: New York University Press, 2000.

Fenton, Norman. *Mental Hygiene in School Practice*. Stanford, CA: Stanford University Press, 1949.

Fernández, Damián. "Cuba and *lo Cubano*, or the Story of Desire and Disenchantment." In *Cuba, the Elusive Nation: Interpretations of National*

Identity, edited by Damián J. Fernández and Madeline Cámara Betancourt, 79–99. Gainesville: University Press of Florida, 2000.

———. *Cuba and the Politics of Passion*. Austin: University of Texas Press, 2000.

———. "Elián as Metaphor: Cuba, Cuban-Americans and the Politics of Passion." Unpublished ms. Miami, January 15, 2008.

———, ed. *Cuba Transnational*. Gainesville: University Press of Florida, 2005.

Fernández-Kelly, Patricia, and Sarah Curran. "Nicaraguans: Voices Lost, Voices Found." In *Ethnicities: Children of Immigrants in America*, edited by Rubén G. Rumbaut and Alejandro Portes, 127–56. Berkeley: University of California Press, 2001.

Ferrer, Ada. "Rethinking Race and Nation in Cuba." In *Cuba, the Elusive Nation: Interpretations of National Identity*, edited by Damián J. Fernández and Madeline Cámara Betancourt, 60–78. Gainesville: University Press of Florida, 2000.

Fiddian-Qasmiyeh, Elena. "Representing Sahrawi Refugees' 'Educational Displacement' to Cuba: Self-Sufficient Agents or Manipulated Victims in Conflict?" *Journal of Refugee Studies* 22, no. 3 (2009): 323–50.

Flores, Juan. *The Diaspora Strikes Back: Caribeño Tales of Learning and Turning*. New York: Routledge, 2009.

Foucault, Michel. *History of Sexuality: An Introduction*. Vol. 1. Translated by Robert Hurley. New York: Vintage, 1988.

Franklin, Jane. *Cuba and the United States: A Chronological History*. Melbourne: Ocean, 1997.

Fraser, Nancy. "Rethinking the Public Sphere: A Contribution to the Critique of Actually Existing Democracy." In *The Phantom Public Sphere*, edited by Bruce Robbins, 56–80. Minneapolis: University of Minnesota Press, 1993.

Frederick, Howard H. *Cuban-American Radio Wars: Ideology in International Telecommunications*. Norwood, NJ: Ablex, 1986.

Gallagher, Patrick Lee. "The Cuban Exile: A Socio-political Analysis." PhD diss., St. Louis University, 1975.

García, María Cristina. *Havana USA: Cuban Exiles and Cuban Americans in South Florida, 1959–1994*. Berkeley: University of California Press, 1996.

———. *Seeking Refuge: Central American Migration to Mexico, the United States, and Canada*. Berkeley: University of California Press, 2006.

García Gallo, Gaspar Jorge. "Educar: Tarea decisiva de la Revolución." *Escuela y revolución en Cuba* 1 (December 1962–January 1963): 4–5.

Gay, Peter, ed. *John Locke on Education*. New York: Columbia University Press, 1964.

Genovese, Eugene D. *Roll, Jordan, Roll: The World the Slaves Made*. New York: Random House, 1974.

Gil, Rosa M. "The Assimilation and Problems of Adjustment to the American Culture of One Hundred Cuban Refugee Adolescents Attending Catholic and Public High Schools in Union City and West New York, New Jersey, 1959–1966." MSW thesis, Fordham University, 1968.

Gonzalez, Joseph J. "The Cause of Civilization: The United States Experience with Nation-Building in Cuba, 1898–1909." PhD diss., University of Michigan, 2002.

González-Pando, Miguel. *The Cuban Americans*. Westport, CT: Greenwood, 1998.

Gorsuch, Anne E. "Soviet Youth and the Politics of Popular Culture during NEP." *Social History* 17 (May 1992): 189–201.

Grau Alsina, Ramón, and Valerie Ridderhof. *Mongo Grau: Cuba desde 1930*. Madrid: Agualarga, 1997.

Grenier, Guillermo J., Lisandro Pérez, and Nancy Foner. *The Legacy of Exile: Cubans in the United States*. Boston: Pearson Education, 2003.

Grenier, Guillermo J., and Alex Stepick III, eds. *Miami Now! Immigration, Ethnicity, and Social Change*. Gainesville: University Press of Florida, 1992.

Guerra, Lillian. *The Myth of José Martí: Conflicting Nationalisms in Early Twentieth-Century Cuba*. Chapel Hill: University of North Carolina Press, 2005.

———. "'To Condemn the Revolution Is to Condemn Christ': Radicalization, Moral Redemption, and the Sacrifice of Civil Society in Cuba, 1960." *Hispanic American Historical Review* 89 (February 2009): 73–109.

———. *Visions of Power in Cuba: Revolution, Redemption, and Resistance, 1959–1971*. Chapel Hill: University of North Carolina Press, 2012.

Gutiérrez, David G. *Walls and Mirrors: Mexican Americans, Mexican Immigrants, and the Politics of Ethnicity*. Berkeley: University of California Press, 1995.

———, ed. *The Columbia History of Latinos in the United States since 1960*. New York: Columbia University Press, 2004.

Gutiérrez-Boronat, Orlando. "Cuban Exile Nationalism." PhD diss., University of Miami, 2005.

Habermas, Jürgen. *The Structural Transformation of the Public Sphere: An Inquiry into a Category of Bourgeois Society*. Cambridge, MA: MIT Press, 1989.

Hagedorn, Hermann. *Leonard Wood: A Biography*. Vol. 1. New York: 1931.

Hall, Stuart. "What Is This 'Black' in Black Popular Culture?" *Social Justice* 20 (Spring/Summer 1993): 111.

Hamilton, Carrie. *Sexual Revolutions in Cuba: Passion, Politics, and Memory*. Chapel Hill: University of North Carolina Press, 2012.

Hanawalt, Barbara A. *Growing Up in Medieval London: The Experience of Childhood in History*. Oxford: Oxford University Press, 1993.

Hansing, Katrin. "Rasta, Race and Revolution: Transnational Connections in Socialist Cuba." *Journal of Ethnic and Migration Studies* 27, no. 4 (October 2001): 733–47.

Harper, Paula. "Cuba Connections: Key West–Tampa–Miami, 1870–1945." *Journal of Decorative and Propaganda Arts* 22 (1996): 278–91.

Harrison, Polly F. "Changes in Feminine Role: An Exploratory Study in the Cuban Context." MA thesis, Catholic University of America, 1974.

Hecht, Tobias, ed. *Minor Omissions: Children in Latin American History and Society*. Madison: University of Wisconsin Press, 2002.

Helg, Aline. *Our Rightful Share: The Afro-Cuban Struggle for Equality, 1886–1912*. Chapel Hill: University of North Carolina Press, 1995.

Henriques, Julian, Wendy Hollway, Cathy Urwin, and Valerie Walkerdine. *Changing the Subject*. London: Routledge, 1998.

Hitchman, J. H. "The American Touch in Imperial Administration: Leonard Wood in Cuba, 1898–1902." *The Americas* 24, no. 4 (April 1968): 394–403.

Hoernel, Robert B. "Sugar and Social Change in Oriente, Cuba, 1898–1946." *Journal of Latin American Studies* 8, no. 2 (November 1976): 215–49.

Honig, Bonnie. "Immigrant America? How Foreignness 'Solves' Democracy's Problems." *Social Text* 56 (1998): 1–27.

Horowitz, Irving Louis. *The Long Night of Dark Intent: A Half Century of Cuban Communism*. New Brunswick, NJ: Transaction, 2008.

Hunt, Michael H. *Ideology and U.S. Foreign Policy*. New Haven, CT: Yale University Press, 1987.

Ibarra Guitart, Jorge Renato. *El Tratado Anglo-Cubano de 1905: Estados Unidos contra Europa*. Havana: Ciencias Sociales, 2008.

Ingalls, Robert. *Urban Vigilantes in the New South: Tampa, 1882–1936*. Knoxville: University of Tennessee Press, 1988.

Jackson, Stevi. *Childhood and Sexuality*. London: Blackwell, 1982.

Jacobson, Matthew Frye. *Barbarian Virtues: The United States Encounters Foreign Peoples at Home and Abroad, 1876–1917*. New York: Hill and Wang, 2000.

James, Allison, and Adrian L. James. "Childhood: Toward a Theory of Continuity and Change." *Annals of the American Academy of Political and Social Science* 575, no. 1 (May 2001): 25–37.

James, Allison, Chris Jenks, and Alan Prout. *Theorizing Childhood*. Cambridge: Polity, 1998.

James, Allison, and Alan Prout. "A New Paradigm for the Sociology of Childhood? Provenance, Promise, and Problems." In *Constructing and Reconstructing Childhood: Contemporary Issues in the Sociological Study of Childhood*, edited by Allison James and Alan Prout, 7–32. London: Falmer, 1990.

Johnson, Walter. *Soul by Soul: Life inside the Antebellum Slave Market*. Cambridge, MA: Harvard University Press, 1999.

———. "Time and Revolution in African America: Temporality and the History of Atlantic Slavery." In *Rethinking American History in a Global Age*, edited by Thomas Bender, 155. Berkeley: University of California Press, 2002.

Jolly, Richard. "Education: The Pre-revolutionary Background." In *Cuba: The Economic and Social Revolution*, edited by Dudley Seers, 166–67. Chapel Hill: University of North Carolina Press, 1964.

Kapcia, Antoni. *Cuba: Island of Dreams*. Oxford: Berg, 2000.

Karabel, Jerome, and A. H. Halsey, eds. *Power and Ideology in Education*. New York: Oxford University Press, 1977.

Keane, John. *Civil Society: Old Images, New Visions*. Oxford: Polity, 1998.

Kelley, Mary. *Learning to Stand and Speak: Women, Education, and Public Life in America's Republic*. Chapel Hill: University of North Carolina Press, 2006.

Kroes, Rob. "American Empire and Cultural Imperialism: A View from the Receiving End." *Diplomatic History* 23, no. 3 (1999): 463–77.

Lao-Montes, Agustín, and Arlene Dávila, eds. *Mambo Montage: The Latinization of New York*. New York: Columbia University Press, 2001.

Leiner, Marvin. *Children Are the Revolution: Day Care in Cuba*. New York: Viking, 1974.

———. *Sexual Politics in Cuba: Machismo, Homosexuality, and AIDS*. Boulder, CO: Westview, 1994.

Lenin, V. I. *On Youth*. Moscow: Novosti, 1969.

Levander, Caroline F. *Cradle of Liberty: Race, the Child, and National Belonging from Thomas Jefferson to W. E. B. Du Bois*. Durham, NC: Duke University Press, 2006.

Levine, Robert M., and Moisés Asís. *Cuban Miami*. New Brunswick, NJ: Rutgers University Press, 2000.

Lewis, Oscar, Ruth M. Lewis, and Susan M. Rigdon. "The Literacy Campaign." In *The Cuba Reader: History, Culture, Politics*, edited by Aviva Chomsky, Barry Carr, and Pamela Maria Smorkaloff, 389–94. Durham, NC: Duke University Press, 2004.

———. "The 'Rehabilitation' of Prostitutes." In *The Cuba Reader: History, Culture, Politics*, edited by Aviva Chomsky, Barry Carr, and Pamela Maria Smorkaloff, 395–98. Durham, NC: Duke University Press, 2004.

Lipset, Seymour Martin. *The First New Nation*. Garden City, NY: Anchor, 1967.

Llanes, José. *Cuban Americans: Masters of Survival*. Cambridge, MA: Abt, 1982.

Llerena, Mario. *The Unsuspected Revolution: The Birth and Rise of Castroism*. Ithaca, NY: Cornell University Press, 1978.

Loescher, Gilbert, and John A. Scanlan. *Calculated Kindness: Refugees and America's Half-Open Door, 1945 to the Present*. New York: Free Press, 1986.

Lutjens, Sheryl. "Education and the Cuban Revolution: A Selected Bibliography." *Comparative Education Review* 42, no. 2 (May 1998): 197–224.

Luzzatto, Sergio. "Young Rebels and Revolutionaries, 1789–1917." In *A History of Young People in the West*, vol. 2, *Stormy Evolution to Modern Times*, edited by Giovanni Levi and Jean-Claude Schmitt, 174–231. Cambridge, MA: Belknap Press of Harvard University Press, 1997.

MacDonald, Victoria-María, ed. *Latino Education in the United States*. New York: Palgrave Macmillan, 2004.

Mackey, William Francis, and Von Nieda Beebe. *Bilingual Schools for a Bicultural Community: Miami's Adaptation to the Cuban Refugees*. Rowley, MA: Newberry House, 1977.

Magnússon, Sigurdur Gylfi. "The Singularization of History: Social History and Microhistory within the Postmodern State of Knowledge." *Journal of Social History* 36, no. 3 (2003): 701–35.

Marx, Karl. *The Early Economic and Philosophical Manuscripts, 1844*. Moscow: Progress, 1974.

Masúd-Piloto, Félix Roberto. *From Welcomed Exiles to Illegal Immigrants: Cuban Migration to the U.S., 1959–1995*. Lahman, MD: Rowman & Littlefield, 1996.

Matos, Huber. *Cómo llegó la noche*. Barcelona: Tusquets, 2002.

Matthews, Herbert L. *Revolution in Cuba*. New York: Charles Scribner's Sons, 1975.

May, Elaine Tyler. *Homeward Bound: American Families in the Cold War Era*. New York: Basic Books, 1988.

McGillivray, Gillian. *Blazing Cane: Sugar Communities, Class, and State Formation in Cuba, 1868–1959*. Durham, NC: Duke University Press, 2009.

Medin, Tzvi. *Cuba: The Shaping of Revolutionary Consciousness*. London: Lynne Rienner, 1990.

Mickenberg, Julia. "The New Generation and the New Russia: Modern Childhood as Collective Fantasy." *American Quarterly* 2 (March 2010).

Miller, Nicola. "The Absolution of History: Uses of the Past in Castro's Cuba." *Journal of Contemporary History* 38, no. 1 (January 2003): 147–62.

Mintz, Steven. *Huck's Raft: A History of American Childhood*. Cambridge, MA: Belknap, 2004.

Mitterauer, Michael, and Reinhard Sieder. *The European Family: Patriarchy to Partnership from the Middle Ages to the Present*. Translated by Karla Oosterven and Manfred Hörzinger. Chicago: University of Chicago Press, 1982.

Monahan, James, and Kenneth O. Gilmore. "How the Kremlin Took Cuba: The Inside Story of a Great Deception." *Reader's Digest*, January 1963.

Montaner, Carlos Alberto. *Fidel Castro and the Cuban Revolution: Age, Position, Character, Destiny, Personality, and Ambition*. New Brunswick, NJ: Transaction, 2007.

Morley, Morris H. *Imperial State and Revolution: The United States and Cuba, 1952–1986*. New York: Cambridge University Press, 1987.

Muir, Helen. *Miami, U.S.A.* Expanded ed. Gainesville: University Press of Florida, 2000.

Ngai, Mae M. *Impossible Subjects: Illegal Aliens and the Making of Modern America*. Princeton, NJ: Princeton University Press, 2005.

Nieto, Sonia. *Puerto Rican Students in U.S. Schools*. Mahwah, NJ: Lawrence Erlbaum, 2000.

O'Brien, Thomas F. *The Revolutionary Mission: American Enterprise in Latin America, 1900–1945*. Cambridge: Cambridge University Press, 1996.

O'Leary, Thomas J. "Cubans in Exile: Political Attitudes and Political Participation." PhD diss., Stanford University, 1967.

Olson, James S., and Judith E. Olson. *Cuban Americans: From Trauma to Triumph*. New York: Twayne, 1995.

O'Reilly Herrera, Andrea, ed. *Cuba: Idea of a Nation Displaced*. Albany: State University of New York Press, 2007.

Ozment, Steven. *Ancestors: The Loving Family in Old Europe*. Cambridge, MA: Harvard University Press, 2001.

Paine, Thomas. *The Political Writings of Thomas Paine*. Middletown, NJ: George Evans, 1837.

Palmié, Stephan. *Wizards and Scientists: Explorations in Afro-Cuban Modernity and Tradition*. Durham, NC: Duke University Press, 2002.

Paterson, Thomas G. *Contesting Castro: The United States and the Triumph of the Cuban Revolution*. New York: Oxford University Press, 1994.

Paulston, Rolland G. "Education." In *Revolutionary Change in Cuba*, edited by Carmelo Mesa-Lago, 387. Pittsburgh: University of Pittsburgh Press, 1971.

Pedraza, Silvia. *Political Disaffection in Cuba's Revolution and Exodus*. Cambridge: Cambridge University Press, 2007.

Pedraza-Bailey, Silvia. "Cuba's Refugees: Manifold Migrations." In *Origins and Destinies: Immigrations, Race and Ethnicity in America*, edited by Silvia Pedraza-Bailey and Rubén G. Rumbaut, 263–79. Belmont, CA: Wadsworth, 1996.

————. *Political and Economic Migrants in America: Cubans and Mexicans*. Austin: University of Texas Press, 1985.

Pérez, Lisandro. "Growing Up in Cuban Miami: Immigration, the Enclave, and New Generations." In *Ethnicities: Children of Immigrants in America*, edited by Rubén G. Rumbaut and Alejandro Portes, 91–126. Berkeley: University of California Press, 2001.

Pérez, Louis, Jr. *Cuba: Between Reform and Revolution*. New York: Oxford University Press, 1988.

————. *Cuba and the United States: Ties of Singular Intimacy*. Athens: University of Georgia Press, 1990.

————. *Cuba in the American Imagination: Metaphor and the Imperial Ethos*. Chapel Hill: University of North Carolina Press, 2008.

————. "Cubans in Tampa: From Exiles to Immigrants, 1892–1901." *Florida Historical Quarterly* 57 (October 1978): 129–40.

————. "The Imperial Design: Politics and Pedagogy in Occupied Cuba, 1899–1902." In *Essays on Cuban History: Historiography and Research*, 35–52. Gainesville: University Press of Florida, 1995.

————. "Incurring a Debt of Gratitude: 1898 and the Moral Sources of United States Hegemony in Cuba." *American Historical Review* 104, no. 2 (April 1999): 356–98.

————. *On Becoming Cuban: Identity, Nationality, and Culture*. Chapel Hill: University of North Carolina Press, 2008.

————. "Protestant Missions in Cuba: Archival Records, Manuscript Collections, and Research Prospects." *Latin American Research Review* 27, no. 1 (1992): 105–20.

Pérez, Louis, Jr., and Rebecca J. Scott, eds. *The Archives of Cuba/Los Archivos de Cuba*. Pittsburgh: University of Pittsburgh Press, 2003.

Pérez Cruz, Felipe de J. *La alfabetización en Cuba: Lectura histórica para pensar el presente*. Havana: Ciencias Sociales, 2001.

Pérez-Firmat, Gustavo. *Next Year in Cuba: A Cubano's Coming-of-Age in America*. Houston: Arte Público, 2005.

Pérez Serantes, Enrique. *La voz de la iglesia en Cuba: 100 documentos episcopales*. Santiago de Cuba, 1960.

Pérez-Stable, Marifeli. *The Cuban Revolution: Origins, Course, and Legacy*. 2nd ed. New York: Oxford University Press, 1999.

Phillips, Henry Albert. *White Elephants in the Caribbean*. New York: R. M. McBride, 1936.

Polletta, Francesca. *It Was Like a Fever: Storytelling in Protest and Politics*. Chicago: University of Chicago Press, 2006.

Porter, Bruce, and Marvin Dunn. *The Miami Riot of 1980*. Lexington, MA: D. C. Heath, 1984.

Portes, Alejandro. "Dilemmas of a Golden Exile: Integration of Cuban Refugee Families in Milwaukee." *American Sociological Review* 34, no. 4 (Aug. 1969): 505–18.

Portes, Alejandro, and Robert L. Bach. *Latin Journey: Cubans and Mexican Immigrants in the United States*. Berkeley: University of California Press, 1985.

Portes, Alejandro, and Alex Stepick. *City on the Edge: The Transformation of Miami.* Berkeley: University of California Press, 1993.

Poyo, Gerald E. *"With All, and for the Good of All": The Emergence of Popular Nationalism in the Cuban Communities of the United States, 1848–1898.* Durham, NC: Duke University Press, 1989.

Premo, Bianca. "How Latin America's History of Childhood Came of Age." *Journal of the History of Childhood and Youth* 1 (2008): 63–76.

Quirk, Robert E. *Fidel Castro.* New York: W. W. Norton, 1995.

Quiroz, Alfonso W. "The Evolution of Laws Regulating Associations and Civil Society in Cuba." In *Religion, Culture and Society: The Case of Cuba,* edited by Margaret Crahan, 55–68. Washington, DC: Woodrow Wilson Center, 2003.

———. "Martí in Cuban Schools." In *The Cuban Republic and José Martí: Reception and Use of a National Symbol,* edited by Mauricio A. Font and Alfonso W. Quiroz, 71–81. Lanham, MD: Lexington, 2006.

Ramos García, Juan. *Operation Wetback: The Mass Deportation of Mexican Undocumented Workers in 1954.* Westport, CT: Greenwood, 1980.

Randall, Margaret. "The Family Code." In *The Cuba Reader: History, Culture, Politics,* edited by Aviva Chomsky, Barry Carr, and Pamela Maria Smorkaloff, 399–405. Durham, NC: Duke University Press, 2004.

Ressler, Everett M., Neil Boothby, and Daniel J. Steinbeck. *Unaccompanied Children: Care and Protection in Wars, Natural Disasters, and Refugee Movements.* New York: Oxford University Press, 1988.

Rhodes, Anthony. *The Vatican in the Age of the Cold War.* London: Michael Russell, 1992.

Richardson, Theresa. *The Century of the Child: The Mental Hygiene Movement and Social Policy in the United States and Canada.* New York: State University of New York Press, 1989.

Richmond, Marie LaLiberte. *Immigrant Adaptation and Family Structure among Cubans in Miami, Florida.* New York: Arno, 1980.

Ripoll, Carlos. *Cubanos en los Estados Unidos.* New York: Eliseo Torres & Sons/Las Américas, 1987.

Roediger, David R. "The Pursuit of Whiteness: Property, Terror, and Expansion, 1790–1860." Special Issue on Racial Consciousness and Nation-Building in the Early Republic, *Journal of the Early Republic* 19, no. 4 (Winter 1999): 579–600.

Rogg, Eleanor M. *The Assimilation of Cuban Exiles: The Role of Community and Class.* New York: Aberdeen, 1974.

Rogin, Michael Paul. *Fathers and Children: Andrew Jackson and the Subjugation of the American Indian.* New York: Random House, 1975.

Rosen, Fred, ed. *Empire and Dissent: The United States and Latin America.* Durham, NC: Duke University Press, 2008.

Rowe, John Carlos. "Elián González, Cuban American Détente, and the Rhetoric of Family Values." In *The New American Studies,* 195–206. Minneapolis: University of Minnesota Press, 2002.

Ruiz, Ramón Eduardo. *Cuba: The Making of a Revolution.* Amherst: University of Massachusetts Press, 1968.

Ruiz, Vicki L. *From out of the Shadows: Mexican Women in Twentieth Century America*. New York: Oxford University Press, 1998.

Salas, Luis P. "Juvenile Delinquency in Post-revolutionary Cuba: Characteristics and Cuban Explanations." In *Cuban Communism*, 9th ed., edited by Irving Louis Horowitz and Jaime Suchlicki, 427–45. New Brunswick: NJ: Transaction, 1995.

Samuel, Raphael. *Past and Present in Contemporary Culture*. Vol. 1 of *Theatres of Memory*. London: Verso, 1994.

Sánchez, George J. *Becoming Mexican American: Ethnicity, Culture and Identity in Chicano Los Angeles, 1900–1945*. New York: Oxford University Press, 1993.

San Miguel, Guadalupe, Jr. *Brown, Not White: School Integration and the Chicano Movement in Houston*. College Station: Texas A&M University Press, 2001.

———. *Contested Policy: The Rise and Fall of Federal Bilingual Education in the United States, 1960–2001*. Denton: University of North Texas Press, 2004.

Schirmer, Daniel B., and Stephen Rosskamm Shalom, eds. *The Philippines Reader: A History of Colonialism, Neocolonialism, Dictatorship, and Resistance*. Boston: South End, 1987.

Schoultz, Lars. *Beneath the United States: A History of U.S. Policy toward Latin America*. Cambridge: Harvard University Press, 1998.

———. *That Infernal Little Cuban Republic: The United States and the Cuban Revolution*. Chapel Hill: University of North Carolina Press, 2009.

Schram, Stuart R., ed. *The Political Thought of Mao Tse Tung*. New York: Praeger, 1963.

Scott, Joan. *Gender and the Politics of History*. Rev. ed. New York: Columbia University Press, 1999.

Shorter, Edward. *The Making of the Modern Family*. New York: Basic Books, 1975.

Skaine, Rosemarie. *The Cuban Family: Custom and Change in an Era of Hardship*. Jefferson, NC: McFarland, 2004.

Skocpol, Theda, and Morris P. Fiorina. "Making Sense of the Civic Engagement Debate." In *Civic Engagement in American Democracy*, edited by Theda Skocpol and Morris P. Fiorina, 1–24. Washington, DC: Brookings Institution, 1999.

Smith, Peter H. *Talons of the Eagle: Dynamics of U.S.–Latin American Relations*. 2d ed. New York: Oxford University Press, 2000.

Smith, Wayne S. *The Closest of Enemies: A Personal and Diplomatic Account of U.S.–Cuban Relations since 1957*. New York: W. W. Norton, 1987.

Solomon, Daniel F. *Breaking Up with Cuba: The Dissolution of Friendly Relations between Washington and Havana, 1956–1961*. Jefferson, NC: McFarland, 2011.

Stargardt, Nicholas. *Witnesses of War: Children's Lives under the Nazis*. New York: Random House, 2005.

Stephens, Sharon, ed. *Children and the Politics of Culture*. Princeton, NJ: Princeton University Press, 1995.

Stepick, Alex, Guillermo Grenier, Max Castro, and Marvin Dunn, eds. *This Land Is Our Land: Immigrants and Power in Miami*. Berkeley: University of California Press, 2003.

Stone, Lawrence. *The Family, Sex, and Marriage in England, 1500–1800*. New York: Harper and Row, 1977.

Suárez, Andrés. *Cuba: Castroism and Communism, 1959–1966.* Cambridge, MA: MIT Press, 1967.

Suárez-Orozco, Marcelo M., and Mariela M. Páez, eds. *Latinos: Remaking America.* Berkeley: University of California Press, 2002.

Takaki, Ronald. "An Entering Wedge: The Origins of the Sugar Plantation and a Multi-ethnic Working Class in Hawaii." *Labor History* 23, no. 1 (Winter 1982): 34–46.

Thorne, Barrie. "Re-visioning Women and Social Change: Where Are the Children?" *Gender and Society* 1, no. 1 (March 1987): 85–109.

Torreira Crespo, Ramón, and José Buajasán Marrawi. *Operación Pedro Pan: Un caso de guerra psicológica contra Cuba.* Havana: Política, 2000.

Torres, María de los Angeles, ed. *By Heart/De Memoria: Cuban Women's Journeys in and out of Exile.* Philadelphia: Temple University Press, 2003.

———. *In the Land of Mirrors: Cuban Exile Politics in the United States.* Ann Arbor: University of Michigan Press, 1999.

———. *The Lost Apple: Operation Pedro Pan, Cuban Children in the U.S., and the Promise of a Better Future.* Boston: Beacon, 2003.

Triay, Victor Andres. *The Cuban Revolution: Years of Promise.* Gainesville: University Press of Florida, 2005.

———. *Fleeing Castro: Operation Pedro Pan and the Cuban Children's Program.* Gainesville: University Press of Florida, 1999.

Truslow, Francis Adams. *Report on Cuba.* Baltimore: Johns Hopkins University Press, 1951.

Wald, Karen. *Children of Che: Childcare and Education in Cuba.* Palo Alto, CA: Ramparts, 1978.

Waldinger, Roger, and David Fitzgerald. "Transnationalism in Question." *American Journal of Sociology* (March 2004): 1177–95.

Wallerstein, Immanuel. *World Systems Analysis: An Introduction.* Durham, NC: Duke University Press, 2004.

Walsh, Bryan O. "Cuban Refugee Children." *Journal of Interamerican Studies and World Affairs* 13 (July–October 1971): 378–415.

Welch, Richard E., Jr. *Response to Revolution: The United States and the Cuban Revolution, 1951–1961.* Chapel Hill: University of North Carolina Press, 1985.

Weldes, Jutta, Mark Laffey, Hugh Gusterson, and Raymond Duvall, eds. *Cultures of Insecurity: States, Communities, and the Production of Danger.* Minneapolis: University of Minnesota Press, 1999.

White, Donald W. *The American Century: The Rise and Decline of the United States as a World Power.* New Haven, CT: Yale University Press, 1996.

Williams, Raymond. "Base and Superstructure in Marxist Cultural Theory." In *Rethinking Popular Culture: Contemporary Perspectives in Cultural Studies,* edited by Chandra Mukerji and Michael Schudson, 407–23. Berkeley: University of California Press, 1991.

Wimmer, Andreas, and Nina Glick-Schiller. "Methodological Nationalism, the Social Sciences, and the Study of Migration: An Essay in Historical Epistemology." *International Migration Review* (Fall 2003): 576–610.

Winsberg, Morton D. "Housing Segregation of a Predominantly Middle-Class Population: Residential Patterns Developed by the Cuban Immigration into Miami, 1950–1974." *American Journal of Economics and Sociology* 38 (October 1979): 403–18.

Woronov, T. E. "Performing the Nation: China's Children as Little Red Pioneers." *Anthropological Quarterly* 80 (Summer 2007): 647–72.

Yaremko, Jason M. "Protestant Missions, Cuban Nationalism and the Machadato." *The Americas* 56, no. 3 (January 2000): 53–75.

Zahra, Tara. *Kidnapped Souls: National Indifference and the Battle for Children in the Bohemian Lands, 1900–1948*. Ithaca, NY: Cornell University Press, 2008.

———. "Lost Children: Displacement, Family, and Nation in Postwar Europe." *Journal of Modern History* 81 (March 2009): 45–86.

Zanetti, Oscar. "American History: A View from Cuba." *Journal of American History* 79, no. 2 (September 1992): 530–31.

Zelizer, Viviana A. *Pricing the Priceless Child: The Changing Social Value of Children*. Princeton, NJ: Princeton University Press, 1985.

Zeruvabel, Eviatar. *Time Maps: Collective Memory and the Social Shape of the Past*. Chicago: University of Chicago Press, 2003.

Index

Association of Cuban Teachers, 193
Association of Rebel Youth, 112, 113
Atheism, 118
Avance, El (daily), 86, 157–58, 163,
    164–65, 174; Bay of Pigs failure and,
    168; Miami edition of, 128, 159–60;
    nationalization of, 128; "Our Cuban
    Visitors" editorial, 146
Avance Criollo, El (Miami exile newspa-
    per), 128, 159–60
Ayers, Bradley Earl, 154

Baldor School (Miami), 192
Balseros (rafters), 204–5, 206
Banco de Seguros Sociales de Cuba, 81
Banes, 30, 37
Barrios Castillo, Leonel, 60
Baseball, 40, 124, 195
Basic Secondary Schools in the Country-
    side, 186
Batista, Fulgencio, 31, 37, 46; dictator-
    ship of, 41–44; fall of, 3, 12, 45; flight
    and exile of, 49, 50, 94; former fol-
    lowers in southern Florida, 123, 130,
    149, 154; violence and repression of
    regime of, 42, 43, 48, 50–52, 53
Batistiano. *See* Anti-Batista insurgency
Bauta: church attacks in, 88
Bauza, Mario, 124
Bayfront Park (Miami), 171, 173–74,
    176–77
Bay of Pigs invasion (1961), 4, 143, 182;
    aftermath of, 172, 173–74, 181, 182;
    doubts about exiles' competence and,
    154, 155–56; expectations for, 114–15,
    154–55, 162–63, 170, 171; failure of,
    93, 115–16, 117, 121, 144, 146, 155 56,
    167–68, 172, 174, 175, 179; landing at
    Playa Girón and, 167; preparations
    for, 151, 154–55, 164, 167–68
Becados (state scholarship students), 101,
    102, 186–87
Bejucal: press burial at, 87
Belén Jesuit Preparatory School
    (Miami), 192

Beléz Technical School, 108
Belgium, 118
Benítez, Conrado, 163
Biaín, Ignacio, 50
Bilingual education (Miami), 190–92,
    194, 201, 203
Boarding school programs (Cuba), 50,
    101–2, 185–87
Bohemia (magazine), 47–48, 50–51, 56,
    58, 60–61, 63–64, 114; Castro educa-
    tion initiatives and, 73; Castro initial
    interview with, 47–48; child-
    dedicated issue of, 101; credibility of,
    48; on Cuban revolutionary Christ-
    mas, 78, 82; exiled editor of, 87–88
Boys and Girls Clubs, 195
Boy Scouts, 37, 195
Boza Masvidal, Eduardo: "Is the Social
    Revolution Being Realized in Cuba a
    Christian One?," 89
Brigadistas. See Antonio Maceo Brigade
Brujería (witchcraft), 29, 51

Cabrera, Raimondo, 21
Camagüey province, 49, 55, 83
Campa, Román de la, 45
Campaña de Alfabetización, 100, 103–5,
    107, 113, 114, 119, 163
Campesinos, 28, 41, 57, 102, 105, 107
Cárdenas Museum for the Battle of
    Ideas, 210
Caruso, Teresa, 43
Casa de las Américas, 124
Castañeda, Carlos, 88; Castro interview
    with, 47–48; child Communist indoc-
    trination reports and, 142
Castillo Fernández, Roberto del, 112
Castro, Fidel, 3–4, 15, 61; anti-Batista
    insurgency and, 43; anti-U.S. rhetoric
    of, 52, 151; arrival in Havana of, 44;
    authoritarianism of, 47, 64, 65, 67;
    Bay of Pigs invasion and, 115–16;
    benevolent paternal image of, 76, 80,
    82, 84–85, 110; Catholicism and, 47,
    50, 65–67, 69, 74, 75, 80, 82, 83, 85,

Missile Crisis (1962) and, 4, 10, 149, 178–79, 183, 184, 211; end of, 204–5, 207; exile media propaganda and, 157–70; family values of, 142, 147; politics of childhood and, 8, 120, 121–47, 158–59; U.S. asylum-seeker policy and, 127–30; U.S. early Cuban policy and, 126–30, 151, 152, 153, 181, 190, 192; U.S. policy shift to Indochina and, 179, 189; as war of propaganda, 127–29, 130, 168

Colegio Belén, 112

Colegio Don Bosco, 71

Colegio School (Miami), 192

College of Cuban Educators in Exile, 171

Columbia Fort prison: conversion into school, 63–64

Comic books, 42

Comic strips, 37

Comités de Defensa de la Revolución (CDR), 111

Comités de Defensa Infantil (CDI), 110–11, 115

Committee of Youth Organizations (Soviet Union), 94

Common-law marriage, 83

Communism, 14–15, 110, 117, 118, 123; Castro initial disavowal of, 47, 52, 55; Castro turn to, 3, 13, 55, 64, 93, 128, 151, 158, 184–89, 211; child indoctrination threat of, 1, 8, 93–95, 132, 137, 139, 163, 184–89, 199, 202; hemispheric threat of, 4, 158–60. *See also* Anticommunism; Cuban Communist Party; Marxism-Leninism; Socialist bloc; Soviet Union

Congress on Education and Culture (1971), 198

"Conozca a Cuba" (song), 42

Consejo Revolucionario Cubano, 155, 172, 174

Conservatism: counterrevolutionary rhetoric and, 109; Cuban white elites and, 26, 32; exile community and, 182, 186, 197–98

Constancia Sugar company, 30

Constitutional Convention (1939), 34, 35. *See also* Cuban Constitution

Coral Way Elementary School (Miami), 190

Corruption, 40–41, 43, 51

Counterculture, 197

Counterrevolution, 1, 2, 4, 15, 92, 104, 106, 107–20; armed confrontations and, 114–15; Catholics and, 13, 107–12, 115, 117, 126, 164–66, 211; Cold War and, 152; components of, 4, 118–19, 211; execution of student and, 108; factors behind, 67, 90–91; failure of U.S.-backed invasion and (*see* Bay of Pigs invasion); goals for, 107–8; illustrious male leaders of, 159; as male-dominated, 110, 159; politics of childhood and, 91, 93, 107–10, 111, 121, 126, 130, 139–40, 148, 164; propaganda and, 109–11, 126, 157–64; student participants of, 108, 112; U.S. support for, 128, 148, 151. *See also* Anti-Castro movement; Exile community

CRC. *See* Cuban Refugee Center

Crisol (publication), 87

Cruz, Milagros, 208

Cruzada Educativa Cubana (CEC), 177–78, 193–95

Cuba in the American Imagination (Pérez), 6–7

Cuban American National Foundation, 204

Cuban Catholic Youth Day, 74

Cuban Children's Program, 129, 141. *See also* Pedro Pan children

Cuban cigar industry, 122–23

Cuban Communist Party, 34, 35, 54, 116–17

Cuban Constitution: 1901, 26, 27; 1940, 34, 36, 54, 64; Castro replacement of, 117

Cuban Educational Crusade (CEC), 177–78, 193–95

Cuban independence struggle, 1, 5, 18, 19, 21–28, 48, 120, 210; cigar workers' role in, 122; heroes of, 21–22, 26, 74 (*see also* Martí, José); Platt Amendment and, 26; race and, 21–22, 27, 28; self-determination and, 31; U.S. military occupation and, 23–24. *See also* Cuban republican period

Cuban Missile Crisis (1962), 4, 10, 149, 178–80, 183, 184, 211

Cuban Refugee Assistance Program, 140, 141, 142, 202

Cuban Refugee Center (CRC), 140, 141–44, 191, 201, 207; child-centered publicity and, 143–44, *144*; "Nine Points" mission statement, 141–42

Cuban Refugee Committee, 140

Cuban Refugee Emergency Center, 140

Cuban Refugee Program, 152

Cuban refugees. *See* Exile community

Cuban republican period (1902–58), 6–7, 26–44, 120; early refugees from, 130; First Republic, 26–33; press suppression by, 86–88; Second Republic, 33–44. *See also* Batista, Fulgencio

Cuban Revolution (1959), 2, 45–64; assured survival of, 184; basis of legitimacy of, 48; Catholic Church and, 73–74; celebration of first Christmas of, 77–82; child-centered rhetoric of, 7, 13, 14–17, 44, 46–57, 60, 64–66, 68, 75, 88, 184–89, 210; civil society and, 66–91, 210; communist turn of (*see* Communism); cultural forces behind, 15; curtailment of freedoms by, 4, 47, 63, 65, 86–88; discontent with, 61; divergence from Martí's moral vision by, 60; economic and social programs of, 50, 53, 67, 75, 89, 90, 97; emotional reactions to, 45–46; end of moderate coalition rule and, 64; exclusive moral paradigm of, 86, 90; exile media's child-centered critique of, 159–60; faded euphoria about, 52–55, 58, 60; fall of Batista and, 45; first Christmas celebration of, 77–82; first emigrants from, 149; first volatile year of, 46–47; gender and, 13; hopes of, 46; initial policies of, 49–50; initial public relations campaign, 50–51, 56–58; legitimacy of, 52; media images of, 48, 56–58, 59, 60–61, 65; minority dissent and, 58–64; moderation promises of, 48; moral imperative of, 49; M-26-7 and, 15, 41, 43, 46, 48, 50–51, 55, 71, 78, 131, 150, 154; provisional government of, 12, 13, 47–49, 53, 55, 63, 69, 73, 210; radicalization of, 13, 15, 54–56, 64, 67, 69, 82–91, 92–120, 211; rioting and looting and, 46; top-down reform campaigns of, 85; undemocratic nature of, 66; U.S. initial response to, 46–47; U.S. rejection of, 151–52. *See also* Castro, Fidel; Castro regime

Cuban Revolutionary Council, 155

Cuban Socialist Party, 32

Cuban Society of Pediatric Medicine, 69

Cuban Teachers Professional Association, 72

Cub Scouts, 37

Dade County (Fla.). *See* Miami–Dade County

Dana, Richard Henry: *To Cuba and Back*, 20

Daycare centers, 13, 185

Defense Department, U.S., 151

Democracy, 31, 50, 60

Democratic Revolutionary Rescue Movement: women's auxiliary, 172–73

Diario de la Marina (daily), 68, 69, 70, 71, 72–73, 74; revolutionary attacks on, 86, 87

Diario las Américas (Miami newspaper), 72–73, 124

Diasporic Cubans. *See* Exile community

Diaz, Isolina, 171

Directorio Magisterial Revolucionario (DMR), 175, 176

(*see* Cold War); conservative values of, 182, 186, 197–98; continuing contacts with Cuba by, 10; Cuban invasion plan and (*see* Bay of Pigs invasion); Cuban Missile Crisis (1962) and, 149, 178, 179; disillusionment of, 181, 183; downward mobility of, 133–34, 152, 170, 182; dreams of liberated homeland of, 153; Elián custody battle and, 184, 206–12; factors in emigration of, 8, 67; first wave of, 126–47, 148, 201, 202; fourth wave of, 204–5, 206; gender roles and, 13–14; generational conflict and, 195–98; "Golden Exile" status of, 3, 146–47; hostility toward, 132–33; improved socioeconomic position of, 189–90, 193; initial divisions among, 150–51; lost hopes of, 178–81; Martí's legacy and, 1, 171; media and, 128, 138–39, 148, 149, 157–70, 182, 191, 205; middle-class origins of, 13, 16, 93, 137; minimal visa requirements for, 127; misplaced trust in U.S. government of, 149; as model immigrants, 141; nation-making project of, 189–90; policies in 1980s of, 204–5; race and, 16, 121, 122–37, 146, 153, 181; radicalized youth of, 197–98; resettlement outside southern Florida and, 142, 202; second wave of, 200, 201, 202, 203; third wave of, 199, 201–4; Two Cubas and, 2, 10, 12, 184–212; unaccompanied minors and, 8, 107, 111, 114, 118, 126, 128, 129, 135, 140, 141, 143, 197, 207; U.S. citizenship of, 204; U.S. encouragement of (1959–61), 4, 16, 122, 126–31, 137–47, 152, 190; U.S. federal funding of, 140, 142, 148, 153, 190, 199–200; U.S. political exploitation of, 148; U.S. reversal of policy and, 179, 204–5

Fair, T. Willard, 201
Family Code (1975), 189
Family values, 4; Castro assault on, 8, 83, 89, 97, 107, 108, 109–10, 186–87, 188–89, 208; Catholics and, 83, 164; Cold War and, 142, 147; Cuban extended families and, 133; Elián custody case and, 207–8; exile media propaganda about, 169, 207–8; generational conflict and, 187, 195–99; middle-class Cubans and, 58, *59*, 92, 121, 137; as patriarchal, 6, 13, 92, 97, 107, 110, 186, 197; U.S.-inspired images of, 58, *59*. *See also* Parents
Fascell, Dante, 200
Fass, Paula S., 1
FBI, 123
Federación de Mujeres Cubanas, 104–5, 188–89
Federación Estudiantil Universitaria, 48
Federation of Cuban Educators, 193
Federation of Cuban Private Schools, 171–72
Federation of Cuban Women, 104–5, 185
Federation of University Youth, 113
Female chastity, 49
Feminine Democratic Union, 160
Feminine University Association in Favor of Peace and Liberty, 160
Feminism, 6, 197
Fernández Puntonel, Juan Alberto, 61, 63
Finca Santa Rica School, 73
First Republic (1902–33), 26–33; leadership ideological differences and, 26–29; Machadato upheaval and, 32–33, 34; race and, 27–29, 30, 34; U.S. oversight and, 26–27, 30
First Student Plenary, 113
Flogar department store (Havana), 114
Florida. *See* Miami–Dade County; South Florida
Fomento, 83
Fontaine, Jim, 143
4-H clubs, 31
Fourth of July, 37
FRD. *See* Frente Revolucionario Democrático

Freedom of speech, 88
Frente Revolucionario Democrático
   (FRD), 153, 155, 156, 174
Frente Revolucionario de Profesores
   Secundarios, 100
Fruit tree planting, 75, *76*

Gagarin, Yuri, 117
Galán, Enrique, 69–70
Galban Lobo company, 69–70
García, Andy, 208
García, Antonio, 194
García Mendoza, Armando, 163
García Sifredo, Armando, 166–67,
   179–80
Gender, 6, 13–14; Castro masculinity
   emphasis and, 188; Cuban American
   norms and, 196; Cuban inequality
   and, 44; female chastity and, 49;
   male-dominated Counterrevolution
   and, 110, 159; rural boarding schools
   program and, 186; women exiles'
   anti-Castro activities and, 172–76,
   182
Generational conflict, 187, 195–99
Geyer, Georgie Anne, 37
Gilbara, 30
Girl Scouts, 37, 195
Gomez Carbonell, María, 177
Gonzáles, Silvio, 107–8
González, Elián, 1–2, 184, 206–12
González, Lázaro, 208, 209–10
González de Chávez Clavero, Mario, 73
Grajales, Mariana, 105
Grave de Peralta, Gabriel and César,
   207–8
Grave de Peralta, Luis, 207–8
Great Depression, 34
Greater Miami Urban League, 201–2
Greene, Juanita, 200
Guaimano Masonic Lodge (Havana),
   39, 40
Guantánamo naval base, 26, 30, 204,
   205
Guaro, 30, 40

Guatamalan refugees, 202–3
Guerra, Lillian: *Visions of Power in
   Cuba*, 7
Guevara, Che, 57, 185
Guillén, Nicolás, 95

Haban Vieja cathedral, 88
Haitian refugees, 202, 203
Hall, Chuck, 132
Hall, Joe, 139, 191, 200
Hall, Stuart, 11
Harrison, N. M., 145
Hart, Armando, 13
Harvard University, 24, 25
Havana Post (U.S. expatriate newspa-
   per), 32, 68, 69, 70–71
Health-care services, 49–50, 65, 68–69
Hernández Rodriguez, Argelio, 114
Hernández Tellaeche, Arturo, 159
Hershey company, 30
Hispanic Americans. *See* Latinas/Latinos
Holidays, 37, 42. *See also* Christmas
Holland, 118
Hollywood films, 37, 58
Homosexuality, 188, 197
Hoy (newspaper), 51, 78, 80, 87, 93–95,
   96, 99; on Operation Toys, 81–82
Hunt, Howard, 153

Ibel Academy (Havana), 112
Illegitimate children, 83
Illiteracy. *See* Literacy
I Love Lucy (TV program), 125
Immaculata Academy (Miami), 192
Immigration and Naturalization Service,
   U.S., 209
Immigration policy, U.S., 4; Anglo-
   American racial views and, 121, 123,
   125, 127; Cold War asylum-seekers
   and, 127–30; Cuban preferential sta-
   tus and, 127, 129–30, 141, 189, 202,
   203; Cuban pre-1959, 122–25, 149;
   Cuban quota (1995) and, 205; Cuban
   second wave and, 199; political refu-
   gee status and, 202–3

Mambi army, 116
Manifest Destiny, 23
Manners, Robert, 20–21
Mariel Boatlift (1980), 199, 201–4
Marinello, Juan, 34, 35, 54
Marist Brothers High School (Miami),
113
Marriage regulation, 83
Martí, José: child-centered language
of, 18–21, 27, 29, 32, 39, 41, 44, 47,
53, 54, 60, 210, 212; CIA-sponsored
propaganda and, 129; competing
claims for legacy of, 1, 5, 6, 60, 65,
90, 95, 96, 105, 106, 109, 116, 185,
197–98; Cuban independence and, 1,
19, 21–23, 25, 28, 29, 33, 34, 36, 46,
53, 55, 60, 63, 122; exile community
celebrations of, 167, 170–71, 176–77,
182; monuments to, 74, 96, 117, 171,
173, 174; political values of, 26, 43,
48, 49, 67, 69, 71, 92, 96, 105, 147,
167, 185, 192
—works of: *Ismaelillo*, 19; *La edad de
oro*, 194; "Nuestra America," 18; *Los
Zapaticos de Rosa*, 19
Marxism-Leninism, 65, 95, 96, 116, 118,
184, 185. *See also* Communism
Matos, Huber, 55, 63, 64, 86, 159
May Day celebration, 117
McCarran-Walter Act (1952), 127
McKinley, William, 23
Media: Bay of Pigs reports by, 167;
Castro initial interviews with, 47–48;
Castro repression of, 67, 86–88, 89;
civil society and, 66, 69–70, 71, 72–
73; Cuban state-sponsored, 13, 48,
53; Elián custody case and, 207–8;
exile community and, 138–39, 148,
149, 157–70, 182, 191, 205; literacy
volunteers and, 106; Mikoyan visit
and, 95–96; on Operation Toys, 80,
81–82; positive reports of Revolution
in, 68; pro- and anti-U.S. messages
in, 56; revolutionary child-centered
images in, 56–58, 59, 60–61, 65;

U.S. child-centered stories and,
128–30. *See also* Propaganda; *specific
publications*
Meet the Press (TV program), 52
Memphis Commercial Appeal (newspaper), 32
Men. *See* Gender
Methodist missionary schools, 30, 31
Mexican-American War (1846–48), 20
Mexican Federation of Democratic
Youth, 160
Mexicans, 124, 127, 190
Miami–Dade County: anti-Cuban backlash in, 203; Batistiano emigrés in,
130–31, 149; bilingual education and,
190–92, 194, 201, 203; Catholic Welfare Bureau, 129, 140, 141; CIA headquarters in, 153; Cuban exile Catholic
schools in, 192; Cuban Refugee
Center, 140, 141–44, 191, 201, 207;
economic recession and, 126, 138,
200; Elián custody case and, 207–8,
209–10; elite Cubans in, 125; exile
community support in, 144–47; exile
media in, 157–70; exile private school
in, 192; expanded flow of Cubans to,
139–40, 199–200; hostility toward
Cuban refugees in, 132–37, 138, 147;
Little Havana section of, 125–26, 131–
34, 208; number of Cuban refugees
in (June 1960), 131; pre-1959 Cuban
community in, 122–25; public school
system of, 134–35, 139–40, 190–92,
194, 195, 200, 201; racial politics and,
200–201
Miami Herald, 87, 138, 145–46,
200–201, 205
Middle-class Cubans: Afro-Cuban community and, 29; American culture
and, 37–38, 58, 59; civil society and,
12–13, 76; Cold War–era values of,
142; conception of childhood of,
38, 92, 97, 118–19; Counterrevolution and, 10, 15, 110, 111, 118–19;
Cuban independence and, 25; Cuban

Progressive education, 24
Progressive Era (U.S.), 24, 30
Propaganda, 12, 157–64; child-centered, 109–11, 115, 126, 129–30, 141–42, 158–59; counterrevolutionary, 107–10, 111, 126, 148–49, 157–58, 164, 182; U.S. Cold War, 127–29, 130, 168
Property confiscation, 50, 67, 89, 90, 97–98
Protestants: Castro policies against, 188; mission schools in Cuba of, 30–31, 35, 69, 118
PSP. *See* Partido Socialista Popular
Public schools. *See* Education *headings*
Public sphere, 6
Puerto, Ramón, 152
Puerto Padre, 30
Puerto Ricans, 18, 124, 190, 191–92; New York City and, 56, 136

Quaker school, 30
Quemado de Güines, 73
Quevedo, Miguel Angel de, 48, 88
Quincena, La (Catholic magazine), 50

Race: Anglo-American views on, 121, 123, 125, 127; anti-Castro movement and, 164; Cuban hierarchy of, 27, 28, 33, 35, 36, 44; Cuban republic and, 26, 34; Cuban Revolution and, 57; exile community and, 16, 121, 122–37, 146, 153, 181; Marielitos and, 203; private schools and, 34, 36; U.S. Cuban policies and, 15, 20, 21, 22, 27, 44, 131, 154, 156; U.S. immigration restrictions and, 127; U.S. segregation and, 123, 125, 136, 200. *See also* African Americans; Afro-Cubans; Mixed-race Cubans; White Cubans
Radio Havana, 117
Radio Swan, 109–10, 115
Rafters (*balseros*), 204–5, 206
Ramírez, Porfirio, 108
Ray, Manuel, 155
Reagan, Ronald, 201

Rebel Army, 47, 49, 55, 57, 84; boys and, 61, 62; former members' exodus to Miami, 131
Rebel Youth, 117
Reciprocity Treaty, U.S.-Cuba (1903), 27, 28
Redistributive programs, 78
Refugees: U.S. Cold War policy and, 127–28, 130. *See also* Exile community
Reno, Janet, 208
Republican-era Cuba. *See* Cuban republican period
Republican Party (U.S.), 204
Revolución (news magazine), 48, 50–51, 71, 87, 98
"Revolución es para los niños, La" (The Revolution is for the children), 1, 7, 45–65, 210
Revolutionary Air Force, 81
Revolutionary Armed Forces, 70–71, 98, 114, 117
Ríos, María Ríos, 42
Rivero, José Ignacio, 86
Rivers, Mendel, 97–98
Rodríguez, Arsenio, 124
Rodríguez, Salvador, 73
Roediger, David, 11
Rollason, Wendell, 139–40
"Rome or Moscow" (pastoral letter), 108
Roosevelt, Theodore, 23
Rotary Club, 37
Rousseau, Jean-Jacques, 19
Rubio Padilla, Antonio, 156
Ruisánchez de Varona, Emelina, 173
Rural areas: boarding schools, 186, 187; Castro welfare projects, 49, 57–58, 83–84; common-law marriages, 83; grassroots efforts, 85; literacy (*see* Literacy Campaign); poverty, 39, 57; scholarship students, 101, 102, 186–87; school facilities, 34, 36, 54–55, 69–70, 84, 85, 101, 185–86; study and agricultural labor program, 185–86; Three Kings' Day celebrations, 80–81

Russia. *See* Soviet Union
Russian Revolution (1917), 14–15

Sacred Heart Church (La Vibora), 112
Sagua la Grande church attacks, 88
St. Mary's Cathedral School (Miami),
    194
Salesians, 70
Salvadoran refugees, 202–3
Sánchez Arango, Aurelio, 159
Sánchez del Castillo, Adrián, 112
Sandinistas, 203
Santa Clauses, revolutionary, 78
Santería, 188
School in the Countryside program,
    185–86
Second Republic (1933–58), 33–44;
    Batista coup and, 41–44; inequalities
    and, 35–36
Segregation, 123, 125, 136, 200
Sexual activity, 49, 106, 186, 188
Shenandoah Elementary School
    (Miami), 175
Sierra del Escambray, 103, 106, 108, 163
Sierra Maestra, 160, 163
SIP. *See* Sociedad Interamericana de
    Prensa
Social hierarchy, 33, 35, 38, 44
Socialist bloc: Castro popularity in, 99;
    Cuba's entry into, 116; U.S. refugee
    policy and, 127. *See also* Communism;
    Soviet Union
Social justice projects, 70–76, 84, 85
Social mobility, 29, 35, 43, 193; Cuban
    exiles and, 133–34, 152, 170, 182, 193
Social welfare, 19, 40, 49, 53–54; chil-
    dren's services, 1, 27, 40, 49–50, 54,
    68–69, 71
Sociedad Interamericana de Prensa
    (SIP), 157–58
South Florida: Cuban pre-Castro im-
    migrants in, 10, 122–23, 149. *See also*
    Miami–Dade County
Soviet Union, 8, 127; Castro alliance
    with, 3, 89, 90, 92–99, 116–17, 118,
119, 120, 121, 137, 151, 211; Castro
    popularity in, 99; children and,
    14–15, 95–96, 99, 103, 111, 116–17,
    128–29, 143, 185; collapse of (1991),
    204, 206; Cuban media favorable
    images of, 93–95; Cuban military aid
    from, 98; Cuban Missile Crisis (1962)
    and, 4, 10, 149, 178–80, 183, 184, 211.
    See also Cold War; Socialist bloc
Space program, 117
Spain, 1, 5, 18, 24, 118; Cuban anti-
    Castro emigration to, 127; Cuban
    Catholic clergy and, 89; Cuban culture
    and, 123; Cuban immigrants from,
    28; surrender of Cuba by, 23, 122
Spanish-Cuban-American War (1898),
    19, 20–23, 31, 33, 131, 151, 154, 181;
    Treaty of Paris, 23, 178–79
Spanish-descent Cubans, 27
Spanish language, 42, 133, 192, 194
Standard of living, 50
State Department, U.S., 158, 179
Street children, 39–40, 41; Castro wel-
    fare policies and, 49–50
Student strike (1961), 108–9
Sugar industry, 27, 28, 30, 34, 69–70;
    stagnation of, 39, 198
Switzerland, 118
Szulc, Tad, 143

Tabaquero communities, 125
Tamarago, Augustín, 63
Tampa (Fla.), 122
Tápanes, Emilito, 51
Taxes, 50
Teachers. *See* Education *headings*
Teller Amendment, 23
Terrero, Mirta, 70–71
Textbooks, 54, 55; Cuban nationalist,
    33, 34; exile community and, 193;
    ideological content in, 101, 160; U.S.
    influence on, 31, 33
Thorne, Barrie, 6
Three Kings' Day, 79–82, 98
Time (magazine), 143

myth as, 137–47; first exiles as, 121, 122, 125; Machadato and, 32–33; private schools and, 25; revolutionary images of children and, 57–58; Spanish immigrants as, 28. *See also* Elite Cubans

Williams, Franklin, 138

Wisconsin, 202

Witchcraft, 29, 51

WMIE (Miami radio station), 193

Women. *See* Gender

Wood, Leonard, 24, 25

Working-class Cubans, 13, 25, 28, 32, 33; anti-Batista youth cadres and, 43; Castro increased purchasing power of, 50; Catholic groups and, 73, 88–89; children of, 38–39, 40; emigration of unaccompanied children and, 118; emigration to Miami of, 118, 121, 122, 203; public schools and, 34–35, 54–55, 185; as Revolution's beneficiaries, 66; support for Revolution by, 54

World Federation of Youth, 103

World War II, 126

Year of Education (1961), 99–107, 119, 163

YMCA/YWCA, 195

Youth (Cuban): as agricultural laborers, 185–86, 188; cadres of, 43, 115, 119, 143; Catholic groups (*see* Catholic youth groups); as intelligence-gatherers, 106, 115, 117, 162; as literacy volunteers, 100, 103–5, 107, 113, 114, 119, 163; malaise (late 1970s) of, 199; militancy of, 143; militias of, 97, 98, 100, 106, 108, 112, 113, 114, 139, 159–60; protests and, 96; rallies and, 14, 61, 62, 63, 65, 74–75, 87, 97, 107–8; student strike, 108–9

Youth (Cuban-American), 196–99

Yucas (Young Urban Cuban Americans), 206

Zayas, Jorge, 157–58

Anita Casavantes Bradford, *The Revolution Is for the Children: The Politics of Childhood in Havana and Miami, 1959–1962* (2014).

Tiffany A. Sippial, *Prostitution, Modernity, and the Making of the Cuban Republic, 1840–1920* (2013).

Kathleen López, *Chinese Cubans: A Transnational History* (2013).

Lillian Guerra, *Visions of Power in Cuba: Revolution, Redemption, and Resistance, 1959–1971* (2012).

Carrie Hamilton, *Sexual Revolutions in Cuba: Passion, Politics, and Memory* (2012).

Sherry Johnson, *Climate and Catastrophe in Cuba and the Atlantic World during the Age of Revolution* (2011).

Melina Pappademos, *Black Political Activism and the Cuban Republic* (2011).

Frank Andre Guridy, *Forging Diaspora: Afro-Cubans and African Americans in a World of Empire and Jim Crow* (2010).

Ann Marie Stock, *On Location in Cuba: Street Filmmaking during Times of Transition* (2009).

Alejandro de la Fuente, *Havana and the Atlantic in the Sixteenth Century* (2008).

Reinaldo Funes Monzote, *From Rainforest to Cane Field in Cuba: An Environmental History since 1492* (2008).

Matt D. Childs, *The 1812 Aponte Rebellion in Cuba and the Struggle against Atlantic Slavery* (2006).

Eduardo González, *Cuba and the Tempest: Literature and Cinema in the Time of Diaspora* (2006).

John Lawrence Tone, *War and Genocide in Cuba, 1895–1898* (2006).

Samuel Farber, *The Origins of the Cuban Revolution Reconsidered* (2006).

Lillian Guerra, *The Myth of José Martí: Conflicting Nationalisms in Early Twentieth-Century Cuba* (2005).

Rodrigo Lazo, *Writing to Cuba: Filibustering and Cuban Exiles in the United States* (2005).

Alejandra Bronfman, *Measures of Equality: Social Science, Citizenship, and Race in Cuba, 1902–1940* (2004).

Edna M. Rodríguez-Mangual, *Lydia Cabrera and the Construction of an Afro-Cuban Cultural Identity* (2004).

Gabino La Rosa Corzo, *Runaway Slave Settlements in Cuba: Resistance and Repression* (2003).

Piero Gleijeses, *Conflicting Missions: Havana, Washington, and Africa, 1959–1976* (2002).

Robert Whitney, *State and Revolution in Cuba: Mass Mobilization and Political Change, 1920–1940* (2001).

Alejandro de la Fuente, *A Nation for All: Race, Inequality, and Politics in Twentieth-Century Cuba* (2001).

Made in the USA
Las Vegas, NV
08 January 2025

15988965R10153